INDUSTRIAL ACCUMULATION IN SRI LANKA

INDUSTRIAL ACCUMULATION IN SRI LANKA

Impact of Policy Shifts

Navaratna dissanayake Samarawickreme

GYAN PUBLISHING HOUSE

NEW DELHI-110002

Industrial Accumulation in Sri Lanka
Impact of Policy Shifts

Rs. 790

ISBN : 81-212-0855-6

Published in 2005 in India by
Gyan Publishing House
5, Ansari Road, Darya Ganj, New Delhi-110002
Phones : 23282060, 23261060, Fax : (011) 23285914
E-mail : gyanbook@vsnl.com
Website : http://www.gyanbooks.com

Laser Typesetting at : Shree Vaishnavi Creations, Delhi
Printed at : Mehra Offset Press, Delhi

Affectionately Dedicated
to
My Wife Chandra

Contents

Preface 9

Acknowledgements 13

List of Abbreviations 15

1. **Conceptualisation of the Problem** **17**
The Transitional Economy of Sri Lanka; The Problem; The 'Fast and Compressed' Growth Path for 'New Nations'; The State and the Economy of Sri Lanka; Summary; Introduction.

2. **The Evolution of An Industrial Sector in Sri Lanka The Initial Phase** **47**
Changing Political Economy; Socio- Political and Economic Forces for Structural Transformation; The Early Colonial Era of Accumulation; The Development of Market Economic Forces; Structural Changes and Private Industrial Accumulation; The Forces of Change in the Late Colonial Era; Post-1931 Developments; Low- Level Private Industrial Accumulation; The Industrial Development Discourse; The State Project of Industrialisation; Post independence Economic Regimes; Conclusions.

3. **Private Industrial Accumulation in Sri Lanka** **89**
Introduction; Compilation of a New Database: Methodology and Limitations; The Plantation Sector; The Construction Sector; The Trade Sector :1; The Finance Sector; The Manufacturing Sector; Changing Pattern of Inter-industry Accumulation; Economic Factors; Growth of an Industrialist Class: Four Classes of Industrialists; The Traditional Industrial Entrepreneur Class; Planning-based New Industrialists; New Industrialists After 1977; Foreign Industrialists; The Private Sector Led Structural Changes; Summary.

4. The Cyclical Behaviour of Industrial Accumulation **127**

Introduction; Hypothesising the Problem; The Overall Trends of Industrial Accumulation; Public Sector Investment; Private Industrial Accumulation; The Economic policy Shift Effects; Variables Determining Investment Behaviour; Economic Policy Shift and Private Accumulation – The Statistical Relationship; Summary.

5. The Slow Growth in Industrial Investment up to 1977 : The Disparate Forces **147**

Introduction; Policy Shifts on Industrial Investment; Phase I (1948 –55): Liberal Market Ideology on Industrial Accumulation; Phase II (1956-64): Shift towards a Planning-oriented; The Composition; The Planning-Orientation; The secondary benefits generated by state enterprises; The Private Industrial Entrepreneur Development ; Phase III (1965 –70): Market-Oriented Economic Forces; Phase IV (1970-77): Intensification of State Intervention; Pro-market and Anti- Market Effects of ISI Policies; The Slow Industrial Growth; Summary; introduction.

6. Industrial Accumulation and Market Forces **189**

Changes in the External Environment; Changes in Internal Environment of Sri Lanka; Transition to Market-oriented Industrialisation - The Stimuli-; Industrial Changes under Neoliberal Economic Policies; The Phase; The 'Tripod Structure'; The Phase II; Dilemmas under Market Orientation; The economic Factors; The External Market for Industrial Products; The Domestic Market for Industrial Products; Forces Hostile to Markets; New Conflicts; Summary.

7. Concluding Remarks **241**

Appendices 251

Bibliography 296

Index 321

Preface

Different nations have achieved industrial status at different phases of time in the past. First generation countries like Britain and Holland took about two centuries to reach that status. The second generation countries like some European countries and Japan reached this status in about a century while Newly Industrialised Countries, the third generation, reached the same status within less than half a century. Some of the countries in the last bloc, though they were prospective candidates for achieving that status, however, failed to reach the full status of industrial development and remain as emerging market nations. Some are yet to reach even that level. The present work deals with the problems faced by the last group of countries that are potential candidates but lag behind due to some intrinsic problems faced by them. Sri Lanka is a good case in point.

The end of the World War II was a watershed in the world econo-political order in the 20th century. The 'new nations', i.e., the post-colonial countries, sought a new economic order under which a 'fast and compressed' path to industrial development was expected to resolve their long standing problems. Most of these countries progressed along a new path based on the new vision buttressed at first by "development economics" and later by 'neo-liberalism'. The new vision has been one of fast building of industrial capacity within these 'new economies' employing borrowed technology, know-how and capital that had already been accumulated in industrially developed countries. However, the 'new nations' demonstrated dissimilar performances of industrial development in their short history regrouping themselves as countries with high, moderate and inadequate economic development achievement. The successful ones are known to have followed the notion of 'tripod structure' - an alliance of state, private and foreign capital - creating dynamism for rapid capitalist industrial development.

Sri Lanka has been one of the countries in the above trajectory of 'new nations' believing in 'new development hypothesis' but endeavouring little to fulfil the 'initial conditions' - the institutional readiness-- required for rapid industrial development. The Sri Lankan government as a 'soft' state was confronted throughout with the problem of balancing the twin objectives of providing welfare services and building-up industrial capacity in the economy.

The post-colonial process of industrialisation set in motion in 1947 was expected to be supported both by the state and the private sector but had to be singularly handled only by the state until the mid-1970s. The private sector endeavoured to accumulate industrial capital only after 1977 under the liberal economic policies of the state. Industrial accumulation in Sri Lanka, therefore, has not been 'fast and compressed' but 'low and slow' with many cyclical vicissitudes. The various economic policy alternatives that were experimented with are to be blamed for the drawbacks of the process, especially, that of failing to manage non-market elements in the system that continuously interfered with the process. This book elaborates the problems encountered and the prospects for Sri Lanka which have been only able to lay the foundation for building conditions for capitalist industrial accumulation -the tripod structure - at least to become an emerging-market nation in the near future.

Chapter 1 provides a review of the development literature on the subject concerned formulating the 'tripod alliance' hypothesis. The remaining chapters are organized for the application of the tripod alliance concept to the concrete situation of Sri Lanka from the colonial era to the present day.

Chapter 2 attempts to analyse the colonial period up to independence and identifies the pressures that built-up in the system for commencing of industrial development. It identifies a conflict between the colonial authority and the local elite on the question of industrial development in Sri Lanka. It draws attention to two policy-considerations that were open to the nation. One was about the possibility of a normal process of industrial growth motivated by market economic forces and the other the relevance and importance of 'political considerations' in the determination of industrial development of the country.

Chapter 3 identifies the path of industrial accumulation under different economic policy shifts. The chapter explains the emergence of new entrepreneur classes that contributed significantly to the process of industrial accumulation in the country.

Chapter 4 develops hypotheses on the cyclical behaviour of industrial development. Kaleckian-type regression equation has been used to estimate the determinants of industrial investment in Sri Lanka. Two types of determinants, namely, the economic and non-economic factors, were identified as explanatory variables that determine cycles of private investment.

In chapter 5, attention is drawn to the role of the state under socialist economic policies. The substantial growth of industrial activity under the planning-oriented industrial strategy was found unsustainable over time. The low surplus-generation of this strategy apparently led to low accumulation.

Chapter 6 describes the process of industrial accumulation under market economics. It commenced successfully with the neo-liberal approach to development with the support of the 'tripod structure'. But, the harrowing experiences of the post- 1983 period had an alarmingly negative impact on industrial accumulation. The forces hostile to market-orientation hindered the process of industrial accumulation that had commenced after 1977. All these made Sri Lanka's industrial accumulation process slower and long-drawn as compared to other successful 'new nations'. The book concludes with the following statement:

> The only "Achilles heel" in the Sri Lankan industrial development process has been the interference of forces hostile-to-the market. The state has a great responsibility in minimising the effects of such forces".

The Sri Lankan experience in industrial accumulation may be the best proxy for explaining the slowness of industrial accumulation in most South Asian Countries not to mention India and Pakistan. This book finds that the Kaleckian hypothesis that "repetition of the well-known historical pattern" --the final submission of the lower middle class to the interests of big business-- (Kalecki, 1972: 162-3) after all is becoming a reality in the Sri Lankan context in the same way that Kalecki has observed in a few other countries. This hypothesis may even be a valid option for explaining economic development of other countries in the region as well.

Acknowledgments

I would like to extend my gratitude and thanks to many people who have contributed to make this work a success. In particular, I am extremely thankful to Professor W.D. Lakshman, Professor of Economics, University of Colombo who took the keenest of interest to see me through this work. It was a heartening experience to work with him, his relentless criticism coupled with wit and humour, and paternal severity at times, but fraternal warmth most of the time. While his constant vigilance has kept me on track, I have also benefited from his extremely critical stance, his demand for thoroughness and detail, and his never ending enthusiasm and encouragement without which this work would not have taken its present form. Despite his heavy schedule of work during the last three years as the Dean, Faculty of Graduate Studies, the Vice-Chancellor, University of Colombo as well as a visiting Professor at the University of Ryukoku in Kyoto, Japan, his interest in this work was never diminished, regularly providing opportunities to meet him or communicating through E-mail.

I am also beholden to Professor Chandra Rodrigo who read through this work and made valuable suggestions. I also take this opportunity to record my grateful thanks to Emeritus Professor B. Hewavitharana who inspired and advised me to study economics at the University. I record my gratitude to Dr. C. R. Abeysekara who helped me to develop the econometric model used in this work. My thanks go to Mrs. Samanmala Dorabawila and Mr. O.G. Dayaratna Banda for helping me to develop a database for the research. I record my gratitude to the members of the staff of the main library, University of Peradeniya, especially to the Senior Assistant Librarian Mr. A.T. Alwis and Library Attendant Mr. K.G. John for their assistance in tracing books. I greatly benefited from the "Ceylon Room" at the main library in collecting information on ancient economic history of Sri Lanka which carries a good collection of material on the subject.

I am thanful to the Department of Economics, University of Peradeniya that stood by me by granting leave and providing with all facilities in the department, helping me to complete my work. I am also grateful to the members of the Department of Economics for their moral support. My thanks are also due to late Mr. S.Selvaratnam for his suggestions and editorial contributions. Dr. V. Kanapathypillai and Sita Kulatunga made their contribution by reading and editing of this work. I thank them too. Professor Punchibanda Meegaskumbura and Professor M. Sinnathamby too helped me in the editorial work to whom I extend my gratitude. Last but not least, I am grateful to my wife Chandra and my two sons, Sachithra and Madhu who supported in all possible ways at all stages of this work.

List of Abbreviations

1.	AEA	Atomic Energy Authority
2.	BOI	Board of Investment
3.	C&P	Chemicals and Pharmaceuticals
4.	CNC	Ceylon National Congress
5.	CP	Communist Party
6.	DFCC	Development Finance Credit Corporation
7.	EDB	Export development Board
8.	EPS	Earnings Per Share
9.	FBT	Food, Beverages and Tobacco.
10.	FDI	Foreign Direct Investment
11.	FIAC	Foreign Investment Advisory Committee
12.	FTZ	Free Trade Zones
13.	GATT	General Agreement on Tariffs and Trade
14.	GCEC	Greater Colombo Economic Commission
15.	GDCF	Gross Domestic Capital Formation
16.	GDFCF	Gross Domestic Fixed Capital Formation
17.	GDP	Gross domestic Product
18.	IDB	Industrial Development Board.
19.	IMF	International Monetary Fund
20.	IPKF	Indian Peacekeeping Force
21.	ISI	Import Substituting Industries
22.	ISIC	International Standard Industry Classification
23.	JSS	Jathika Sevaka Sangamaya
24.	JVP	Janatha Vimukthi Peramuna
25.	LSSP	Lanka Sama Samaja Party
26.	LTTE	Liberation Tigers Tamil Elam
27.	MFA	Multi-fibre Arrangement

28. MMI Miscellaneous Manufacturing Industries
29. MNCs Multinational Corporations
30. NDB National Development Bank.
31. NICs Newly Industrialised Countries
32. NIE New Institutional Economics
33. NSB National Savings Bank
34. OECD Overseas Economic Development
35. OIE Old Institutional Economics
36. PA 'Peoples' Alliance'
37. PERC Public Enterprise Restructuring Committee
38. PMES Public Manufacturing Enterprises
39. PTC Presidential Tariff Commission
40. S&T Science and Technology
41. SEC Security Exchange Commission
42. SLFP Sri Lanka Freedom Party
43. SMI Small and Medium Industries
44. SMIB The State Mortgage and Investment Bank
45. SMS Sinhala Maha Sabha
46. UNP United National Party
47. WTO World Trade Organisation
48. WW World War

1

Conceptualisation of the Problem

1.1. The Transitional Economy of Sri Lanka

Sri Lanka was a British colony for about 150 years[1]. Prior to this, it had a predominantly agriculture-based subsistence economy. The British were able to change the system from an 'agricultural economy to a plantation market economy' extracting economic opportunities of the island (Kumari Jayawardena, 1972). The Colebrooke Commission in 1833 provided the necessary legal framework to assist this change and proposed various reforms for the establishment of a 'plantation market economy'[2]. The most outstanding feature of the 'plantation market economy' was the neutrality of the state; the state confined itself to the provision of basic facilities for capitalist economic development.

The 'plantation market economy' changed the structure of the ancient village organisation, and transplanted a dual economic system which consisted of a modern and a traditional sector. Of the modern sector, the two important sub-sectors, the plantations sector in the hills and the urban commercial sector close to the capital grew side by side in this new economic environment. Associated with the 'plantation enterprise', many related activities too grew over time in this system[3].

The Sri Lankan polity underwent a process of transformation in the 20th century. This transformation had two different aspects. First, there was a process of transformation in the political structure. The change was from colonial status to increasing self-government. The nucleus of the change apparently was the middle-class element, the elite, who received a western education. However, the divisions among elite groups into conservative, moderate and radical led gradually to intra-group competition to gain political power. This political competition intensified after independence. Secondly, there was a gradual transformation in the economic structure over the long period from private sector-dependent plantation economy towards an economy dependent on state industrial development and in more recent years to a private sector-dependent industrial development.

Sri Lanka gained independence from British rule in 1948. The post-independent political economy of Sri Lanka underwent two interrelated processes of change, i.e., at the political and economic levels. Politically, the policies of democratically elected governments based on divergent econo-political ideologies influenced the change in the political process of Sri Lanka. The political party system comprised basically two broad coalitions; the United National party (UNP) assumed a liberal democratic, right-of-centre approach, while the Sri Lanka Freedom Party (SLFP)-based coalitions adopted social democratic policies, thus assuming a left-of-centre approach.

Economically, the post-independence growth process in Sri Lanka commenced as recommended in contemporary 'development economics'. There were three distinctive policy changes in this process. First was the interventionist industrial policy of the state. It continued for about two decades starting in the late 1950s; some call it 'State capitalism'[4]. The interventionist policy contributed to the development of a capitalist industrial base providing an initial boost to the slow phase of private accumulation. Secondly, dominance of market economics in industrial development was evident since 1977 with the introduction of neo-liberal economic policies in the country. This process continued and even intensified in the early part of the 1990s to meet the challenges posed by 'Globalisation'. Finally, there was evidence once again of an infiltration of social welfare policies into the formal economic strategy under the neo-liberal economic umbrella, especially, after 1994.

Evidently, the overall industrial formation in the post-independent period was cyclical. Industrial development under the interventionist policy during the period between 1956 and 1977 was relatively high[5]. But, the contribution of the private sector to industrial accumulation during this period was quite low. State enterprises contributed substantially to the industrial formation during this period. It ultimately reached saturation in the mid-1970s. However, industrial development under state patronage was a low self-growth generating process assisted by intermittent capital transfers by the state (Hewavitharana, 1986).

Private industrial accumulation in the second phase after 1977 was high under the free market economic environment. Industrial accumulation took off effectively in this second phase entering a self-growth generating process. But, the process could not continue for long. Once again, the volume of industrial real fixed assets fell in the economy especially after 1983 because of the influence of factors that were beyond the control of the system. In all, Sri Lanka's industrial accumulation lagged behind that of other countries in Southeast Asia. Moore (1992) ascribes this to certain weaknesses in both the 'state structure' as well as the 'economic structure'.

1.2. The Problem

'Small nations' — small developing countries as well as some small developed countries — are highly vulnerable to changes taking place in the international economy[6]. The degree of vulnerability of many small developing countries, immediately after their independence, was very high. These nations, after identifying their most important national objectives of the time – an alternative path of development different from the colonial path— drew up their own political strategies. Most governments formulated policy agendas in pursuit of a 'fast' and 'compressed process' of industrial development[7].

Doubts, however, have been cast upon the capacity of 'small nations' to achieve their ambitious goal of 'fast and compressed process of industrial development', given the poor state of economic, political and social conditions of these countries. The query which is valid even for today is, whether a typical 'small country' with no developed 'investment climate' —the industrial infrastructure, industrial know-how and industrial resources— can set forth a programme of achieving a process of 'fast and compressed industrial development' given the rapidly changing international economic order. Putting it another way, this raises doubts as to whether a 'small country' with given specific 'initial conditions'[8] that shape subsequent development' could achieve steady industrial accumulation in a relatively short period of time (Adelman, 2001:126).

Sri Lanka has been a case in point. Sri Lanka being a small nation has had a long-term vision of transforming its old plantation-based economic sub-structure, following a dynamic path of industrial development. It drew up different planning strategies over the past half-century to achieve the 'fast and compressed process' of industrial development quite in line with other 'small nations' in the region.

The experiences of 'new nations' in respect of industrial progress are highly varied[9]. Sri Lanka's progress, in particular, has been slow compared with that of certain other 'small nations'. The industrial accumulation process of Sri Lanka, which continued for about half a century, apparently, produced amorphous results; sometimes it has been slow and at other times stagnant. The process altogether was cyclical. Sri Lanka appears to have been unsuccessful in accessing the 'compressed path of industrial development' suggested by theory. Instead, Sri Lanka seems to have followed an alternative path of industrialisation involving a longer period. In all, Sri Lanka was a late starter of industrial development as well as a slow mover to different levels of industrialisation compared with other 'new nations'. Sri Lanka, therefore, is a 'late-late developer'[10] within the 'small nations' bloc.

The question may arise as to what factors contributed to the low-level industrial achievements of Sri Lanka compared with the achievements of certain 'new nations' in the East Asian bloc. In this regard, there have been a few studies which attempted to explain the causes for slow-growth of industrial capitalism in the colonial period. De Silva (1982: 474-5) believes that 'in the colonies, the effects of imperialism were to develop and strengthen the role of merchant capital and to stifle its transformation into industrial capital'. Kumari Jayawardena (2000) describes that some forces were behind the behaviour of bourgeoisie in the dominant plantation economy of Sri Lanka causing them to specialise in the accumulation of mercantile capital as a source of achieving political and social power. Comparing and reviewing the works of the above two scholars, Jayasuriya[11] summarises that '... the mercantile character of the new bourgeoisie structurally constrained their ability to transform into industrial capitalists'. But, the developments that took place in the fields of politics and economics in the second half of the 20th century have been quite different from those of the colonial era. It, therefore, raises doubts as to whether the above explanations could satisfactorily describe the changes, especially the transition of entrepreneurs towards industrial accumulation in the post independent era. Perhaps, the postcolonial industrial development may be explained through other factors, in addition, to the above.

Obviously, the main cause of the failure to achieve a high rate of industrial growth in post independence period may not necessarily be the ineffectiveness of actors, the entrepreneur class, engaged in economic activities. The success in entrepreneurial capacity of Sri Lankan investors was well proved by their past records as plantation entrepreneurs. Their degree of proficiency should not, therefore, be underestimated. This class of entrepreneurs, local as well as foreign, has demonstrated exceptionally high accumulative capacity under plantation development. They exhibited enormous dynamism and enthusiasm in the transplantation of a new agricultural system in the hills. The foreign and indigenous capitalist class exploited opportunities open to them by undertaking high-risk investment in plantations. Their success in plantations accumulation may be attributable partly to the harmonious relations which prevailed among foreign, local and state capital in the environment created by the state under the *laissez-faire* policy that prevailed at the time. In fact, Sri Lanka had fulfilled certain 'initial conditions' (types mentioned in note 8 above) under the plantation economic environment.

Certainly, industrial achievements of Newly Industrialised Countries, (NICs) have been remarkable. These countries have been able to realise high rates of industrial development under the 'compressed path of industrial development' specified by theory. It is argued that the socio- politico-economic environment and the dynamism of actors in the system have been the main causes for the above success. It is said that three different classes of investors —indigenous, foreign, and state capital— the important 'tripods structure' harmoniously contributed to the transformation of these countries[12].

'Development theory' was helpful to these countries in the formalisation of policies to facilitate transition. It insisted on the dominance of market forces in the mobilisation of resources towards productive investments and work towards a weakening of non-market forces in the system[13]. The East Asian States, so-called 'hard States', fulfilled these conditions in their early phases of development as these states had the capacity to strengthen market forces and minimise such pressures produced by non-market elements in these systems. Adelman (2001:127) finds that "... by 1973 the overwhelming majority of countries that were institutionally more developed in 1950 had become either newly industrial countries (NICs) or industrial countries, while none of the countries at lower levels of socio institutional development had become NICs". In the later phases, these countries intensified market economic activities in their economies under the influence of 'neo-liberal economic theory' for improving firm-level efficiency.

South Asian countries were structurally different from East Asian countries in the bloc of 'new nations'[14]. One of the problems faced by these countries has been their slowness in for fulfilling prerequisites of the 'development theory' because of the presence of certain unfavourable elements in econo-social structures. These countries were unsuccessful in implementing programmes of modernisation in the socio-economic environment[15]. The change in the socio-economic environment in favour of market economic forces was the main prerequisite of the 'neoclassical economic foundation'. Economic theory insists that the improvement of economic efficiency within firm-levels is a requirement for a 'fast' and 'compressed development'. The other requisite that South Asian countries have failed to institute was the promotion of active collaboration among state, domestic and foreign capital to achieve a high rate of capitalist industrial accumulation. The non-market forces including the institutional structure appear to have over-intervened in the system relegating market forces to a secondary position in the economy[16].

Two important features of the process of industrialisation of 'new nations', therefore, require attention when assessing progress: (1) appropriateness of the objective function of these nations —the 'fast and compressed process of industrial development' and (2) adequacy of institutional arrangements and socio-political structures in achieving the said objective[17]. The latter is more useful for understanding the behaviour of market forces in these countries. Zysman (1996:177) has correctly pointed out that market economies of these countries consist of institutions and rules which permit them to function and to shape 'how buying and selling and the very organisation of production take place'. The institutional environment of these countries thus reshapes the markets and their functions. Jayasuriya (2000: 2), therefore, holds that 'markets cannot be isolated from the wider ensemble of political and economic power'. Citing the work of Steinmo et al. (1992), Jayasuriya (2000) suggests an approach of 'historical institutionalism'[18] that he claims is more appropriate to explain the behaviour of markets and other institutions of these countries. For him, 'a comprehensive understanding of economic behaviour is possible only within the wider context of political and institutional structure' (Jayasuriya, 2000:2).

1.3. The 'Fast and Compressed' Growth Path for 'New Nations'

The literature on the theoretical foundation necessary for conceptualising the problem of accumulation of 'new nations' is rich and extensive. Basically, two broad directions of theorisation of accumulation may be found in the literature. One is the generalisation of circumstances based on historical events. The other is the identification of explanatory variables influencing the behaviour of industrial accumulation for building theoretical models on a cross sectional basis. In the search of a path of industrial development for 'new nations', complete reliance on historical precedents or experiences of other countries, however, may be narrow and misleading. It may be hard to find predetermined (or ahistorical) set of conditions or variables, which would always lead to the same or similar results in the future. As Lim (1988: 477) says there are no universal models or panaceas for successful capitalist development that are applicable to every country. The literature on industrial accumulations of other nations, however, may furnish some information pertaining to necessary and appropriate conditions for industrial accumulation. A literature survey on industrial accumulations of other nations can provide satisfactory theoretical rationalisation on explanatory variables and trends of industrial growth processes relevant to the 'new nations'.

The present study is carried out in two stages: the first is an examination of theoretical foundations to explain why some countries have achieved industrial development sooner than others. The second is the search of empirical evidence for justifying any such theoretical rationalisation. The latter will be attempted according to the following broad classification of countries, depending upon their degrees of industrial achievement in the mid-20th century.

The historical industrial experiences of different countries can be classified into four different types[19]. The countries in the West like Britain and Holland, which achieved industrial development a long time ago, fall into group (a). Countries like Germany, France, Russia, Italy, and probably Japan, which developed industries in the late 19th century, may be categorised into Group (b). The countries, which are described as Newly Industrialised Countries (NICs) like South Korea, Hong Kong, Singapore, and Taiwan, and 'emerging market economies'[20] like Malaysia, Thailand, and Indonesia which achieved high industrial development in the recent past, are placed in group (c)[21]. Lastly, the South Asian countries like India, Sri Lanka, Bangladesh, and Pakistan, which are in the lowest rung of the ladder of industrial development, are placed in group (d)[22]. (There are many countries in other continents falling into the above four groups which are not mentioned above).

Can 'small nations' enter 'fast and compressed' processes of industrial accumulation? It was the central problem faced by 'new nations' as well as by development economists in the post World War period. The relevant literature throws up two basic hypotheses concerning potential industrial processes. One is the capitalist development process which is unique and that late comers have to follow the same process as the forerunners. The other proposition has been that 'new nations' can secure an alternative process of industrial development which is shorter and quicker.

The first proposition was held by Classical Marxists, at one end, and Stage theorists at the other, suggesting that 'there is universality' in capitalist development 'from which economies are incapable of deviating' (Harris et. al., 1998:2). The 'stage theory' of W.W. Rostow (1961) presents an historical explanation of the process of industrial development. The industrial development in developed countries in group (a) above provides a historical 'example of a successful process' in the long history of over 100 years.

Rostow spoke of the relevance of 'stage theory' for developing countries as a process of industrial development. However, the stage theory – which some call "path dependencies"[23] or "gradualism", is said to be unsatisfactory for providing much guidance to the problems of 'new nations' and therefore is of little relevance to the needs of these countries (Kuznets, 1961; Rosovsky, 1965; Higgins, 1959; Myrdal, 1968; Meier, 1970). One reason, as critics argue, is that the 'initial conditions' on which industrial development was achieved by 'pioneers' in the past are different from those of 'latecomers' embarking upon industrial development in the post WW II period[24].

Another was the longer time path of industrialisation of the 'pioneers' primarily guided by competitive market forces. Indeed, the main objective of the 'new nations', was to achieve a 'fast and compressed industrialisation'. But the forces at work in the latter countries, however, were completely different from those of the former. Markets were virtually non-existent or grossly imperfect in these countries (Myrdal, 1970). Griffin (1970:18) therefore, advised that 'the poor countries of today need not follow the same path toward prosperity, as did the industrial nations. [The goals of the new nations] may be different; their means are certainly superior'.

Development economists of the post-WW II period rejected the free market economic option —the neoclassical economic foundation— as non-attainable. They provided numerous reasons why there would be poor performance in new nations in achieving their main objectives. Balogh (1966) points out that monopolistic characteristics of sectors and consequent distortions of commodity and factor prices would undoubtedly disturb such free market allocation of resources in these economies. Dudley Seers is cautious about the relevance of mainstream economics in explaining changes in economically underdeveloped countries[25]. He finds that, 'neoclassical economics' '[does] not have a great deal to offer by way of useful advice'.

Meier insisted on an alternative approach to explain changes taking place in these countries. He was not content with 'neoclassical economic foundation' as it ignores the importance of *different social systems and economic structures* in developing countries. He thinks that the existing theory '...[may] have to be altered to make the theory more immediately relevant to countries that have a different social systems and economic structures...'(Meier, 1970: 87-88). For economies with different *structures* of *social systems and economic institutions* the free market policies may be of little relevance, which could only lead to intensify 'frictions' — frictions between social and economic institutions in the system[26].

These economies were regulated by different economic and non-economic forces which tended to distort the process of allocation of productive resources. Therefore, the main challenge for 'new nations' after their independence from European colonial rule was to develop institutional prerequisites for a free market economy, which could gear the reallocation of scarce resources gradually towards capitalist industrial development. These economies therefore required a structural and institutional transformation supportive of the development of market forces.

'Development theory' as it evolved in the post-World War period indicates an alternative approach to the process of industrial development of 'new nations'. Although, both the market and the state were the main actors in this 'development theory', the most important role was assigned to the state to undertake structural changes in the production processes of these countries (Stern, 1991:250). This alternative approach grew alongside Keynesian and Polanyian[27] perception of bringing the state to the forefront of economic policymaking (Myint, 1971; Boyer, 1996). In fact, the foundation of 'development economics' was the old theme of classical theory of capital accumulation, blended with a greater role assigned to the state. Bell (1987) and Wade (1990) highlighted the infiltration of classical concepts and modern ideas[28] into 'development economics' in the post Second World War period[29].

Professor Gerschenkron's (1962) 'historical analysis' added a new dimension to 'development theory' searching for a 'compressed' path of industrial development for 'new nations'. Gerschenkron compared the historical patterns of industrial development of some European countries with different degrees of backwardness (Gerschenkron, 1962). Countries like France, Germany, and Russia, belonging to the second generation (group b), achieved industrial development in a shorter period than the first group of countries (group a). These countries were economically backward in different degrees and, therefore, the level of industrial development they achieved too varied.

Gerschenkron's 'theory of relative backwardness', role of the state, and 'borrowed technology' in the given state of private accumulation added new insights to 'development theory' and the shortening of the industrial processes of 'new nations'. His postulate, that 'latecomers' are in a more advantageous position than the 'pioneers' because of the latter's ability to access new technology and know-how, became the new theme of 'development economics'. According to Mouzelis (1994), the most important part in Gerschenkron's contribution was his concept of the 'state'. He finds that the state is the most powerful institution which could guide the path of economic development of 'new nations'. For Mouzelis, (1994: 127) 'the structure of the State' is the one which determines 'why late developers with comparable starting-points and resources have performed so unevenly within the world economy'. Harris holds that the role of Gerschenkron's state was to compensate for the lack of prerequisites for industrialisation. Such prerequisites were what enabled some such economies to 'catch up' (Harris et. al., 1995:9). The state, therefore, has been the most important institution in 'high-speed industrialisation' of these nations (Gerschenkron, 1961:16-21). Its role ought to be to act as a balancing force to avoid possible frictions among different institutions that arise in the process of modernisation.

One important role of the state was to correct market failures that were by-products of colonial economic policies. Some states relied on pragmatic political considerations in allocating resources towards the new process of industrial development which hitherto were made on pure economic considerations. The pure economic considerations may be misleading and unrealistic in situations where markets are distorted and oligopolistic in the 'new nations'. Some, therefore, argued that the decisions regarding reallocation of resources needed to be taken outside the market mechanism (Griffin, 1970; Agarwala at el., 1958:330; Meier, 1970: 333; Myint, 1971:13, Bell, 1987:820; Srinivasan, 1989). Structuralists 'de-emphasised the importance of relative prices as means of affecting both distributive and productive outcomes', and emphasised 'state interventionism' in these countries. They were concerned with the 'growing evidence of the importance of non-price variables in affecting (or in explaining the absence of) economic responses in developing countries' (Colclough, 1993:3).

A strong state with its 'visible hand', however, can intervene in economic affairs to provide the 'prerequisites' for economic, social and political changes in these systems for structural transitions (Colclough, 1993:2). Perhaps, the 'visible hand' of the state in 'new nations' is more powerful and effective than the 'invisible hand' of the weak market system in making decisions for transition. Subsequently, such a state can play a role in promoting competitive environments and market forces in economies to intensify reallocation of resources towards industrial development.

'Development theory' served as a bridge between the old economic practices implemented in economies of 'new nations' and the growing market-oriented economic concept embedded in the world economic order. In its early phases, the 'development theory' with the influence of Old Institutional Economics (OIE) and Latin-American structuralism associated with the work of writers like Raul Prebisch developed alternative strategies and institutions to effect gradual and peaceful transitions toward a market-oriented economic system[30]. The OIE, bringing the state to the economic forefront, emphasised the need for developing strategies to minimise frictions between non-market and market forces when economies move from an agricultural base towards fast industrial development. Frictions are likely to arise with the formation of a new labour force, a new investment climate facilitating foreign capital and inflow of foreign resources for fast industrial development.

The OIE, in this regard, emphasised the promotion of market-oriented economic structures via reforms in non-market institutions in these economies. Myrdal, an OIE supporter, was of the view that social and economic reforms in developing countries were fundamental requisites for an effective transformation towards market-orientation. Myrdal advocated 'the need to use pricing policy rather than direct controls' in the economy. Streeten (1993:1282), interpreting Myrdal, mentions that "[w]e thought it important for the government to organize markets so that they work efficiently, but we did not confuse price *policy*..."

'Development theory' under the structuralist influence advocated that the state should '[play] the role of the Schumpeterian entrepreneur as well as intervene in existing markets' for rapid industrial development (Srinivasan, 1989:4). In a state of poor private industrial investment, the 'big push' theory assumed a need of 'a high minimum amount of industrial investment in order to 'jump over the economic obstacles to development'[31]. The theory envisaged the public sector investing a considerable amount of funds in the economy to provide the initial capital formation necessary for 'compressed industrial development'. It also wanted to provide venture capital for new enterprises and to support the "thrust industries"(Shapiro et. al.1990: 874). Many developing countries incorporated the concept of 'big push' and the active role of the state in their development strategies in the 1950s (Bardhan, 1984).

However, 'development theory' was criticised for its limited exposure to the important concept of 'technological transfer', one of the main ingredients of Gerschenkron's thesis (1962) in capitalist development. In practice, 'development theory' tended to place emphasis more on the role of the state but little on the transfer of technology which ought to come from developed countries. Perhaps, the rigorous interventionist policies of the state may be counterproductive to the extent that they could go against the policies of the private sector discouraging inflow of foreign direct investment, the source of transfer of new technology to 'new nations'. In practice, most developing nations in the past tended to advocate inward-looking policies favouring the choice of 'appropriate technology', 'intermediate technology', and 'labour-intensive technology' (Schumacher, 1965; Sen, 1972). This advocacy may have been the result of the scarcity of financial resources available to these countries to import superior technology from the West as they suffered from balance of payments problems (Higgins, 1959:195).

Generally, the historical circumstances result in change in the significance of existing theories and approaches bringing about new theories and concepts challenging the old ones. Keynesian economics thus lost its momentum especially after the 1970s as 'the Keynesian compromise has in recent years not delivered the same results as during the 1950s' (Boyer, 1996). Similarly, the traditional 'development theory' was able to offer very little to the persistently lagging industrial accumulation in 'new nations'. The state-centric development programmes, concentrating on import substitution industrialisation, suffered from certain setbacks in the 1960s due to internal and external bottlenecks. The inward-looking characteristics of the above strategy posed limitations on their capacity to earn foreign exchange to finance import requirements[32].

'Development theory' underwent a process of change in the 1970s. The change was prompted by the recession that the world and its economic order experienced in the late 1960s[33]. The slow economic growth in these countries was attributed to low productivity of resources, and economic inefficiencies at firm-levels. This resulted in their low level of competitiveness in the international market. Most countries switched over to an alternative strategy of neo-liberal-microeconomics in the late 1970s for minimising costs of production at firm levels (Parkin et. al., 1997:549-51). Thus, the 'neo-liberal synthesis' has become the dominant economic policy in industrialised as well as industrialising countries in the post-1970s. The Western financial Agencies also favoured the neo-liberal economic strategy as a source of promoting global competition and cost minimisation (Manor, 1991).

The new option in the 1980s, the 'neo-liberal paradigm', was also subject to much criticism, especially on its relations with the neoclassical theory, its capacity and shortcomings as a refutable theory of economic development. In fact, Toye's (1993) answer to his own question " "Is there a new political economy of development?" brings out many issues about the integrity of neo-liberalism as a theory and a refutable proposition. He summarises his arguments saying "[w]e argue that major features are an unrelievedly cynical view of the state and a sharp disjunction between that view and the political requirements for the adoption of liberalization policies in the economic sphere" (Toye,1993:321). We do not attempt here to explore these criticisms in detail as it is beyond the purview of this study. Instead, we discuss the practical significance of the neo-liberal approach as an alternative approach which could be used in industrial development in 'new nations'.

The neo-liberal economic policy, the macro and micro-level liberalisation of economic activities of an economy, was intensively applied in NICs, in the late 1960s producing structural changes and raising efficiency at firms-level[34]. The export-led industrial development of these countries benefited substantially from liberalisation policies. These economies grew to such an extent that it was called an "*East*

Asian miracle" by the World Bank. The *miracle* for Rowen (1998) was "getting the economic fundamentals right"[35] in these economies. In Taiwan, for example, the economic reforms of the late-1950s and early 1960s shifted policy emphasis from the state-owned sector towards the private sector providing property rights and various other fiscal and financial incentives (Haggard, 1998:83). Wade interprets, in detail, Taiwan's industrial boom as an outcome of the adaptation of neoclassical policies with an "outward orientation" especially after 1958 (Wade, 1990:52-3)[36]. The end-result of this dominance of market economics in the 1980s was that 'development economics has been absorbed back into the mainstream, and now enjoys no separate existence' (Bell, 1987).

The market economic dominance may be viewed as a dynamic move to attract economic agents —the private sector, foreign investors, and the state— into already developed industrial structures of these countries to bond them with collective responsibility for attaining a high level of efficiency. Market economic forces ensure the economic utilisation of scarce resources at micro levels and, thereby, at macro level, to improve the overall efficiency and competitiveness in the system. In such an optimal blend, the private sector and the state sector are to share economic activities harmoniously and productively to generate, extract, and accumulate surpluses in industrial activities. The new 'export-led development strategy', is a product of the above system with a market-orientation of production and distribution.

The new market-state interface paved the way for a favourable 'investment climate' for foreign entrepreneurs to invest funds in these countries. The countries that joined in the process of globalisation benefited substantially from technological transfers[37] coming from developed countries (as stipulated by Gerschenkron). The 'Multinational corporations (MNCs) [played] a pivotal role in the cross-national flow of goods, capital and technology' under the neo-liberal economic order[38]. Foreign direct investment (FDI) through MNCs served as a source of external finance alternative to foreign aid and to internal sources of funds (Clark at el., 1996).

The new system continues as a typical "tripod structure' of development combining indigenous private capital, foreign capital and state capital in such a way that it would produce optimum industrialisation for these countries. In this structure, the state serves as the balancing force and the leading partner in the partnership of the three pods –the state, domestic and foreign capital. The range of the state-market interface under this economic strategy, however, is too wide. The degree of dominance swings favouring state dominance at one time and market dominance at other times in search of an optimal combination. In practice, such swings took place in 'new nations' —NICs— in the latter part of the twentieth century.

Industrial development under neo-liberalism based on the concept of minimal state intervention took a new turn, in the late 1980s. Now the economists insisted the 'state to be back in'[39] the economic forum of these nations. Skocpol (1985) argues that the state should play its role to eliminate 'market failures' while the market should play the role to eliminate 'government failures' bringing the economy to a balance. For Boyer, the state is still an important institution in the modern economy as the political priorities have to be set by the government and this function of the government cannot be replaced by 'any other mechanism, especially not markets' (Boyer, 1996: 86)[40]. It appears that the economists now attempt to find a balance between the two strong actors, the state and the market for a desirable and a congenial relationship between them in the system for a faster growth of industrial accumulation.

Pereira (1993) argues that the state and the market change cyclically in their involvement in developing economies. At one time, the former becomes strong and at another time the latter while the former becomes weak. Eventually, both the market and the state function in a collective and friendly environment ensuring equilibrium. Boyer (1996) foresees that '[the] twenty-first century will probably experience a genuine social and political engagement of markets with networks, associations and local communities along with renewed state intervention'. He poses the question as to whether the state and market are going to have a new engagement for the twenty first century?

In sum, the theoretical foundation envisages that a country in the 'new nations' group may be a prospective candidate for entering into a 'compressed process of industrial development', if the country follows the process of adjustments specified by the above conceptualisation. A country requires an initial fulfilment of conditions proposed by 'development theory' to develop a favourable 'investment climate' for industrial development. This requires the promotion of market economic forces in the system weakening non-market forces which are hostile to development. Given the problems of the external sector faced by the country, it would start initially with an inward-looking policy of import-competing industrial development—the second best approach. The state is responsible for the provision of institutional changes, proper guidance and leadership to the industrially weak economy by way of providing infrastructural facilities and incentives for the private sector (including foreign capital) to engage in industrial activities. The state could also get directly involved in economic activities in the system.

The country needs subsequent switch over to an outward-looking policy of export-led industrial development in the medium phase without allowing the initial phase of import-substitution strategy persist too long. In this transition, the state needs to reduce its degree of intervention in the economy and allow market forces to mobilise scarce resources on competitive market signals. This undoubtedly results in greater economic efficiency. The 'neo-liberal economic policies' have a role to play in raising production efficiency of resources for greater competitiveness at micro firm-levels.

The process, based on competitive market forces, may help industrial development to reach a self-growth generating status, earning surpluses and accumulating them in the industry like in countries that are already developed industrially. At maturity, both the market and the state may play their respective roles in maintaining a harmonious relationship in the system. The crucial institution in the above capitalist industrial process in a new nation is the state; the dynamic state could co-ordinate socio- political economic activities of the economy to reach the above mature status under the leadership of competitive market forces.

Have all countries in 'new nations' followed the path of capitalist industrial development and prospered as envisaged by the above conceptualisations? If not, what factors contributed to the failure to achieve a significant industrial development in those countries? These two questions are empirically important for appraising the validity of the conceptual foundation developed above.

The 'new nations' continued their industrial accumulation practices in a highly favourable international environment[41]. Most of them started initially with a focus on an inward looking approach of import substitution[42]. This policy approach was acceptable to 'development economics'. In some countries, the private sector participated effectively in industrial capital formation under the protective environment created by the state. The state itself engaged in industrial capital formation under different degrees of intervention in these countries.

State intervention in most economies took two forms. First, they introduced new institutions into the system to challenge the prevailing colonial value bases that were counter-productive to the changing economies. Secondly, under the policy of interventionism the state participated in industrial formation as 'big entrepreneurs' of public enterprises. The state entered in various economic activities to provide infrastructural facilities to the system to assist the policy of import substitution. It also provided protection to private industrialists by erecting tariff walls and providing various stimuli. This was aimed to have promoted a new class of private entrepreneurs in these countries. Later, certain countries among the 'new nations' changed their emphasis to an outward looking policy of 'export development' guided by neo-liberal policy.

Meier in his introduction to the "Frontiers of Development Economics" (Meier et. al., 2001:1) examines the past development records of poor countries. He concludes: '[a]lthough the development record exhibits many successes, there are also failures and disappointed expectations'. This book provides information on how 'new nations' (countries in groups (c) and (d)) have experienced varying degrees of success in achieving a steady industrial development during the last four decades. Some have been successful in this endeavour (countries in group (c)) and others have been either moderately successful as in the case of countries in group (d), or unsuccessful in achieving their desired objectives. Evans et al. (1985), Wade (1990), Evans (1979), and Bell (1995) also provide successful stories of the former groups and Jenkins (1995), Bhambhri (1989) and Mukherjee (1989) and Sen (1982) give explanations for the moderate success of Indian industrialisation. Particularly, some East-Asian countries were the successful ones which acquired high rates of industrial accumulation over a short period of time. South Asian countries, however, achieved only a moderate success in their endeavour.

Obviously, 'the search for a single-cause, and hence a single-remedy, theory of development' for such variations is 'likely to be either completely or partially incorrect' (Adelman, 2001:130) Adelman believes that '[e]conomic development is a highly multifaceted, nonlinear, path-dependent, dynamic process...'. For Adelman (2001:130), it '...involves systematically shifting interaction patterns among different aspects of development and therefore requires predictable changes in policies and institutions over time'. Meier (2001:3) using his matrix of 'Development Thought' describes that current researches on causes and remedies for low level development have taken new directions in explaining "institutional failures". They speak of "getting institutions right", "complementarily of government and market", and "social Capital" in economic systems.

Although, South Asian countries have implemented "well-designed economic policies" they, however, have achieved only limited success in political and economic transformation favourable for industrial accumulation. One reason for the deficiency may be the 'initial conditions' of South Asian countries, which have not changed sufficiently to suit basic prerequisites of theories. Adelman (2001:126) emphatically expresses that '[I]nitial conditions shape subsequent development' of countries. She cites Abramovitz (1986) to explain the initial levels of social capability[43] of different European industrialist nations during the 19th century. Adelman (2001:127) argues that **"institutional readiness for capitalist economic growth is key to economic development"**. She describes that those developing countries in the 1950s that were institutionally more advanced were the ones that benefited most from the growth impetus imparted by import demand from OECD countries during the golden era of economic development'.

Adelman, (2001:127-28) highlights the importance of '[t]he initial degree of government political autonomy' in the process of economic development of these countries. The autonomy of the state means the capacity of the state to formulate independent official goals and strategies suitable for the nation. The 'states [are] conceived as organisations claiming control over territories and people'. These 'goals are not simply reflective of the demands or interests of social groups, classes, or society'. The capacity of the state, therefore, is its ability to 'implement official goals, especially against the actual or potential opposition of powerful social groups or in the face of recalcitrant socioeconomic circumstances' (Skocpol, 1985:9). Have the institutional structures[44] of South Asian countries changed dynamically to ensure 'the autonomy of the state' to implement official goals of these nations independently?

Many explain that the conditions in South Asia to be different in perspectives. The different schools, for example, institutionalists, neo-Marxists and neoclassical political economists, give different explanations to the problems faced by South Asian countries. Bardhan (1989) provides a summary of different versions of these explanations. He (2001) points out two major shortcomings: (a) 'the persistence of dysfunctional institutions in poor countries' and (b) 'a more complex and nuance role of the state, to deal with the need for coordination'. Viewed from Myrdal's perspective, these countries are all 'soft states' ruled by democratic governments[45]. '[T]he state does not optimize anything, neither public welfare nor self-interest. It compromises, attempts to resolve conflicts, manages bargaining between groups, occasionally leads'... declared policies are not implemented or not enforced'... Streeten (1993), therefore, finds that the behaviour of these states may thus be best explained by what is called a 'common-sense theory'. This theory insists that these governments are 'neither monolithic nor impervious to pressures for rational and altruistic policies'.

Some Marxist-oriented analyses, for example, explain the process of economic development in India as different from the mainstream explanations (Sen, 1982; Bhambhri, 1989; Bardhan, 1984; Haggard et al., 1992; Duncan, 1995). Most of these studies are concerned with the degree of complexity of relations and interactions between the state and the social classes or 'interest groups' in industrial development in the Indian polity. Jenkins (1995) provides a critical account of various analyses upon Indian economic development. The popular theme of analyses has been the rent-seeking behaviour of the most powerful economic groups in the controlled Indian economy who have 'a little incentive as political elites to favour reform' (Jenkins, 1995:4). Jenkins himself provides an alternative view on the dynamic behaviour of the state. To him the 'political dynamic of economic adjustment' of Indian economy in the recent past has led to a new dynamic path of the Indian capitalist economy under the prudent practice of the state which diverted the emphasis of the big business class towards growth[46].

1.4. The State and the Economy of Sri Lanka

Sri Lanka's progress along the path of Industrial accumulation has been very slow. This slow process of industrial development may not be exactly on par with that of any other South Asian country. The Indian experiences, in particular, is quite different. The best possible explanation thus may be the sort of a common-sense theory[47] described by Streeten to explain the functions and the characteristics of Sri Lankan economy. Different factors determine the behaviour of the state regarding the formation of economic policies and their implementation. It is necessary, therefore, to understand the forces that operate within the system which determine the pace of industrial accumulation.

Historically, the causes for the slow transition of capitalist development from plantations to industrial accumulation in Sri Lanka were many. These range from socio-politico-economic forces to state intervention which tended to intervene in the generation, extraction and accumulation of surpluses in industry. These forces were at work for a long period in the form of a *process*; certain forces operated in an interconnected and causal fashion in this system. It is therefore important to understand the principal forces that controlled the main structure and their 'causal relations' in the process of industrial accumulation of Sri Lanka. The most important task, therefore, is to understand the relations between the state and economic structure comprising the private sector.

A small country like Sri Lanka, which was under colonial rule for a long period, and therefore had inherited a colonial economic structure was, largely, externally dependent[48]. The external sector, the leading sector, experiencing deficit balance of payments on most occasions, was a threat to the smooth functioning of the internal sector, especially after the 1950s. This caused the internal economy to adjust regularly to the changes taking place in the external sector. In this economy, the internal sector was characterised by the existence of the state, and two other sub-elements –the working class and the political elite class– which produce feedback to the state and the economic structure .

The state was entrusted with an important role in the process of industrial development. It intervened in the economy directly and indirectly, effecting changes in the economic structure whenever necessary. The economic structure comprised the private and public sectors engaged mainly in agricultural and industrial activities. Sectoral composition of this economy and the level of involvement of the state and private sectors determined the structural characteristics of this economy. These characteristics determined the intensity of accumulation in plantation, domestic agriculture, manufacturing, and service industries of the economy.

In the Sri Lankan context, the state is not an autonomous actor. It is a quasi-autonomous institution in the system. The state is influenced by non-economic factors, especially, two elements, the social (class) structure (or the pressure group structure)[49] and the elite structure[50]. The social structure comprises the household sector of different economic, social and cultural entities. The different income earning groups classified according to classes or categories are included in the social structure. Although the working class is a significant element in the Sri Lankan polity, it is, nevertheless, not as powerful as in India. The middle class element is much more predominant. Equally true is the fact that the upper middle class or the well-to-do class is powerful in this polity.

The elite structure comprises different groups of elite who hold different political ideologies and social relations with others in the society. Like in India, they are very strong in the political, social and cultural fronts. Politically, they are divided into camps as conservatives, moderates, and radicals. The elite are the 'prime movers' who bring new ideas, and ideologies into the system. They receive feedback from non-market as well as market sources and transfer them to the authority, the state. In the past, they provided the leadership in the struggle against the colonial power. Their voice had been powerful in the State Council and later in the Parliament.

The state and the economic structure are inter-linked with feedback of these two elements —the social class structure and the elite structure. The changes that take place in the state structure influence the changes taking place in the economic structure e.g., changes in the pattern of accumulation in different periods. Changes in the economic structure affect the societal structure in different ways. The favourable or unfavourable effects on the society may produce pressures within the system, which transmit itself into the elite structure in this underdeveloped small economy. The elite structure could influence the 'state' structure through political elite. For example, the political elite joining in different political camps influenced the state structure[51] . The feedback continues producing different results, short term and long term ones, changing the economic base of this country.

The relations between the state and the economy changed during the first half of the 20th century. The equilibrium in the state of relations that existed in the 19th century between the state and the economic structure based on plantations had to face various problems from internal and external political and economic environments in the first half of the 20th century. The relations that changed during this period led to the change in the configuration of the state and the economic structure. New institutions developed within the system to change the relations both at the state level and the level of the economic structure. A new strategy — industrial development— was the outcome of friendly relations between the state and the economic structure prevailed in the middle of the century.

The following simple system diagram may best explain this

behaviour of a small economy. The elements in the diagram are inter-connected; thus, the feedback also flows both ways. Sri Lanka being a small country is subject to constant interference of the external environment which changes the internal economic environment. The change in the internal economic environment affects the societal structure which in turn is transmitted to the state through the elite structure. Thus, it is a two-way process. The internal economic structure is affected by the changes taking place in different cells as well as in the external environment. Changes that take place in the internal economic environment, in turn, affect the external environment in the second round. Likewise, the elements in the system diagram are interconnected producing feedback effects. This dynamic system diagram may be employed to explain the changes (in inter and intra- period) in the capitalist development process in Sri Lanka taking into account the changing behaviour of forces in the system. Wright (1993) and Birch (1993) have developed models to explain the relations between the state and the economic structure in a political system. Those models helped to develop this diagram.

This simple model may best explain the change in complex characteristics of Sri Lanka's polity over time. First, it provides an understanding of the different roles of individual participants in the decision making process and the relations. The dominance of non-market elements in the system is a common characteristic in the early phases after independence which is explained by lines linking the two upper sub-cells. It results in the state functioning as a quasi-autonomous state in the decision-making process. This situation, however, changed over time. In the latter phases, especially after 1977, the market forces become prominent and the influence of the above elements on the decision-making process declines gradually over time. The relations between the two-sub-cells with two core cells —the state and the economic structure— in the model thus become neutral and ineffective. This long-term change in relations is normal and is necessary for a 'new nation' to continue with the process of capitalist industrial development. The slow process of change of the above relations thus determines the slowness of the industrial path of some 'new nations'.

1.5. Summary

This chapter develops the following conceptual framework highlighting the problems faced by the 'new nations', Sri Lanka, in particular.

FIGURE 1.1. MODEL OF DETERMINATION OF RELATIONS

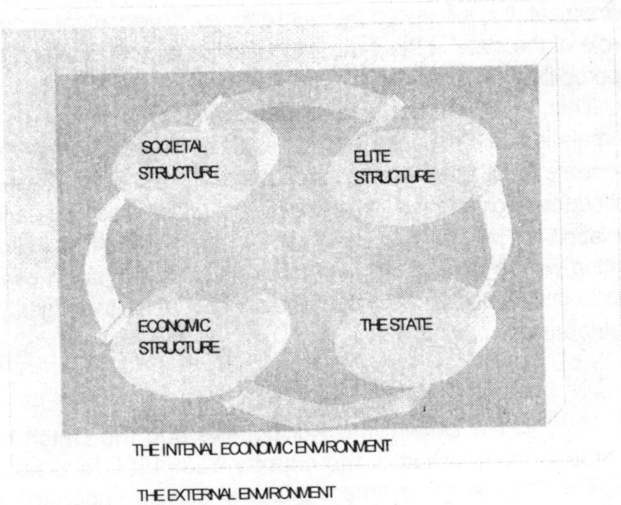

"Under the post-World War capitalist development, the 'development theory' insisted on a process of industrial accumulation for small nations, like Sri Lanka, with the initial participation of the state in the transition. It was the state and certain favourable non-market forces (and not precisely the market factors) under the 'Old Institutional Economics' that brought about changes in the colonial heritage in the initial stage of industrial development of these countries. The dynamics of the capitalist development process —the market— may take over this process at some point of time to enable it to dominate the process of industrialisation and to set limits on the state and non-market forces. The 'neo-liberal economics', would, subsequently, gain momentum over 'development economics' which coordinate economic activities in search of an optimum growth path towards industrialisation. In this effort, the state capital collaborates with local and foreign capital for a steady process of accumulation. The former assumes a 'balancing force' in the 'tripod structure'. The future growth process would continue with neoliberalism providing due recognition to the state".

Empirically, it was found that the successful and 'compressed' paths of industrial accumulation are associated with alliances of domestic capital, foreign capital and state capital in the processes of capitalist development. The Sri Lankan path of industrial accumulation apparently was a longer one than the standard short processes supported by theories of economic development. It is influenced by overextended 'development economics' and the role of the state' without adjusting itself to the neo-liberal requirements at appropriate junctures.

This work attempts to understand the process of industrial accumulation in Sri Lanka and to explain the factors that have been responsible for different accumulation practices over time. The next chapter will therefore look into the 'initial conditions' under which Sri Lanka laid the foundation for industrial accumulation in the mid-1940s. Following this, attention will be paid to the pattern of industrial formation over the long range to understand and establish the concept of its 'prolonged process' of industrialisation.

Notes

1. Prior to the British, the Portuguese and the Dutch ruled over the Coastal areas of the country from 1505 to 1796.
2. The colonial government adopted certain important measures to strengthen the process of development of plantations in the island. Among them, the establishment of the concept of private property rights, Labour Ordinance of 1865, and the development of infra-structural facilities may be mentioned as having produced an impact on the domestic economy.
3. Mainly the supportive ones like trade, finance, manufactories, and transport. With the development of infra-structural facilities, mini-towns, towns and urban centres developed and these were linked with the Capital City and the main harbour. The activities related to transport, engineering workshops, and plantations-related industries in the urban sector produced a demand for workers with different skills.
4. For example, Uyangoda (1992).
5. Gunasinghe discusses the merits and demerits of this policy. He states that ' This experiment had a certain degree of success, in terms of economic growth in the initial period of its application -especially during the period of 1956 to 1965 where the state was able to build up a certain industrial base' (Gunasinghe, 1990:3).
6. The use of the word 'small nation' is based on the familiar 'small country assumption' in international trade literature where the country concerned faces given import supply prices and export demand prices abroad. Corden uses this concept in his

analysis (Corden, 1977, 18). This concept is commonly used to highlight different characteristics of these countries (Harberger, 1998).

7. The term 'compression of the industrialisation process' is employed to explain skill accumulation in relevant industrial field (Chenery et. al. 1989:336). We use this term to imply industrial development in a relatively short period of time.
8. Adelman holds that a country should have a 'preindustrial sector well endowed with trained labor and entrepreneurs; governments that protected private property, enforced private contracts, and acted to free domestic commodity and labor markets; and leaderships responsive to capitalist interests that adopted trade, transport, and education policies which fostered technological progress...' Adelman says that European countries that had achieved economic growth by the end of 19th century had acquired these initial conditions. Another definition for the word 'initial conditions' is 'basic prerequisites for easy start of industrialisation'. (Myrdal, 1970:54-5; Clark at el., 1996:169).
9. For skocpol 'the dismantlement of colonial empires gave birth to dozen of "new nations" which before long revealed that they would not simply recapitulate Western liberal democratic patterns in their political organisation or policy choices' (Evans et al., 1985: 6).
10. This is a term used by Nicos Mouzelis to identify certain countries in the developing world (Mouzelis, 1994: 126).
11. The book review by Kanishka Jayasuriya on Kumari Jayawardena's book appeared in E-mail network distributing information on current research and other information related to Asia coordinated by Dr. Siri Gamage, University of Queensland (2001 March).
12. Akira speaks of the manner in which the 'Tripod' structure played an important role in capital accumulation in Thailand (Akira, 1989) and Evans describes similar experiences in Brazil (Evans, 1979).
13. The non-market elements may be cultural, social and political behaviours which intervene in the economic activities of people and the state. Many have written on this aspect (Myrdal, 1970; Streeten, 1993).
14. The 'new nations' bloc comprises all countries which obtained independence from colonial powers after WW2.
15. Modernisation means many things to many people. In its broadest sense, 'modernization may be thought of as how far a society has come from pre-industrial or how far it still has to

go to become post-industrial'. But in a practical sense '...modernization involves changing people as well as artifacts, resources, and leadership' (Khan, 1979: 114).

16. For Rowen (1998) 'Institutions are the humanly devised constraints that structure human interaction'.
17. Mouzelis emphasises the 'actual structure of the state that is the most crucial aspect for understanding why late developers with comparable starting points and resources have performed so unevenly within the world economy' (Mouzelis, 1994: 127).
18. Jayasuriya (2000) interprets this as '[r]ather than adopting a static and abstract view of markets and cognizing economic behaviour as independent of historical experience and institutional context, historical institutionalism conceives of markets as a structure that is determined by a complex historical past'.
19. 'Early eighteen-century British industrialisation was based, [Amsden] suggests, upon *invention* as a source of improved productivity. Here, enterprise, embodied in the small firms of the individual entrepreneur was regulated through *laissez-faire*. A second period of nineteenth-century industrialisation of Germany and the United States based upon *innovation* and enterprise embodied in the large-scale managerial firms was regulated by 'infant industry protection'. East Asia is part of a third twentieth century period of industrialisation based upon 'borrowing technology from more technologically advanced societies, or what may be called *learning*'. In the absence of novel technology, borrowed technology is incorporated into production to reach the highest equivalent levels of international productivity in this third period' (Amsden, 1990:14-16 Quoted in Cowen al. et. 1996: 429).
20. Prominent scholars use this expression to identify this group of countries from others. See Masson et al. (1999) and Collignon et al. (1999).
21. Rowen regroups the fast-growing countries into another four groups. Japan is in group one. South Korea, Taiwan (two former colonies), Hong Kong, and Singapore are in group two. Thailand, Malaysia, and Indonesia are in group three. China is in group four (Rowen, 1998:2)
22. Some loosely include Sri Lanka, India and Pakistan in the group of 'emerging market economies'. We maintain that these countries still maintain lower rates of growth compared to those 'emerging market economies'.

23. Steve Chan and Cal Clark call it the "path dependencies" that is the past influence comes from historical structuralism. See p.167, in "Do MNCs Matter for National Development? Contrasting East Asia and Latin America" (Clark et. al, 1996).
24. We use the same terminology used by Bell to denote industrial countries as 'pioneers' and underdeveloped ones as' latecomers' (Bell, 1987:818).
25. "The Limitations of the Special Case", Bulletin of the Oxford Institute of Economics and Statistics, 25(2), May 1963.
26. The rational behaviour of agents in the neoclassical system is a prerequisite for the market economy to yield desired results. This would hardly find in behaviours of economic agents in these countries.
27. He emphasised the role of the state in economic affairs. Polanyi, Karl (1946), The *Great Transformation*. Traduction francaise. Paris: Gallimard, 1983.
28. Bell noted that 'while the classical influence is still strong, development economics has come to absorb a good deal from other fields that are noticeably 'modern'' (Bell, 1987:819).
29. 'Development economics thus restored capital formation to prominence, which having been at the heart of economic theory from the eighteenth century to the First World War had then been displaced by issues of efficient resource allocation' (Wade, 1990:9)
30. Import substitution strategy was to reduce the adverse impact of poor performance of the external sectors of these countries.
31. Meier (1995:345) (quoted in Rosenstein-Rodan, 1943:204-7).
32. The fixed exchange rate policies furthered the anti-export tendencies of these economies.
33. During the late 1960s and 1970s, the rising inflation was coupled with a slowing down in long-term growth and rising unemployment- the stagflation. The oil crisis also disturbed the world economic order.
34. This is only one interpretation. Scholars like Hart-Landsberg (1993:109) and Mouzelis (1994:144) argue that the *dirigiste* characteristics of the state and the initial influence of Japan helped these countries to adapt neo-liberal policies successfully. A review on *The Rush to Development: Economic change and Political struggle in South Korea* by Hart-Landsberg in *Journal of Contemporary Asia,* 25 (3), 1993: 414 –419 provides an alternative view about Korea's development state.
35. Some fundamentals are: Macroeconomic stability, openness, the allocation of resources, property and other economic rights,

physical capital, human capital, technology (Rowen, 1998:5-7).

36. Wade explains the measures that Taiwan has taken during the seven-year period as (1) exchange rate policies favourable for export (2) reduction of protection (3) export promotional policy (4) encouragement of foreign investment.
37. East Asia incorporated 'borrowed technology' into production to reach the highest equivalent levels of international productivity (Amsden, 1990:14-16 Quoted in Cowen al. et. 1996: 429).
38. It has become the key element in the international political economy featured by the 'rising globalisation of production processes, interpenetrating of national product markets, interlocking holding if financial assets and diffusion of manufacturing technology' (Clark at. el., 1996).
39. Skocpol (1985) uses this term to signify the importance of the state in economies.
40. Boyer identifies the following areas where the government should intervene: education and training, access and financing of healthcare, production of knowledge i.e. innovation which are the core of economic growth (Boyer, 1996:86).
41. The Bretton Woods system provided a stable international financial system for 25 years. The industrial countries were booming. The US provided a large, relatively open market for the products of these countries (Rowen, 1998:1-3).
42. Helen Hughes (1995:88) discusses about how economic growth has been achieved in East Asian "7"and talks about the contribution of statist and import substitution ideologies to the development of these countries.
43. The system without conflicts. The capability of the system to facilitate good social-relations i.e., the industrial relations in workplaces.
44. Scholars ((Moore, 1985: 224-30; Lakshman, 1997:20; Abeyratne, 1998:71-77)) have highlighted the social, cultural, legal, and administrative structures and their degree of stagnation in Sri Lanka's polity.
45. The literary meaning of the word "soft" may not be counted here as Streeten warns (Streeten, 1993:1282). Soft states also go in for military violence, both internal and external. They, on one occasion, implement rigorous interventionist policies and on other, market oriented policies. The Sri Lankan State is a good case in point.
46. Baru points out that because of the large amount of public investment in the economy by the late 1970s a new capitalist

class grew which had been the driving forces for change in the mid-1980s. Jenkins quotes Sanjaya Baru (Jenkins.1990: 8).

47. Gunnar Myrdal's notion of the South Asian "soft state," in which declared policies are not implemented or not enforced, fits into this picture (Streeten, 1993:1290).
48. The import-export economic structure was dependent upon external markets. The changes taking place in the latter markets directly affect the former. This pattern was in existence in several continents; Asia, Africa and South America, and is identified as external dependency by many Scholars (Evans, 1979; Weeks, 1985).
49. Moore describes the power of different classes in the Sri Lankan polity. He refers to the struggles of the peasant class i.e., land to the tiller programme (p.61), and the nature of the Sri Lankan polity (Moore, 1985:204).
50. 'Sri Lanka has long had a highly developed bourgeois class'. ...The Sri Lankan political system is so much the creation of the upper stratum of this bourgeoisie, here termed 'the elite'...(Moore, 1985:206).
51. Such influences on the state by Marxist elite were very common in the 1930s and 1940s, and even after Independence (Moore, 1985:214-219).

2

The Evolution of An Industrial Sector in Sri Lanka The Initial Phase

2.1. Introduction

The pre-British period of Sri Lanka's history was characterised by a twofold[1] economic and political structure. After capturing the country, the British laid the foundation for a new economic order based on market economic principles inclined towards laissez-faire. The private investors, comprising mainly foreign capitalists, exploited the new opportunities that opened up in Sri Lankan soil. They gradually effected drastic changes in the economic structure. The new economic structure comprised the modern sector of plantations, ancillary industries and services, and the large rural sector of traditional agriculture, fishing, and cottage industries. The emerging class of foreign and indigenous entrepreneurs successfully effected accumulation of wealth in plantations, commerce and finance on a competitive basis.

The plantation economy opened up various avenues of earning to those engaged in plantation enterprise as well as those in ancillary economic activities related to plantations. A substantial part of this income went back to markets in the form of consumption expenditure. Over time, this resulted in the development of consumption practices influencing the entire economic machinery: production, resource allocation and distribution of goods and income. The other consequence of the plantation economy was the urbanisation process, which resulted in the formation of mini-towns, towns, cities and 'urban centers'.

Some processing industries associated with plantations flourished over time within this economic structure. Moreover, a small group of indigenous manufacturing entrepreneurs progressed with a small capital base, enjoying the benefits of the market economy. Since the late 19th century, a new class of educated elite emerged within this system, linked, particularly, to the group of indigenous entrepreneurs.

Certain conditions that arose in the twentieth century, especially after World War I, contributed to the initiation of industrial activities in Sri Lanka. Many forces were at work in producing this result. Most importantly, the diminisning prospects of the plantation economy after WW I was the main factor that led to the emergence of economic imbalances in the system. The political elite and the representatives of the politically conscious working class were engaged in a discourse over the policy of industrial development for overcoming the growing crisis in the system.

A moderate industrial development got under way with the state's participation in industrial activities during WW II. A new class of private entrepreneurs contributed largely to industrial development in this new environment. Even after the war, this process continued, opening a new path of industrialisation, which was shared by the state and the private sector. Indeed, it was essentially a 'state-led process of industrialisation' artificially motivated by underlying conditions.

This chapter is organised within the framework of the model developed in chapter 1 to study the interactions between the external sector and the internal sector in the determination of the economic structure, state policies and social structure. The chapter will inquire into causes and effects of changes in the external sector on internal economic and political structures, placing special emphasis on the development of various forces in the system over the years. (See figure 1.1 in chapter 1).

An attempt will be made here to understand the process of industrial development in Sri Lanka paying attention to the following. (1) the initiation of an industrial sector; (2) market and non-market factors which influenced industrial development in the colonial economic environment; (3) forces in the move towards industrial development and their strength; (4) changing response of the state towards industrial development, and finally (5) the character of changes in the economic structure.

2.2. Changing Political Economy

The plantation economy of Sri Lanka reached the peak of prosperity by the first quarter of the 20th century. The political economy based on the policy of laissez-faire instituted the machinery necessary for this maturity providing a legal framework for private ownership, favourable state policy for private investment and flexible import-export framework which strengthened private accumulation of wealth. The system maintained a balance between internal and external sectors coordinating financial flows between them. The colonial government was responsible for maintaining a favourable investment climate for private accumulation. This developed a dual economic structure in which the plantations became an enclave sub-system in the broad framework of the traditional agrarian economy.

These conditions changed with the beginning of the 20th century. Certain contradictions developed within the system, some of them being by-products of the system itself. The educated elite who emerged through this system began to revolt against the system with the assistance of the suppressed groups, the religious movements and the working class. The colonial government made many adjustments in the power structure, accommodating more and more local personnel at the decision making level. But, the pressure of these contradictions remained until independence that was granted in 1948.

The two World Wars disturbed the import export network of the British Empire. In Sri Lanka, in particular, these wars produced serious imbalances in macroeconomic variables like price levels, employment levels, balance of payments and more particularly on the welfare levels of the people. The adverse effects of the Great Depression of the 1930s were severely felt by the urban population whose living standards deteriorated because of severe unemployment in urban areas.

2.3. Socio- Political and Economic Forces for Structural Transformation

The transformation from feudal economy to plantation accumulation and then to industrial accumulation was a long process in which many forces interacted to determine the pattern of accumulation. The nature of this process may vary from one country to another depending upon the nature and strengths/ weaknesses of underlying forces (Bagchi, 1987:797-9). The different characteristics of these forces are determined by the changing pattern of social, political and economic environments of individual countries.

In the process of transformation of social, political and economic structures in Sri Lanka since the 19th century, three main interacting forces were significant. (1) The political forces associated with 'interest groups' (or pressure groups) working for self-determination (2) the economic forces, which brought about new pressures on the development of industries along with the plantations and (3) the social forces that influenced the setting of new targets and priorities for the new economy. These forces were active on an elementary basis separately and collectively to meet internal and external challenges of the 20th century. The working of these forces, in the short term as well as the long term, in response to changes taking place in external and internal environments determined the nature of political economy of the 20th century.

We examine here the nature and strength of, and interactions and interdependence among these different forces which evolved in the system as by-products of the plantation economy. This will be done in three stages. First, an attempt will be made to understand the nature, strengths and weaknesses of these forces. Second, the responses of different groups to the changes in external and internal development will be explored. Third, the changes in relations that took place between the state and the economic structure as a result of these changes will be discussed. In discussing the forces of change, the focus will be on market forces and non-market institutional forces (including the working class pressures and political forces)[2]

This historical process of transformation from plantations to industrial accumulation will be studied according to a rough periodisation as follows: (a) the early colonial regime of accumulation, (b) the late colonial regime of accumulation (the first half of the 20th century), a regime which continued until independence and (c) the post-independence regimes of accumulation. The period (a) covering the 19th century will be examined briefly, (b) and (c) will be dealt with, in detail, in chapters 5 and 6.

The above periodisation of the process of accumulation will help to establish the view that different forces, which developed in the system in different periods, have contributed to the determination of different relations between the state and the economic structure. It can be seen that the configuration (value system and goals) of the state as well as of the economic structure was subject to change as a result of forces which developed in the system in different periods. Some of these forces were exogenous and others endogenous.

2.4. The Early Colonial Era of Accumulation

The politico-economic system in the early colonial period fostered congenial and cordial relations between the state and the economy. The goals and priorities of participants of these two segments were more or less the same. The economic activities covered production and distribution of products of plantations, other agricultural services and manufacturing industries.

Basically, there were at least three important interest groups who played different roles in Sri Lanka's economic structure: plantation capitalists both local and foreign, the class of indentured labour[3] and others including the farming population in the rural agricultural economy. The others referred to here were the actors in the informal sector whose contribution to the determination of change in the polity was not seen to be particularly important. The state and the economy were harmoniously operating within the existing environment of social relations; the forces influencing change in the economic structure had been weak until the last quarter of the 19th century[4]. This permitted dominant groups to realise their own goals.

The objectives of the Colonial State and that of dominant economic actors (the foreign & local capitalists in the plantations sector) were almost identical in the above economy. The state practised the policy of laissez-faire allowing the market mechanism to determine the mobilisation of economic resources. The state while not interfering in the economy provided the basic infra-structural facilities to promote economic activities of the private sector[5].

In the latter part of the 19th century, the working class had gradually become politically conscious[6]. Yet, the class structure (with social relations of production) was in a very primitive state; only the urban working class was organised in the form of trade unions which exercised their power on a few occasions. However, the labour force could produce only a marginal impact on existing relations between the economy and the state. Evidently, the state and the bourgeoisie were relatively strong at least until WW I so that they were able to keep trade unions at bay[7].

Industrial accumulation was a non-issue in the given economic environment. The colonial government showed no special interest in promoting industrial accumulation in the island. It may be because of the Imperial policy of not encouraging any production in the colonies which were likely to adversely affect the interests of dominant classes in Great Britain[8]. Its interest was to promote agriculture and some processing industries which emerged as complementary by-products of plantations. The foreign and local capitalists found little economic advantage in undertaking major industrial activities on Sri Lankan soil. Whatever the industrial activity that remained in Sri Lankan soil was restricted to cottage industry.

2.4.1 The Development of Market Economic Forces

Under the given politico-economic environment, certain developments took place in the economic structure facilitating the economic transformation from old feudal orientation to new market orientation. The British, in pursuit of their colonial interests, promoted a broad economic strategy[9] to transform the existing economic structures of the colonies into a new import-export framework[10]. Correspondingly, stimuli were provided for the establishment of a network of markets linking each with the cosmopolitan market at the 'centre'. The principal market for the produce of the colonies was established at the 'centre'. This market was dependent on peripheral markets to the extent that raw materials and other primary products were to come from sub-markets in all colonies to this market.

The prices of these products were determined in this competitive market framework. The prices of tea, rubber, coconuts, plumbago etc., were relatively high at this time. This encouraged foreign capitalists to invest their funds in these products in the colonies. Within the free market economic environment, foreign and local capitalists responded favourably to these market signals[11]. They mobilised their productive resources to manufacture plantation-products such as coffee, tea, rubber, cocoa, coconuts, and mineral products like plumbago, exported them to the market at the 'centre', and earned large profits. A part of the profits of the foreign capitalists was reinvested in the plantations. Some local capitalists who owned subsidiary industries relating to plantations and others who owned plantations too reinvested their profits in the industry.

These new economic conditions paved the way for the development of new consumption habits among the people of Sri Lanka[12]. It subsequently influenced the establishment of a 'local market' for commodities. The local capitalists largely spent their earnings on consumer goods in this market. A small proportion of the wage income of unskilled plantation workers from South India[13] (the coolies) came back to the market to purchase essential items like food, as good part of their income was remitted to their kith and kin in South India. The domestic traditional sector maintained a very low level of transaction in the market. The markets for finished goods, wage goods, consumer durable and intermediate and investment goods began to grow with the growth of the plantation economy.

The supply of consumer goods to this market was met mainly through imports. A large number of traders were engaged in import trade. Proceeds from exports facilitated the importation of a variety of goods. These goods were distributed to a chain of internal market outlets through an internal network of distribution. Goods sold in these markets were food, drinks and nicotine, raw materials and manufactured goods, which were imported from other countries.

Food, drink and tobacco accounted for about 47.5 percent of total imports, on average, during the early years of the 20th century. Some items of food, drink and tobacco, for example, rice, curry stuffs, sugar and cigars were imported for the consumption largely of workers and peasants[14]. On the other hand, fish, meat, cheese, coffee, milk powder, butter, potatoes, drinks, aerated water, spirits, liquor, confectionery etc., were imported for the consumption of affluent classes of people. Machinery and raw materials like fertiliser, seeds, tea chests etc. were imported to meet the production requirements of plantation industries[15]. Other imports like tanning substances, hides and skins, coal, fire clay, raw cotton etc., were used in domestic home industries such as weaving and spinning, brass work, iron work and so on.

There has been an increase in the household demand for goods in the local market over time. For example, the proportion of the above goods in total imports grew over the first half of the 20th century and remained thereafter at a high level of 37.1 percent. These goods were manufactured elsewhere, mainly in Britain or in other parts of the British Empire, and brought to Sri Lanka for people in the 'plantations enterprise,' especially, for the affluent classes. The local capitalist class and their dependents demanded these goods at the local market.

All in all, the market economy expanded rapidly in Sri Lanka during the 19th century largely as a result of 'the plantation enterprise'. The domestic markets for the above types of goods, particularly, the consumer goods grew substantially during the 20th century. While the volume of goods transacted increased over time, new commodities too were introduced. A long list of items was imported involving large sums of money each year to satisfy the growing demand in local markets (see Table 2A1.1, Appendix 1). The household items that were becoming popular in the market were earthenware, porcelain-ware, glassware, electric goods, clothes, apparel and chemicals and service generating items like vehicles, tyres, sports items and papers. These were standard income-elastic commodities.

2.4.2. Structural Changes and Private Industrial Accumulation

'Economic structure' of this country in the 19th century was characterised by the coexistence of plantation (agricultural) industries and some manufactories[16]. The processing activities of the plantations industry paved the way for the establishment of some manufactories. The most notable one was the processing industrial base required for agricultural exports. Plumbago, for example, became an economic product with high profit margins and it required a certain amount of processing before shipment. Associated with these, some engineering workshops were opened to undertake repairs and provide maintenance facilities for plant and machinery used in processing industries. These processing industries experienced rapid growth until the beginning of the 20th century because of healthy world market conditions for plantation and other export products[17].

There was an old 'home industrial base' consisting of indigenous cottage industries even before the British conquest. It produced indigenous industrial goods for the informal local market —pottery, handlooms, silverware, iron goods and carpentry products —[18]. Local craftsmen or artisans who were operating on a small scale manned these enterprises. Capital employed was small and technology utilised was traditional and sometimes primitive. They were able, therefore, to generate only small surpluses for growth purposes.

Since the end of the 19th century, the growing market economy paved the way for the development of a light industrial-base to manufacture and supply certain commodities to the local market. These "new industrialists"[19] endeavoured to cater to the local as well as foreign demand for these goods[20]. They supplied items to the local market that were uneconomical to be imported from foreign countries. These included products like furniture, textiles, carts, rickshaws, arrack, engineering equipment, electricity generators etc. (see table 2A1.2, Appendix 1 for details). They supplied products like furniture to the home market as well as to the foreign markets.

Furniture and textiles were important industries that expanded over the years[21]. Distilling arrack for local and foreign markets was yet another profitable industry[22]. Local capitalists developed this industry by reinvesting a part of their huge surpluses derived from distilling arrack. The new light-industry sector grew slowly as it was subject to constraints like the non-availability of expertise, limited market, and their inaccessibility to commercial sources of capital and limited entrepreneurial talent[23].

The newly born light-manufacturing sector may be viewed, in a way, as training ground for the small industrialists in the home industrial base to accept challenges generated by the new market environment. Some industries like weaving and spinning, coir mills, and tiles and bricks, which existed earlier, grew under the market economic environment and developed to reach the level of light manufacturing industries. A few industries like furniture and textiles were operating on a large scale. The census carried out since 1901 provides information about these light industries, and the number of employees engaged in them, thus enabling us to map out how the relative significance of this sector evolved in the Sri Lankan economy. The Census records demonstrate that the industrial labour force was concentrated in a few broad industrial categories: textiles and coir, hides and skins, metals, ceramics, chemical products, food industries, drugs, furniture, and building materials to name some of them.

The proportion of industrial labour concentrated in the main industrial groups in each period is given in Table 2.1. Obviously, the first four categories of the table are related to the home industrial base and could be treated as traditional industries in which category 1 and 3 accommodate a relatively large labour force. Others were light industrial categories of medium scale — the newcomers to the industrial sector. The Ceylon Blue Books provide some information on a number of medium sized factories and industries[24].

Table 2.1. Labour Share in Each Industry

Item	*1911* %	*1921* %	*1946* %	*1953* %
1. Textiles	21.8	23.7	14.0	11.0
2. Wood and Baskets	0.0	0.2	0.3	0.1
3. Hides and Skins	25.6	26.7	7.7	0.0
4. Metals	0.0	0.2	0.3	0.1
5. Food industries	12.0	16.5	16.7	48.9
6. Furniture	0.1	1.1	3.0	4.3
7. Ceramics	5.6	4.0	4.6	3.1
8. Chemical Products	4.3	0.4	0.7	1.8
9. Building Industries	7.5	5.6	12.8	9.1
10. Others	23.1	21.6	39.9	21.6
TOTAL	100	100	100	100

Sources: Census of Ceylon: Reports.

However, the data in Table 2A1.3, Appendix 1, suggest that the growth of the light industrial sector over this long span of time was not very significant, in terms of number of factories.. The number of industries had increased from 8 in 1875 to 44 industries in 1938. The addition of new industries to the existing pool in each period was also not very significant as shown in row 2 of Table 2A1.3, Appendix 1.

These point to the fact that the new economic structure that was established by the British in the 19th century produced only limited structural change in the system. In this economic structure, labour enrolment in the agricultural sector was high and the proportion of industrial labour in the total labour force had remained almost constant, around 11 percent, over the long period. The distribution of productive labour force among different sectors of the economy over a long range of time follows, more or less, a uniform pattern with a slight slant from the agricultural to the 3rd and 4th sectors in subsequent periods.

TABLE 2.2. Distribution of Productive Labour Force by Type of Occupation

Type of Occupation	*1901* %	*1911* %	*1921* %	*1946* %
1 Agricultural Occupations	65.1	64.4	62.2	52.9
2 Industrial Occupations	10.6	10.7	12.0	11.0
Goods production (1+2)	75.6	75.1	74.2	63.9
3 Trading, Commerce and Finance	20.5	21.4	18.1	21.1
4 Other services	3.9	3.5	7.7	15.0
	100.0	100.00	100.00	100.00

Sources: Census of Ceylon, 1901, 1911, 1921 and 1946

2.5. The Forces of Change in the Late Colonial Era

At the beginning of the 20th century, the stable pattern of capitalist accumulation that had prevailed in the 19th century came under threat. There were symptoms of transformation in the political, economic and social environment of Sri Lanka. The changes in the internal and external economic spheres produced interactions determining changes in the environment.

The internal environment consisted of many groups of actors with different interests —the Colonial State, a new class of political elite, foreign and domestic capitalists, nascent industrialists, the working class in both the estate and urban sectors and, finally, those in the traditional rural sector. Among them, the state and the alliance between foreign and domestic (non-industrial) capitalists exerted a great deal of influence on the polity during the 19th century. The influences of the others were marginal.

The internal environment changed in the 20th century as a result of both direct and indirect influences of different forces in the system. The urban economy grew parallel to plantations in the latter part of the 19th century. The towns developed with trading and commercial activities and later with the creation of administrative units. The urban centres helped the smooth functioning of the plantation economy by providing commercial, financial, transport and port services[25]. These facilities contributed, in turn, to the accumulation of commercial and plantation capital. The plantations and commercial activities indirectly paved the way for the concentration of population in urban areas which took place gradually since the late 19th century[26]. The economic activities that developed in urban centres helped to accommodate and provide employment opportunities to the migrant population.

The plantation economy experienced a slowdown in growth since the beginning of the 20th century[27]. At the same time, the urban economy was growing at a moderate rate as implied by Table 2A1.4 in Appendix 1. This development of urban centres was later found by the colonial government to be counter-productive to the stability of the plantation economy[28]. The fast growth of urban population as an outcome of migration to cities —the side effects of the plantations and market economy— led to the intensification of urban issues and problems[29]. The urban centres became the platform from which the elite as well as the working class organised and co-ordinated their activities.

The process of strengthening class consciousness among workers had spread ever since the late 19th century and continued to grow in the first two decades of the 20th century (Jayawardene, 1972). A number of strikes were organised by trade unionists and these were, however, brought under control by the authorities[30]. Industrial relations or employer-employee relationships were seen to deteriorate gradually.

The emergence of a new class of political elite was a significant development at the beginning of the 20th century[31]. This group gradually became the dynamic force (an important variable in our diagrammatic model, FIGURE 1.1) in the system, the force which was responsible for bringing about necessary changes in the political economy The new class was still a minority in the Legislative Council, but outside they were establishing their position as a class and were exerting pressure on the colonial rulers for political reforms[32]. However, the colonial rulers were able to ignore their agitation at least in the first two decades of the 20th century.

In the early decades, relations between the class of political elite (including the new class of nascent industrialists) and the working class remained at a very low level. Also, there was no significant degree of articulation of interests between the nascent industrialists and those of the political elite at least in the early decades. The reason may be that the early political elite arose from plantation and commercial sectors and their economic interests were associated still with plantations[33]. Given this background of interests, the first generation of political elite, conservative by nature, did not engage much in matters relating to structural changes in the economic sphere.

The notion of 'industrialisation' was familiar to the political elite ever since the turn of the 20th century. Some members of the elite campaigned for active participation of the potential local industrialists in industrial development. *Anagarika* Dharmapala was the first of this kind who envisaged the development of local industries simultaneously with agriculture, taking examples from the experience of other countries like India and Japan[34]. He rejected the export-based economy which he thought was only a plot to stop the expansion of industrialisation of Sri Lanka. The business elite - the local capitalists - however, showed little response to these calls; a few of them commenced some industries but most of these industrial activities proved unsuccessful[35].

In the first couple of decades of the 20th century, the idea of industrialisation appeared in the arguments of political elite concerning future development programmes. Mr. Ponnambalam Arunachalam at the inaugural presidential address of the Ceylon National Congress in 1919 underscored the importance of industry in future development programmes of Sri Lanka[36]. He spoke of the importance of industrial, agricultural, commercial and technical education as future development strategies for Sri Lanka. Industrialisation was becoming the trump card in the struggle for economic liberation. Some members of the political elite stressed the concept of industrialisation in the struggle against colonial power.

The external environment began to influence the internal environment considerably during the 20th century. Particularly, World War I was a watershed and a turning point in the relations among main actors in the internal environment (Figure 1.1, Chap.1), especially between the leaders of the government and leaders of the economy. The war produced a wave of disturbances in the external economy. The disturbances in international trade obstructed the smooth flow of imports and exports of the island. The low volume of exports and the drop in export prices associated with the war led to a fall in the export revenue of the country (The Ceylon Blue Books, 1925:R 3; 1938: S 4). The resulting drop in foreign exchange earnings (in real terms) was a major blow to the stability of the import-export economy.

The repercussions of the changes in the external environment were many. In the short run, these produced an adverse impact on the state affecting economic activities and social classes in turn. The war disturbed public finances. Government revenue from foreign trade grew only marginally as the value of foreign trade dropped. This caused the state to practise thrifty spending on public works[37]. It resulted in an increase in unemployment. The market forces responded adversely to these changes in the urban sector. Prices of consumer goods rose as a result of scarcity caused by the curtailment of imports. The rise in domestic price levels, coupled with the increase in the rate of unemployment, was detrimental to the living standard of the people, especially in the urban sector[38].

From a long-term perspective, these developments, especially, the drop in foreign prices of cash crops and the growing unrest of the working class, adversely affected the long-term stability of the 'economic structure'. The plantation economy started showing signs of instability[39]. There was a slow down in the growth process of the old plantation economy and a change in expectations of foreign capitalists about the future of industry (Corea, 1975:75).

The first two decades were a period of strengthening and building up of a national leadership to take up challenges of the time, mainly, political[40]. Political consciousness of the elite led to the formation of a (nationalist) movement for self-determination. The individual elite-politics took a new turn after the 1920s. There was a tendency among them to group into camps. This marked a turning point in the relations between the Colonial State and the political elite. Three main camps, more or less, developed among them on class lines. One camp consisted of members who aligned themselves with the working class to follow a radical approach, demanding political and economic independence[41]. Others in the conservative extreme believed in gradual constitutional reforms. An intermediate group[42] was seen gradually emerging within the system, emphasising the interest of the peasantry in the rural economy[43]. The radical elite promoted class-consciousness among workers under the umbrella of the Young Lanka League since the 1920s (later, Ceylon Labour Union (in 1922) and was followed by the formation of Lanka *Sama Samaja* Party in 1935[44]).

This divided political elite (radical, moderate and conservative) and the urban working class were powerful forces of change in the 20th century political economy. Some of these social groups realised the limitations of the export economy and market forces relating to plantation industry[45]. They began to speak of the importance of manufacturing industries as a desirable alternative strategy to plantations. The war, thus, paved the way for a demand for structural change and diversification of the economic base.

Conflicts were seen developing gradually at the State Council level between the colonial rulers and the country's domestic political elite. The former advocated the development of agricultural industries (purely on the basis of comparative economic advantage) while the latter emphasised the importance of manufacturing industries. The latter's pro-manufacturing stand was based both on political and economic considerations. Some members of the political elite agitated in the Legislative Council for the promotion of local manufacturing industries and wanted the government to adopt a new policy of agricultural and industrial development in place of plantations[46].

The political elite was greatly influenced by the economic development of contemporary Japan and India. They wanted the government of Sri Lanka to follow the path of Japan and 'come first and start industries' as a gesture of providing assistance to the private sector[47]. Some local leaders challenged the position taken by the colonial government with respect to the investment of funds (surpluses) in securities abroad to earn higher commercial returns in the short run. They, instead, argued for a policy of investment in local industries for long term returns.

However, the pressure for structural change was relatively mild in Sri Lanka compared with other countries in the region[48]. Sri Lanka's major emphasis was on the achievement of political independence, whereas, in India, it was the reform programme based both upon political and economic objectives. Indian leaders, for example, had been fighting for the protection of local industries since the early 1920s[49]. Sri Lankan politicians never thought of tariff protection as a pre-requisite for the development of industry until the late 1930s[50]. There were speeches in the Legislative Council for industrial development from individual members but these did not represent a collective and co-ordinated voice for change[51].

World War I was a significant landmark in Sri Lanka's industrial history. It made policy makers understand the vulnerability of the classical export economy to external vicissitudes. The local leaders as well as the colonial government were forced to look for alternative economic strategies, possibly industrialisation. The colonial government, however, axed all prospective proposals for industrialisation at the legislative council by evaluating them on criteria of commercial profitability, power, market size, availability of resources etc. However, the debate about political considerations vs pure economic considerations in evaluating the viability of new industrial projects continued[52]. The local political elite favoured the former while the colonial leaders preferred the latter.

2.5.1 Post-1931 Developments

The forces generated within the system after 1931 were strong so as to exert pressure on the state to develop alternative economic policies suited to the new politico-economic order instituted by the Donoughmore Commission. The Donoughmore reforms produced lasting effects on the political system. They changed the balance of power in the State Council strengthening the local representatives as against the foreign members. The reforms changed the composition and power distribution of the legislature in favour of the local leaders[53].

Clearly, two forces were at work until independence. The first one was the political force for the transfer of political power from colonial to local leaders. The local leaders who were becoming more and more powerful in the domain of politics were able to form a counter-force to the colonial leadership. Secondly, parallel to the above developments, a force emerged in the system to change the economic structure by way of superimposing the manufacturing industry on the existing stagnant plantation base[54].

A change was witnessed in the objectives sought by the political elite. The political elite saw in the universal franchise introduced under the Donoughmore Constitution opportunities to articulate their position of paying greater heed to rural interests[55]. The electoral processes opened up new problems and prospects. The problems faced by rural voters[56], the growing unemployment in the urban areas (partly due to the rural to urban migration for better living conditions[57]), generally poor living conditions (See 2A.5, Appendix 1) and the need for social overhead expenses were matters requiring attention of the local elite.

The structure of the political elite itself changed as a new force. 'Pressure group' or 'interest group' politics intensified specially after the 1930s. Initially, the conservative faction led by Sir D.B.Jayatilake and Mr.D.S.Senanayake had the majority in the Ceylon National Congress. According to Doric de Souza these were 'men of good families' elected to the State Council in 1931(Lerski, 1968:23). There was a process of re-grouping of political elite into different ideological camps (Moore, 1985). This has been the start of a gradual move towards a political party system which grew after independence gradually coming to dominate the economic, political and social life of the people of Sri Lanka[58].

Broad group interests (instead of individual interests) began to dominate political and economic policy decisions. The major groups, those of Ceylon National Congress[59] (CNC), consisting of the conservative elite, could obtain many ministerial portfolios under the Executive Committee system[60]. Moving away from total reliance on plantation agriculture, the members of CNC gradually changed their economic policy stances toward the diversification of the economic structure. They began to incorporate food crops and industries into policies pertaining to the agricultural industrial base.

The second group, a radical Marxist group gained influence in politics around 1935[61]. A few of them were elected to the State Council and they served as a strong opposition to many Ministers who came from the ruling National Congress. This radical group, who popularised socialist ideas within the polity, dominated the Council debates. They also developed close links with rural voters (Amunugama, 1994). Marxist influence was evident inside as well as outside the State Council, and their protests produced a decisive impact on economic and political developments in the latter part of 1930s. The Marxists found that it was necessary to awaken the political consciousness of the people to prevent the State Council from remaining primarily the instrument of the affluent class. These radical political groups agreed upon a policy to completely overhaul the existing economic base and priorities[62]. They advocated nationalisation of foreign interests.

A third moderate group grew up around some persons who were earlier with the CNC but later formed their own organisation. This group led by Mr. S.W.R.D.Bandaranaike soon 'engaged in manoeuvres to exploit the opportunities opened to them' under the Donoughmore reforms (Amunugama, 1995). They gave high priority to problems in the rural sector. Amunugama writes that 'Bandaranaike was busy building up the Sinhala *Maha Sabha* (SMS) which intended to work as a definite party inside as well as outside the State Council' (Amunugama, 1994:ix).

The Great Depression of the early 1930s and subsequent disturbances to the marketing of Sri Lanka's products in foreign markets caused problems of economic management. Deficits emerged in foreign trade for the first time in Sri Lanka's history. Trade related problems thus began to cause shortages in the local market. The rate of unemployment too increased. All these led to a lowering of the standard of living[63] of the people, particularly in urban areas. The condition was further aggravated by the outburst of the Malaria epidemic in the early 1930s[64].

The most important factors that were responsible for the changes that took place in the process of economic management were the issues in the urban sector. As discussed earlier, the urban population was growing fast in the first part of the 20th century. The urban working class, their standard of living and the level of employment were the issues that drew attention of the political leaders. In particular, the incidence of unemployment among the urban youth and the poor living standard of the people were the major issues addressed by the political elite in and outside the State Council in the 1930s[65].

The new forces that developed in the spheres of politics and economics seemed to have disturbed the relations among the working class, the elite and the state, thereby producing varying impacts on the economy (as explained by figure 1.1, Chap.1). The local and foreign capitalists lost interest in the plantations mainly because of political interference and the drop in profit margins of the industry[66]. Hence, foreign investments in plantations as well as in commerce diminished during this period. The capital that left the plantations, however, had not moved towards industrial accumulation in Sri Lanka. Foreign investors appeared to have found that Sri Lanka was not a suitable location for private investment in manufacturing as high commercial returns for the investments were not forthcoming.

The majority of the political elite thought that the social and political criteria along with pure economic considerations had to be taken into account in the choice of investment[67]. They advocated a policy of active participation of the state in promoting investment opportunities in manufacturing industry. The local capitalists welcomed this perception of the political elite. They were of the view that incentives that were offered to manufacturing industry by the Ministry of Labour, Industry and Commerce were not sufficient.

2.6. Low- Level Private Industrial Accumulation

The new economic conditions after the WW I inspired two main categories of entrepreneurs to engage in economic activities in Sri Lanka. One group was the conservative investors who preferred risk-free investment and invested surpluses in sectors like land and commerce. The traditional bourgeoisie intensified their investment of surpluses (e.g., from rubber industry) in the acquisition of estates. They purchased the plantations sold by non-resident tea estate owners who left Sri Lanka before the war (Ceylon Year Book, 1948: 14). Capital accumulation by this class in plantation & commerce was considerable by the middle of this century. For example, the value of the plantation enterprise by 1924, estimated on a rule of thumb basis, was around Rs. 41,292,120, of which about Rs. 8,214,202, i.e. 20 percent, was supposedly to have been owned by this class[68]. A part of plantations owned by foreign investors seemed to have been acquired by domestic capitalists in the 1940s. This group did not convert their capital in plantations and commerce into manufacturing. Rather, they used the returns of their capital from plantations on speculative purposes (buying real estate-land and property in Colombo) and in commerce[69].

The other was the new class of light manufacturing industrialists who took certain risks in investing funds in new industries[70]. The post-WW I new economic conditions inspired this indigenous industrialist class, i.e., the local 'compradore bourgeoisie' to engage in light industries in a very small way[71]. The Great Depression in the 1930s, followed by World War II, provided unique investment opportunities for the private entrepreneur class. This class, identified as the 'national bourgeoisie'[72], raised the initial capital through involvement in 'various industries related to the war-efforts financed by the Government'. They were involved in providing timber, constructing warehouses, temporary dormitories for soldiers and prisoners of war and supplying provisions for the army thereby accumulating substantial capital.

The economic atmosphere during the war was very favourable for private industrial accumulation. The strict control over foreign trade through import licensing and quotas created a state of scarcity of commodities in the local market[73]. The exorbitant spending habits of thousands of servicemen in the island plus the expenses incurred by the Imperial government on war-activities produced an effective demand for goods in the local market[74]. The result was the formation of a favourable price structure which encouraged new industrialists (the inflation rates in 1942 and 1943 were 34.4 and 19.5, respectively, see 2A1.7, Appendix 1). This situation permitted the 'national bourgeoisie' to engage in industrial production successfully.

Three broad categories of industries, which emerged in the system, exploited the new opportunities. They were the private light industries, cottage industries (with the assistance of the state) and the public sector large industries. Exploiting favourable market conditions, the private sector industrialists established some new industries especially, in the following areas[75]:

> Basket supply, Brass foundering, Bricks and tiles, Brushes & brooms, dyers, Furniture, leather products, lime manufacturing, Matches manufacturing, Mat and Matting manufacturing, Rattan work, Soap, Tile manufacturing, Electroplating, Weaving, Manufacture of Disinfectants, Paper manufacturing, and Tin manufacturing, Saw milling, moulded rubber goods, batteries, eau-de-cologne, packing chests, toilet goods,

plywood, hosiery, lacquered goods, glass, ink, sealing wax, hand made papers, twine, biscuit manufacturing, rebuilt tyre manufacturing, rubber products, boot products, and a host of other items. Some of these have survived as permanent peacetime units[76].

The cottage industrialists assisted by the state in establishing field units, engaged in subsidiary industrial activities like textiles weaving, sericulture, coir goods, pottery, mats, *hana* (local hemp) products, hand-made paper, *wetakeiya*, and palm leaf products, fiber products, rattan goods, twine, carpentry work, needle work etc.

The rise of the domestic industrial class did not continue at the same tempo for long. Its growth gradually subsided into a slow pace due to internal politics and weak market conditions during the post-war period. With the gradual resumption of free flow of imports to the island, prices and profit rates of these industries dropped[77]. The new entrepreneurial class, discouraged by the lack of protection for their infant industries, resorted to hold a low profile in the business hierarchy[78]. Some allied with politicians and sought different types of concessions.

2.7. The Industrial Development Discourse

The local capitalists, retaining its compradore bourgeois character, continued to purchase plantation estates sold off by their foreign counterparts. This sector generated moderate returns for the capital invested in them. The market for manufactured-goods was dominated by imported items[79]. The industrial infrastructure itself remained undeveloped[80]. Consequently, there were no stimuli for transferring capital from plantations to manufacturing industry.

The investment practices of the capitalist class were appraised differently by different parties of the political elite. The conservative political elite, the members of the Ceylon National Congress, supported the capitalist class in their investments in plantations and commerce[81]. The non-conservative political elite groups, in particular, the Marxists, were against the conservative elite and criticised the behaviour of the domestic capitalist class openly. The radical-Left proposed a policy of industrial capital accumulation based on complete participation of the state[82]. They supported a development strategy based on socialist principles to solve problems like unemployment and the poor living standards of the people.

Indeed, the moderates as well as conservatives were convinced of the necessity for change in the economic structure towards manufacturing. They felt the need for the provision of effective assistance by the state for industrial development programmes of the private sector[83]. However, the 'state-aided industrial development' of the Colonial State in the 1930s was meant only to supply infra-structural assistance to the private sector[84]. The Ministry of Labour, Industry and Commerce took measures to provide scientific research, train labour skills, supply cheap power, open up avenues of credit for local entrepreneurs and to revitalise the share market of Sri Lanka.

In practice, the provision of incentives to the private sector by the state to promote manufacturing industries produced little result. The private entrepreneurs responded slowly to these signals. As a result, there was an element of sluggishness in private industrial development during this period. The state viewed this as a lack of enthusiasm on the part of private entrepreneurs to form industrial enterprises on a large scale. As a new move, the state established certain model industrial enterprises in the late 1930s to encourage the private sector.

The system was once again disrupted by the shock of World War II and confusion of its aftermath. The war situation necessitated an ad hoc policy of industrialisation under the initiative of the state in the form of a contingent plan to provide goods needed for the war economy. As a result, the government opened up some eight industries[85] to produce miscellaneous items to the system[86]. The war economy thus witnessed experimentation of another model of industrial development – 'state enterprises in a market economy'. In fact, this model was quite different from that of the radical option which emphasised the need for the state to undertake industrial accumulation in a socialist economic context. Importantly, the war economy introduced a new element called 'state capital' into the process of industrial development in a capitalist market framework.

The post-war economic conditions have led different factions of political elite to come to a consensus about an alternative economic strategy. There was a consensus among them to initiate a 'project of industrialisation' expeditiously. This desire of elite was well expressed in their speeches in the State

Council at the time of the debate on the 'Industrial Corporation Bill' of 1944[87]. Many State Counsellors argued for the development of industries as an essential prerequisite for the achievement of economic progress. Some argued that 'the progress of the country, its place in the civilised society was to be judged by the extent of industrialisation achieved. '[I]f the country wants to progress, if it wants a higher standard of living for its people, rapid industrialisation was very essential' (Dudley Senanayake in Hansard, 1944:437). Perhaps, this was the outcome of the long campaign of the elite in the past for industrial development of the country. It led to the formulation of a general plan to carry out 'the project of industrialisation'[88].

The post war 'project of industrialisation' of the political elite came out as a "report on Industrial Development and Policy" in 1947. It was a combination of slogans of 'state-aided industrialisation' within a market economic environment and 'direct state participation' in industrial development as was the case during the wartime. Opinions did not differ much among representatives of different 'interest groups' with regard to the formulation of the industrial project and its ultimate objectives.

The private sector-oriented industrial development, earlier stressed by some CNC supporters, lost its credibility as an economic strategy because of the criticisms directed against possible monopoly practices that could develop with the prevailing non-competitive market economic environment[89]. The mild reformists in the State Council advocated a "state-led" industrial policy (which was different from 'state-aided' policy). The Marxist option was not strongly reflected in the project owing to their limited representation in the State Council during the 1940s when the project was initiated.

The outstanding feature of elite politics since WW II is the change in their approach to national issues. Political parties with different ideologies were formed. Individual politics was replaced gradually by party politics. The formation of the Lanka *Sama Samaja* Party (LSSP)(1935), the Communist Party (CP) (1943), the United National Party (UNP) (1946) and the Sri Lanka Freedom Party (SLFP) (1951) can be noted in this regard. While the UNP stood for private sector-oriented industrial development, the Marxists in the LSSP and the CP favoured an industrial development through state capital. Later, the SLFP began to espouse an intermediate position and promoting a mixed economic system.

The decades after World War II (especially after independence) witnessed the development of new forces in the system combining political, economic and social issues. The growing disequilibrium experienced during this period in the external sector had some influence on the emergence of these new forces.

2.8. The State Project of Industrialisation

The accidental wartime participation of the state in industries brought about a new dimension into the process of industrial development. As discussed earlier, it led the State Council to embark upon a dialogue on the theme of industrial policy in the post-war general plan for economic development. The changing outlook of local as well as global political dimensions after the war inspired this dialogue. The change of outlook was a product of war-related uncertainty and world-wide changes in political economic priorities.

The post-war economic reforms in developed as well as developing world were centred on two alternative propositions, namely, industrialisation and structural change (a) through market economic principles and (b) through socialist mode of planning. India, for example, chose a mixed economic model based on planning principles with the collaboration of the private sector[90]. These Indian economic policies have influenced the designing of the 'state project of industrialisation' in Sri Lanka.

The objectives of the 'state project of industrialisation' in Sri Lanka were the promotion of economic development and the provision of employment opportunities through industrial development'[91]. This was aimed at raising the standard of living of the people by 'increasing the national wealth and by preventing the flow of money from Ceylon to foreign counties'[92]. The constraints that the project was likely to face too were identified[93]. Limited participation of the private sector was anticipated to be a potential bottleneck, and limitation of the state machinery to promcte efficiency in state-aided industries was identified as another impediment.

Though industrialisation was the main projects of the state, there seemed to have been no clear consensus among political leaders as to how the project was to be implemented to achieve the desired goals. This question of the mode of implementation of the project was engulfed in class politics since the early

1940s. Industrialisation for whom and by whom was the theme over these years and this problem was continually debated throughout the industrial history of Sri Lanka.

Two basic issues dominated arguments in the 1940s regarding the 'general policy of industrialisation'. One was the control of industries and the other was the ownership of enterprises. Some favoured the introduction of various controls over industrial development. Learning from the experience of other countries, particularly India, it was the general opinion that some industries needed to be left entirely in the hands of the state[94]. 'Some basic industries like power, heavy industries i.e. steel, cement and the industries which provide the necessities of life should be state-owned'. 'With regard to non-basic industries, the government was expected to undertake industrial research, publish those research results, establish pilot factories, and provide whatever help is necessary for private capital to increase the natural wealth'. It was felt that these industries were required, exclusively, to be owned and controlled by the state in the greater interest of the society[95]. All others were handed over to the private sector.

The manner in which *ownership* of industry was viewed was as varied as the political ideologies of the political elite itself. The issue of ownership was debated at the State Council level on the bill of Industrial Corporation where the members freely expressed their views opposing private sector dominance in the industrial development in Sri Lanka. The transformation of state enterprises that were established solely because of the exigencies created by the war into joint ventures or into public companies was the focus of the debate. Majority of members was of the opinion that this transformation would eventually end up in a monopoly of few capitalists[96].

There was, however, a sort of consensus among the Council members that both the state and the private sector needed to be involved in the implementation of the project. The difference, however, remained in the degree of involvement by each party in the process of industrialisation. The report on industrial development and policy by the Ministry of Labour, Industry and Commerce summarised the outcome of the debate on the question of ownership and the control of industries which had hitherto been established. Taking more of a democratic and conventional stand, it proposed an industrial plan[97] for Sri Lanka and suggested some measures[98] for the implementation of the plan.

After independence, the political party system that evolved incorporating all existing ideological bases began to address new issues on a bi-partisan basis. The political parties developed own manifestos addressing current issues under the framework of individual party ideologies and offered packages of solutions to problems. All parties in their manifestos gave 'the state project of industrialisation' significant recognition.

2.9. Post independence Economic Regimes

This section provides an overview of different economic regimes that prevailed in the post-independence era. Since independence, several economic regimes came into existence under the influence of different political ideologies of political parties which eventually developed 'into a unique bi-party system with two broad groups contending for ruling power' (Lakshman, 1973:16). These political parties were in power at different periods and implemented their own economic programmes to promote the process of industrial accumulation. In analysing the effects of economic regimes on economic development, the critiques have divided the period after independence to different segments[99]. We adopt a periodisation quite similar to that of others but is specific to the process of capital accumulation.

The first is the period between 1941 and 1956 where the 'colonial elite'[100] who had faith in market-oriented economic policies exerted their influence on the determination of economic policies. This regime continued until 1956, followed by a new regime constituting 'nationalist elites' who exerted tremendous pressure on the decision making process, thereafter. This second phase was characterised by the implementation of new strategies based on 'socialist-oriented economic policies within the mixed economy'. This phase lasted for about 8 years from 1956 until 1964.

In the third phase between 1965 and 1970, the economic regime re-introduced market-oriented economic policies and sought for active co-operation of the private sector in the process of economic development. In the fourth phase during 1971-77, the 'nationalist elite' brought in planning-oriented economic policies for the second time, the strategic theme of which was known as 'socialist policies with inward looking approach'. In the fifth phase, from 1978 to 1985 and from 1989 to 1994, market economic policies with an export-led development strategy came into being under a 'free and liberalised market economy'. The regime after 1994 was primarily concerned with 'market economic policies with a human face'.

The above periodisation could be summarised in the following form relating to different types of economic policies implemented by various political parties.

1952 - 55: market-oriented economic policies,
1956 - 64: planning-oriented economic policies,
1965 - 70: market-oriented economic policies,
1971 - 77: market-hostile economic policies
1978 - 85: market-oriented economic policies,
1986 – 89: period of internal conflicts,
1990 - 94: market-friendly economic policies, and
1994 - 98: market and employee-friendly economic policies.

The period 1986-89 was quite different from the rest as ethnic problems and JVP[101] insurrection disturbed the political and economic stability of the country. A detailed analysis of the impact of the economic regime on accumulation will be carried out in later chapters. This brief account is only an attempt to provide background information.

2.9. Conclusions

The relations between the state and the economic structure underwent a series of changes over the 20th century. The relations that prevailed in the 19th century between the state and the economy were disturbed by the changes in the internal and external politico-economic environment. Externally, the wars impaired the import-export machinery. Internally, the relations changed in part as the state was subject to change its configuration, values and composition, and in part, changes took place in the economic structure. The influence of the political elite, the process of urbanisation and the deterioration of economic conditions had been responsible for these changes.

One cycle of investment in plantations reached saturation point and another cycle of investment in manufacturing emerged in the system in the late nineteenth century and grew slowly over the years. The new investment cycle was slow in progress until the end of the 1940s. There were no stimuli from the economic environment for it to grow independently. Unlike in plantations the natural resource endowment was not supportive of the new sector to prosper autonomously, and it had, therefore, to rely very much upon the state for it to grow out of infancy.

The political elite, realising the dynamic characteristics of the industrial sector, promoted it at the State Council level as the potential leading project of the economy. But, the private sector did not show much enthusiasm to take part in manufacturing until the late 1930s. This situation changed in favour of the industrial sector in the late 1930s. The deteriorating economic conditions and the worsening prospects of plantations led the state to directly participate in industrial activity. The war conditions stimulated the private sector to participate in manufacturing activities on a fairly significant scale.

Industrialisation became basically a state project. The new project required the effective participation of all parties, the public and the private sectors. From its inception, the effective participation of the private sector in the project was determined by the dominance of many factors, both economic and non-economic in the system. It would therefore be interesting to observe how the new sector would grow in the new econo-political environment after independence. One thing, however, is certain from past experience that the state would have to shoulder all burdens until at least the project reached maturity and could survive on its own.

The process of industrial accumulation after independence took many turns. Its path has been highly cyclical. The two major partners, the state and the private sector, who were not having a common programme, acted differently in different phases. The next chapter elucidates the changing pattern of private accumulation in different sectors of the economy under changing conditions. The chapter will identify the attitudes and preferences of the private sector in involving in the industrial development of a small nation.

Notes

1. One was the Sinhala Kingdom in the interior of Sri Lanka and the other was the foreign dominated coastal belt.
2. There can be others like social forces but those will be incorporated into the above because the purpose of the study is economic. Again, there can be interactions among these

forces to build a common force which can also be integrated into the analysis as the study proceeds.

3. The class of labour comprised seasonal migrants from India whose strength as a class was practically nil.
4. Kumari Jayawardena (1972) says that the political consciousness in the labour force was very low until 1920s.
5. Institutions were developed to transfer the feudal structure to a market economy. A communication network was developed constructing a road and railway network. Postal services, educational and medical facilities were provided. Facilities were provided to assist the migration of Indian Tamils into the plantations sector. Rigorous labour laws were introduced in 1862 to facilitate the exploitation of labour force to make surpluses (DE Silva, 1981).
6. Kumari Jayawardena (1972) gives an account of the growth of class-consciousness among the labour and the political consciousness among the elite.
7. For example, the State using the Police controlled the strike at Caves & Co. in 1892. Similarly, the strikes in railway and transport sectors were controlled in the same manner (Jayawardene, 1972).
8. This position was taken by Mr. T.H. Chapman, the chairman to consider the development of Ceylon's resources. "Sessional Papers" VI- 1921, Development of Economic Resources of the Colony, P4.
9. The British colonial economic strategy was to promote the production of raw materials in colonies and export them to the motherland for the industries at home. The finished products were to be sent back to the colonies in which process the colonialists were able make double profits from the operation.
10. The Coolebrooke Commission's recommendations led to the creation of a market economy in Sri Lanka through the advancement of capitalism and elaboration of its administrative and judicial structure during the 19th and 20th centuries (Roberts, 1979:159).
11. There were about 22 indigenous planters by 1874 according to Fergusion's Ceylon Directory, 1875. But this has grown to about 224 (non-European Land owners) in accordance with names and sizes of land in 1927 (Roberts,1979:166).
12. The consumer class comprising foreigners and local personnel

who were benefited by the growth of the plantation economy, was prepared to spend their incomes to consume not only the locally-produced goods but also those imported goods both essential and luxury.

13. For example, the Indian plantation labourers, railway construction gangs, carters and other workmen demanded commodities including Arrack. (Roberts, 1979:169).
14. The list of goods and the expenditure on them is given in Ceylon Blue Books, from 1901.
15. Some raw materials imported under this category were: Coal, fireclay, precious stones, semi- precious stones, wood, timber, raw cotton, cotton waste, textile materials, gums, oil & fats, geese, vegetable oil, hides & skins, dry salt, rubber canes, ivory, fertilizer, seeds, shells, tanning substances.
16. The word 'manufactories' was used in Furguson's Directory (1875) to denote industries with a relatively large labour force and with certain machinery which used power. This new manufacturing sector in the 1870s employed about 1297 total effective horse power engines, 90 steam engines, about 19,861 men and boys, 16 practical engineers and 56 managers (Ferguson, 1875:676).
17. There has been a rapid growth of tea, rubber and coconut factories and engineering sheds since the beginning of the 20th century. The Ceylon Ferguson's Directory and the Ceylon Blue Books provide information on the magnitude of these industries.
18. By 1975 a substantial number of factories in the following categories existed according to Ferguson.

1. Handlooms	1027	2. Mat and grass bags	560
3. Potteries	587	4. Silversmiths' shops	1197
5. Blacksmiths' shops	865	6. Carpenters' shops	1726

Source: Ferguson's Directory, 1875: 676.

19. A few Sri Lankan capitalists had enrolled in the organised light industrial ventures. ' These enterprises are witness to the increase in specialisation and the linkage between specialisation and urbanisation '. Some of these were engaged in printing and in the manufacturing of aerated water, Matches, Candles etc. They were new to industrial development and had no experience as a class of industrial bourgeoisie like in India. The lack of experience and independent motivation with

regard to industrial development caused the local bourgeoisie to accumulate capital mostly in plantations and commercial sectors following their foreign counterpart.

20. In addition to the major cash crops the following things were also exported by Sri Lanka in the year 1900 :

    Raw materials

    textiles (cotton), metal and chemicals, dyeing and tanning materials

    Manufactured Articles

    Textiles- Apparel, cotton, lace and nets

    Metal (other than machinery)

    Brassware, copperware, hardware, carriages and carts, furniture, glass and glass ware, mats, mat bags and baskets.

    Source: Ceylon Blue Book, 1900: 62.

21. H. Don. Carolis & sons started their furniture business in 1860 in a small way and began to supply furniture to planters and for export to Asia. The furniture was manufactured according to European styles. A team of expert carpenters from Moratuwa was employed and a firm of steamed furniture work was started in Slave Island. About 250 skilled workmen were employed in it. It possessed a well-trained staff. Michael Roberts (1979:165) gives some information on the development of new trades in the plantation areas for the supply of furniture, timber, barrels, arrack, railway sleepers and telephone poles etc. These have provided opportunities for sawmill owners and timber dealers to engage in these trades. He has also given a list of names of the people who were engaged in these professions and their degree of success.

22. By 1975 there were about 158 arrack distilleries in Sri Lanka according to Ferguson's Ceylon Directory. Patrick Peebles has estimated that the arrack renters of the year 1896- 97 made a net profits of some five to six million Rupees (Peebles, 1973).

23. The Banking Commission, 1935, highlighted the problems faced by the local industrialists some of which were the shyness of capital, unavailability and laziness of the domestic investors.

24. The following are some products manufactured under the broad industrial headings:
    Ceramics :
    Items like glass, fancyware, glass bangles etc.
    Chemical products:
    Matches, explosives, aerated water, Mineral water, refined vegetable oil, soap, candles, perfume and drugs etc.
    Food industry:
    Bakeries, Biscuit manufacturing, confectionery work, sugar manufacturing, Distiller, brewing etc.
    Dress industry:
    Tailoring, dressmaking, shoe-making etc.
    Furniture:
    Cabinet making, Carriage makers and painting, furniture making etc.
25. Michael Roberts in writing on the question of the early city centers mentions that ' the steadily increasing population within the South-Western region with Galle and Colombo serving as growth centers as the beginning of urbanisation were witnessed' (Roberts, 1979:163).
26. Country Monograph series No.4, the United Nations, 1976, Economic and Social Commission for Asia and Pacific, on the Population of Sri Lanka provides some details about the formation of towns and cities in Sri Lanka and factors of urbanisation.
27. The slackening of the rate of expansion caused mainly by the 'cessation of foreign investment associated with a change in the international economic position...' (Corea, 1975:83.)
28. Counter-productive in the sense that the growth of urban centers became the battle ground for the struggle against the colonial practices which were opposed by workers and the radical groups.
29. Urbanisation created a huge demand for social overheads, housing and communal amenities, including sewerage, water supply, street lighting, tramway and telecommunications (De Silva, 1981: 75).
30. A few Strikes were organised in 1906, 1912 and in 1923, 1927 and 1928 showing the growth of strength of the working class (Jayawardene, 1972).
31. The special features tof the elite were (1) power: political,

economic, and holding of office (2) Status: distinctive life-style, high social status and access to the valued intellectual and cultural activities (Roberts, 1979:153). Moore writes on Sri Lankan elite (Moore, 1985:205- 230).

32. For example, there were only *three* local members out of *seventeen* members in the Legislative Council (two Sinhalese and a Muslim) in 1900.
    In 1910, only *five* (two Sinhalese, two Tamils and a Muslim) members out of *seventeen* members in the Legislative Council.
33. The members of the political elite like F.R.Senanayake started with arrack renting and switched on to plumbago mines and plantations whose interests were on agriculture (Roberts, 1979). De Silva refers to Henry Maccullum's writing (1910), on the emergence of a new elite 'who were anglicanized, received a western education and were alienated from the people' (De Silva, 1981:327).
34. *Anagarika Darmapala* urged the local industrialists to participate in industrial activities. He was influenced by the development in Bengal and Japan during the period. Simon *Hewavitharana* and *Edmond Hewavitharana* pioneered the promotion of industries locally. They formed industrial schools formed a scholarship fund to train industrialists abroad.
35. The book on 'All Ceylon Industries, Eastern Province Manual', 1st Exhibition, March 1922, Colombo by Wesleyan Mission Press, Baticaloa, provides some industries which were operated successfully during the period between 1911 and 1922. Some of these industries were weaving, brass work, Iron work, Pottery, Baskets, Mats, Jungle ropes, Preserved food, Carpentry, Needlework, Gold & Silver work, Vegetable etc.
36. The Ceylon National Congress (1919): 12.
37. The Statement made by the Governor at the Legislative council elaborate this curtailment of expenses for the purpose of War needs "Ceylon Sessional papers", 1916. See also the Address by the Governor William Henry Manning, Proceedings of the Legislative Council of Ceylon, June 8, 1922, See "Ceylon Sessional papers", 1922.
38. See Economic and Social Development of Ceylon, 1926 -1950, (a Survey).

39. 'A decline in export has its inevitable repercussions on domestic investment, the cessation of foreign investment etc., (Corea, 1975:88).
40. Basically, two long-term objectives have loomed largely in the behaviour of the political elite. (1) The gaining of political independence and (2) the achievement of economic independence, and in the later stages the ' industrialisation.'
41. The important person in this category was Mr. A.E.Goonasinghe who formed the Ceylon Labour Union in 1922 as a new model trade union which helped him in entering into the political arena. The new political elites tried focus to social and economic problems of the masses (De Silva, 1981:398-400).
42. Peiris (1958: 4) in his book gives importance to this group in class politics. He asserts that this class was politically inefficient up to 1931. Its momentum of growth effectively started since the Donoughmore reforms.
43. Mr. S.W.R.D.Bandaranaike took the lead in this direction, using *Mahajana Sabas* 'sought to revitalise the rural areas and to politicise the peasantry', (De Silva, 1981: 398).
44. Amarasinghe (1998:7) provides a detailed account on the formation of LSSP.
45. In the Legislative Council some political elites have openly expressed their views regarding the limitations of the plantations economy. For example, Mahadeva (Hanzard, 1926:845-846).
46. For example, F.A.Obeyasekara (*Hansard*, 1926:1546).
47. For instances, D.B.Jayatilaka (*Hansard*, 1926: 1615).
48. In India, the pressure generated in the system for promotion of some industries was strong ever since the mid-nineteen century (Chaudhuri, 1939).
49. The appointment of the Indian Fiscal Commission to study the prospects of granting tariffs protection to industries was a new development, (Chaudhuri, 1939:369-379).
50. Some measures were adopted to adjust some tariff duties in order to assist certain industries like tobacco, soap and safety matches. These industries were provided partial protection (Peiris, 1994).
51. 'The demand for industrialisation by the local leaders was seen by the colonial government largely as an expression of nationalist emotions.' (Oliver, 1957: 9) .

52. Some critics assign the political considerations and leadership to the success of Japanese industrialisation (Bagchi, 1987:799)
53. But power over crucial areas i.e., Finance, was with appointed officials representing colonial government.
54. Fred. V. Taylor analysing the situation in the 1930s asks 'Why that every body in Ceylon today is interested in the *economic restructuring* of the Island? ' His explanation to it is that ' the reason is to be found in the present economic conditions of Ceylon. Of the major industries in Ceylon, the tea industry is just paying its way. The Coconuts industry struggling for existence and the rubber industry is worse than not paying which will take the place of the sinking industries ' (Nicholas, 1933 :146).
55. Marxists like S.A.Wickremasinghe, N.M.Perera, Phillip Gunawardene and moderate leaders lik S.W.R.D.Bandaranaike and A. Ratnayake arose through the support of rural voters.
56. The living standard of the rural population, health problems, landlessness, irrigation problems and employment problems were some new issues that have to be addressed by the political elite.
57. Mr. A. E. Goonasinghe has said that 'There are hundreds of men who come into the town asking for jobs to do simply because their villages cannot provide them with a means of living, with even a day's meal', (Hansard, 1932 :2941).
58. The conservative group believed in liberal democratic philosophy. The Marxists (formed the Lanka *Sama Samaja* Party (LSSP) in 1935), believed in 'Marxian Socialism' strongly favoured State enterprises and State controlled economy. The moderate group (formed the Sri Lanka Freedom Party (SLFP) in 1951) believed in 'social democracy' on a mixed economic base.
59. It, however, was dissolved in 1947 a new political party - the United National Party was established.
60. Don Baron Jayatilake, Senanayake, Obeysekara, Kotalawela, Jayawardene were the pioneers concerned with the growth of agriculture. Their interest was to be self-sufficient in food and to promote irrigation facilities. See in ' Social and Economic Changes' 1931-1947(De Silva, 1981).

61. Starting from A.E.Goonasinghe with the Lanka Youth League, the pioneers N.M. Perera, S.A. Wickremasinghe, Philip Gunawardene, Colvin R.de Silva etc., with 'the 'Suriya Mal movement' formed "the first Ceylon political-propaganda Center for full independence" p.250, Ludewyk is quoted by George Jan Lerski. 1968.
62. The policies are documented in the manifesto, which includes i. an introduction of a National Public Works programme, by the Government ii. a policy of industrial development iii. Socialist economy etc. (Lerski, 1968: 48).
63. See 'Economic and social development in Ceylon', 1951.
64. Malaria Epidemic 1934-35 took some 125,000 lives (Lerski, 1968: 6).
65. The main economic struggle of LSSP was against the plague of unemployment. N.M.Perera pointed out that ' this is the inexorable social law of capital accumulation' (Lerski, 1968:48).
66. The anti-capitalist and nationalist forces began to surface within the system. Estate labour was becoming powerful in the post 1931 era.
67. In State Council Debates, S.W.R.D.Bandaranaike, (Ceylon Hanzard, 1944: 461), Also (Lerski, 1968: 21);.
68. This estimate was done in the Furguson's directory on the Ceylon Planting Enterprise and it was modified to separate the share of the Sri Lankan Capitalists (Ceylon Ferguson's Directory, 1925: 26).
69. Samarakkody spokes on nationalisation of Estates (Ceylon Hansard, 1957:2519-20).
70. Mr. Sundaram in his report to the State Council in 1933 mentioned that private sector manufacturers of printer's ink, soap, candles, cordials, preserves, pencils, matches, tea chest, perfumes, distemper have appeared for assistance. Mr. A.E.Goonasinghe mentioned some names of the industrialists who sought assistance (Hansard, 1939).
71. Michael Roberts draws a distinction between the indigenous (compradore) bourgeoisie and the foreign Compradore Bourgeoisie in Sri Lanka. (Roberts, 1979: 153).
72. Mick Moore (1985:212) discusses the development of a National Entrepreneurial Class in Sri Lanka.
73. The control of imports was necessitated for the conservation

of shipping space and foreign exchange. Some food items e.g. rice, consumer goods like textiles and other raw materials like paper, chemicals for various products and cotton yarn for weaving were subject to control (Ceylon Year Book, 1948:117). At the same time, the wartime breakdown of navigational transport facilities deterred the flow of imports to the island and artificially created a State of scarcity in the local market.

74. In Sri Lanka the Imperial Government seemed to have spent about Rs. 400 million by 1944 on the war-effort (Ceylon Year Book, 1948).

75. Secondary information on these industries is difficult to trace. However, as a substitute the records maintained by the Ferguson's Ceylon Directory can be utilised to observe the developments during the wartime economic atmosphere. The names of some popular industrialists are also given in the Colombo trade lists:

    Fernando G. P, Uttamadasa & Co., Jinadasa and sons, Don Theodoris & sons, Ceylon Cottage industries, the Hydraulic Bricks & tiles works, the Terrazzo Tile works, Brush and broom factory, various furniture Companies (by 1950 there were about 41 such Cos.), Ceylon safety matches manufacturing Co. Ltd., Ceylon Industrial Development Co., Colombo match works, Swadeshi Industrial works Ltd., the Match works, Don Carolis & Sons Ltd. Fernando S. P and Co., Electroplating and Iron works, Borella Textiles School, Ceylon Spinning and Weaving Co., Colombo Biscuit manufacturing Co., Maliban Hotels, Wahids paper factory, Dickinson & Co.Ltd., Richard Peiris & Co. Ltd. Rubber industries ltd. Singer Sewing machine Co., Ceylon Tin Manufacturers, Ceylon Tyre Co., Ceylon Tyre rebuilding Co., General Tyrecraft & Motor Co. etc.

    Sources: Ferguson's Ceylon Directory (1935, 1938,1941, 1944, 1946, 1947, 1950). Ceylon Year Book, 1948.

76. Ceylon Year Book, 1948.

77. There was a general tendency to remove all controls and to bring the economy back to the competitive base. 'By the end of 1946, imports were in large quantities'. For detailed information on the relaxation of control see p.11, Ceylon Year Book, 1948.

78. Ferguson's Directory does not maintain the names of some companies which were maintained in the directory during War period. This may be either due to the deliberate drop of these names by the Directory or due to the non-existence of these companies when the trade lists were being compiled. Some examples related to 1956 can be cited:
In Leather manufacturing, Seneviratna Tanneries and Chrome Leather Cos. do not appear in the directory.
In Tiles Manufacturing, Hydraulic Bricks & tiles Works and Trust Brand tiles do not appear (Ferguson's Directory, 1943; 1945; 1956).
79. The import of consumer goods like textiles, leather products and other light manufacturing items from East Asia and India at cheap prices weakened the local manufacturers of accessing to the newly growing local market for these goods (Peiris, 1994).
80. Smallness of the market, absence of organised manufacturing industrial base and the lack of a resource base, particularly, the under-developed share market were the major reasons for the underdevelopment. Industries Commission report in 1922 and the Banking commission in 1935 highlight these shortcomings.
81. The policy of the Jayatilake - Senanayake leadership was the 'collaboration with imperialism and defence of the existing socio- economic structure'. (Lerski, 1968: 22).
82. LSSP Publication No.2, (Lerski, 1968).
83. The industrial policy document highlighted the role of the state as a promoter of industries. It distinguishes the role of the state in three directions: (1) Provision of technical assistance and scientific research facilities (2) Provision of financial grants and subsidies to the development of industries (3) Opening the credit market to the local industrialists with the state-aided banking facilities (Ceylon Hansard, 1935).
84. See the report of the Industries Commission, 1922. The Banking Commission (1935) has identified these constraints and recommended extending the credit market for the small and medium scale industrialists. It suggested forming a state-aided bank to assist the above groups.
85. The State stepped into the hitherto closed field of 'Commercial undertakings' and established several major industrial ventures

during the war years. Factories were set up for the manufacture of coir (1940), leather- boots and shoes (1941), plywood (1941), quinine and other drugs (1943), steel re-rolling (1941), plywood (1941), paper (1942), glass (1944) and ceramic (1944) (W. D. Lakshman, 1976).

86. See the State Council debates on Industrial Corporation (Ceylon Hansard, 1944: 425).

87. Mr. J.R.Jayawardene outlined the project proposal (the industrial plan) in which he divided the industries into 'Key industries', Heavy industries and consumer goods industries. He talked about the industries held by the State and those by the private sector (Ceylon Hanzard, 1944:652).

88. The demand for a comprehensive plan for industrialisation goes back to the 1930s. Mr. Amarasuriya (Galle) proposed a motion in the State council in 1937 demanding that ' consequent to the increase of unemployment in the country the government should take immediate steps to introduce a well-considered scheme of State-aided industrial development'. In 1944, Mr. J.R.Jayawardene requested the State Council to submit a complete plan for industrialisation. In 1945, Mr. J.Tyagaraja made a similar demand for a plan (Ceylon Hansards, 1944).

89. Mr. J.R.Jayawardene vehemently opposed the idea of handing over the State factories to a Public Company. Mr. Aluvihare, Mr. S.Samarakkody, Mr.Dudley Senanayake, Mr.C.W.W. Kannangara, Mr. S.W.R.D.Bandaranaike, Mr.A Ratnayake and other prominent members opposed the bill. They criticised the capitalist practices (Ceylon Hanzard, 1944: 427-471 and 650-650).

90. Anupam Sen quoting ' the plan of Economic Development of India ' (known as Bombay Plan) p.5, (Signatories to the plan were: J.R.D.Tata, G. Birla, Shri Ram Purshottomdas Thakurdas, Ser Ardeshir Dalal, John Mathai, A.D.Shraff and Kasturbhai Lalbhai) (Sen, 1982:.92).

91. Mr. J.R.Jayawardene making an ' excellent speech and the sentiments' pointed out that the pure private profit motivated industrial plan to this country would be unacceptable and an industrial plan based on the humanitarian point of view needed to be developed. The objective ' to increase the standard of living for the people by providing better food, clothing and so on must take into consideration what industries this little

country of our can develop' (The Ceylon Hansard, 1944: 651).

92. Parliamentary Debates (Ceylon Hansard, 1948: 1045).

93. Mr. S.W.R.D.Bandaranaike in his deliberation has identified the difficulties faced by the industrial programme in Sri Lanka in 1944. '.... the general difficulty of having to compete with established industries outside, the difficulty of taking certain steps to which Imperial interests have been opposed definitely in the past, difficulties of the foreign markets. In this light of such a possibility let us examine this proposal' (Ceylon Hansard, 1944: 461).

'One of the problems facing many countries today is that created by the fact that Big Business, large-scale industries have come under the control of one or two corporations or families. It has been stated that most of the international problems that have arisen through out the world were accentuated by the fact that Government was unable to control Big business in the countries concerned. We have also heard it Stated that in Japan.'.., Mr. S. Samarakkody (Ceylon Hansard, 1944: 436).

94. The Minister of Labour, Industries and Commerce has classified the industries in to four groups (1) which should be treated as basic, (2) the industries should be run by the State, (3) the industries need to be State-aided and (4) those should be left entirely to the private sector.

95. Mr. J. R.Jayawardene cited six main industrial groups in his deliberations on industrial corporations, namely, key industries, in heavy industries, essential consumer goods industries, luxuries consumer good industries and cottage industries. He argues that the first two can not be assigned to private-ownership, as they will create problems hence they should be withheld by the State. Other industrial groups can be assigned to private ownership (Ceyion Hansard, 1944 : 652).

96. For example, Mr. Bandaranaike, Mr. Aluvihare etc.

97. It has stated the objective of the future industrial plan in page 14 as the maximum economic utilisation of available resources -human and material. 'It must in the result bring about a higher level of employment and a higher standard of living based on a larger national income'.

98. The main propositions have been that the state should involve

itself in the industrial development partly as a supplier of industrial infrastructure and partly as an institution to participate directly in industries like basic industries and monitoring the private sector. It should take measures to protect infant industries from foreign competition and provide fiscal assistance.

99. Some of those who use periodisation were, for example, Nanayakkara et al., (1993), Rajapathirana (1988), Jayasundera (1986), Atapattu (1997), Lakshman (1997).
100. The Sri Lankan ruling elite is described by Sivananda Patnaik as the 'colonial elite' who were associated with the UNP 'who had interests and aspirations for the development of a free economy with scope for foreign private capital investment', and the 'nationalist elites' associated with the SLFP 'who were guided by spirit of nationalism' (India Quarterly, 1980).
101. Janatha Vimukthi Peramuna (JVP) is a Marxist political organisation consisting of youths.

3

Private Industrial Accumulation in Sri Lanka

A Quantitative Survey

3.1. Introduction

Political independence in a 'new nation' is expected to pave the way for making innovative policies for national benefits. Colonial rulers of Sri Lanka in preparing the country for political independence around the Second World War period adopted many measures to set up an independent political and economic system. This endeavour was continued after independence too. In the previous chapter, we referred to the way in which the economic environment changed gradually over a long period. The socio-political environment too changed gradually to suit the needs of the new economic structure.

Sri Lanka's process of industrialisation, a collaborative project of the public and private sectors, took different turns over the long period after independence. Different political-economic regimes were involved in this process demonstrating that different interest groups have influenced its course. The three partners — domestic entrepreneur class, the foreign investor class, and the state— participated in it in different capacities sometimes in market-friendly and at others in market-hostile environments.

In this chapter, we study the trends of change in the economic structure of Sri Lanka paying special attention to private industrial accumulation. In the appraisal of industrial accumulation after independence, we must keep in mind that the economic structure at independence was predominantly agricultural and that the share of manufacturing was almost insignificant. However, the different forces that emerged in the system after independence brought about pressures to diversify the agriculture-based economic structure to include a strong industrial segment in it. Lakshman identified these pressure groups and the impact of these on development in his brief account of the political economy of different regimes (Lakshman, 1973:15-16).

The first part of this chapter provides an account of the methodology adopted in the present study. A brief description of the areas of private capital accumulation since independence has to be followed by a detailed analysis of the pattern of accumulation in plantations, manufacture, trade, finance and construction industries.

The most serious problem encountered in this research was the lack of continuous data series to study trends in capital accumulating behaviour of the above sectors. The data series available on capital accumulation in each of the above sectors appears to be incomplete. The serious deficiency is the lack of continuity and uniformity of such data. The databases that are maintained by government and non-governmental organisations on capital accumulation in each of the above sectors suffer from periodic lapses of data. Similarly, these institutions use different sources and bases in preparing the above databases which make the databases incomparable. Therefore, the primary task of this study is to develop a consistent and reliable database to explain the long-term behaviour of capital accumulation of individual sectors of the economy. We developed a reliable database compiling information available in audited final accounts of the corporate sector into a standard format designed by the IMF. The new database enables an inter-industry analysis which helps to explain the long-term movements of private investible funds among different branches of the economy.

Importantly, our analysis reveals that there has been a transfer of funds from other sectors of the economy to the manufacturing industry over time. This study will examine the strengths and weaknesses of the process of private industrial accumulation. Furthermore, the chapter will attempt to identify the features of contradiction in the private industrial accumulation. For example, the private sector before 1977 even with a favourable market environment and profit margins that were advantageous to the private industrial accumulation showed only moderate enthusiasm for industrial accumulation. On the whole, in the long term the trend of private accumulation appears to be slow and cyclical. The path of industrial accumulation in Sri Lanka has been relatively long compared to the process postulated by theory and the experience of some other countries, especially, the NICs. The causes for the lengthiness of the path will be discussed in detail in chapters 5 and 6.

3.2. Compilation of a New Database: Methodology and Limitations

The purpose of this section is to develop a statistical database for the study of the long-term industrial behaviour of private and public sectors in the period 1952-97. Historically, several forms of private establishments participated in industrial activities over the period ever since the early years of the 19th century. Those were the cottage industries, small-scale, medium-scale and large-scale industrial ventures which were primarily formed with indigenous capital. Some large-scale industries that evolved in the structure after the early part of the 19th century grew into a corporate sector in the later period. These may be classified into two broad categories, i.e., unlisted and listed companies (or quoted and non-quoted companies). The state also formed its own manufacturing enterprises since the 1940s and intensified industrial formation after independence, in particular, after 1956.

The compilation and maintenance of broad databases on socioeconomic variables of the economy have been the primary responsibility of certain institutions like the Central Bank, the Department of Census and Statistics, and a few other establishments[1]. The Central Bank maintains a database on Gross Domestic Capital Formation (GDCF) in private and public corporations and the government and public enterprises. The methodology adopted by the Central Bank is to estimate yearly values of GDCF as described in table 6 in its Annual Report, 1998. Accordingly, GDCF is a product of two broad items, namely, Gross Domestic Fixed Capital Formation GDFCF and the change of stocks of private and public corporations, government and public enterprises. The information on these is collected from various sources, namely, government subsidies given to the agricultural sector, construction indexes, estimates based on imports and information available in the Government Budget[2].

The data on economic activities of the private sector available in the above sources are not comprehensive enough for our work. The database is deficient in terms of continuity and regularity in record keeping. One shortcoming is the lack of detailed information of entrepreneurs, volumes and types of their investments, profit levels, and employment opportunities[3]. Another is the difficulty in finding a detailed and continuous series of data on long-term investment activities of public and private enterprises. The information on GDCF is provided in terms of aggregate values on sectoral basis. Therefore, the detailed information on firms or individual sectors like plantations, manufacturing, finance, trading and construction is not available. The national databases, therefore, provide only a limited coverage.

The necessity arises therefore to develop a comprehensive database covering micro as well as macro level information on investment in all broad industrial groups of the economy. But, a comprehensive survey of all forms of industrial activities with a long-term coverage is quite cumbersome and costly. Therefore, a sample of enterprises in the corporate sector, particularly, the listed companies sector is the main source of information on private industrial formation used for this study. The sample was based on the following structural pattern of the private sector enterprises:

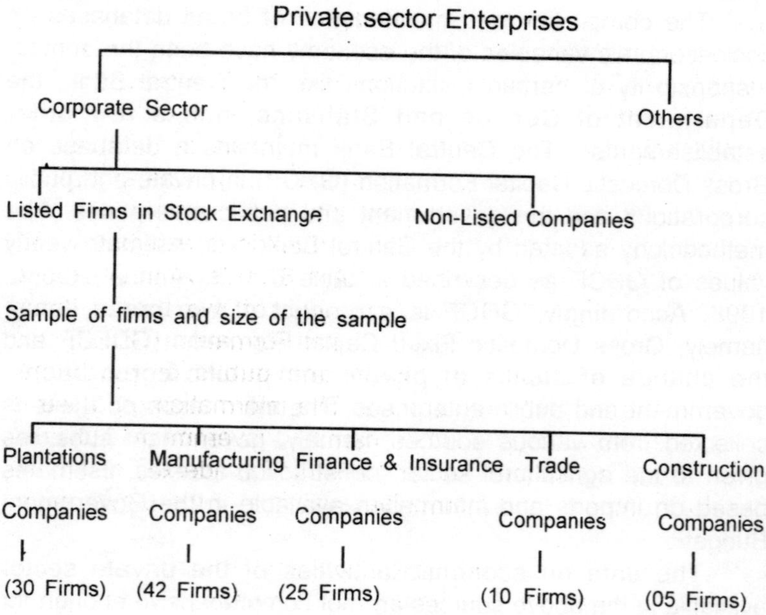

The behaviour of these enterprises can be considered to be the best proxy for explaining the behaviour of the private sector. The listed-companies group appears to reasonably represent the activities of the private sector in Sri Lanka in terms of the intensity of capital utilisation[4]. The total capital employed by listed companies in plantations, manufacture, trade and finance accounts for approximately 30 to 40 per cent[5] of the total private capital invested in Sri Lanka in 1956, 1965 and 1970. This rose to 60 and 62 per cent in the years 1990 and 1993, respectively[6].

Different areas of investment such as plantations, trade, finance and construction are taken into account for the empirical investigation of investment[7]. The accumulation practices of these branches may be compared with the pattern of fixed assets formation in the manufacturing industry over the years. The methodological base for the collection of data will thus be the representative samples (and in some instances the total populations) of individual sectors. For example, of about 129 listed companies operating in the plantation industry 30 (that is about 23 per cent) are sampled to study the accumulation behaviour in this industry. All listed firms in manufacturing, trading, and finance are also taken into account in this study.

As part of this study, we collected a continuous series of information on the volume of investment made by private entrepreneurs, changes in these magnitudes over time, profit margins of different industries, different sources and uses of capital of these firms and so forth. The information on the above variables is found in annual financial statements published by private and public enterprises. The office of the Registrar of Companies and the Department of Archives have a complete set of annual statements of the above enterprise-categories for the entire period concerned. The Colombo Stock Exchange prepares a Handbook of Listed Companies incorporating financial statements of listed private companies. However, the stock exchange does not carry the complete series of Handbooks going back to the early periods.

The financial statements (profit and loss accounts and balance sheets) of individual firms of the above broad industrial groups are aggregated into a single sectoral profit & loss account and a balance sheet using the standard format prepared by the IMF[8]. These aggregate sectoral final accounts have been prepared for a period of 45 years from 1952 to 1997. The data have been deflated using the implicit GNP deflator adjusted to the base year 1956.

A few shortcomings might still exist in the measures that we developed to assess the long-term trend of capital formation. Some of them are:

(1) qualitative changes are disregarded and only the quantitative changes in the capital stock are considered ignoring the technological effects as well. The qualitative changes, in fact, upgrade the level of productive capacity of productive enterprises[6].

(2) The best deflator to use in our analysis would be a price index of investment goods. However, in the absence of such a price index, we use the Implicit GNP Deflator for this purpose.

(3) The treatment of depreciation in computing net values of fixed assets is another problem. Out of alternative methods of depreciation, the standard practice of firms, namely, the straight-line method is employed here.

(4) The revaluation of fixed assets and the inflation of values of fixed assets from one period to another are other problems. The revaluation practice became common only in the latter part of the 1970s.

The procedure of computing values of items, e.g., fixed assets, in different sectors may be described in the following form:

$$\sum_{f=1}^{n} \frac{X^t_{if}}{P^t} = \frac{X^t_{i1}}{P^t} + \frac{X^t_{i2}}{P^t} + \frac{X^t_{i3}}{P^t} + \frac{X^t_{i4}}{P^t} \text{.........} + \frac{X^t_{in}}{P^t} \quad (3.1)$$

X^t_{if}: Value of ith item in final accounts of firm f in year t. The ith items may be, for example, fixed assets, inventory, profits, dividends, tax, savings or paid-up capital.

P^t: Adjusted GNP Deflator in year t.

$$RV_i = \left(\frac{\sum_{f=1}^{n} \frac{X^t_{if}}{P}}{F} \right) \quad (3.2)$$

$$ARV_i = \frac{RV_i}{GDP_t} \quad (3.3)$$

Where,

RV_i : Real Value of the ith item of an average firm in the industry (e.g., per firm real investment).

ARV_i : Real value of the ith item of an average firm as a ratio of Gross Domestic Product in year t ,GDPt.

The accumulation of capital of a firm could conceivably be measured[10] in any of the following forms:

(1) The summing up of year to year changes in total investment. (These are 'uses' of funds in accounting terminology).

(2) The summing up of changes in internal finance, short term net liabilities, long term liabilities and equity capital. (These are 'sources' in accounting terminology).

Putting this in a different way as an identity:

Δ Total Investment=Δ Internal Finance+Δ Net Short-term Liabilities+Δ Long-term Liabilities+ Δ Equity Capital

where Δ Total Investment is analogous to capital accumulation effected during two consecutive years. The total investment is the sum of investment in fixed assets, other investments, and inventories (circulating capital).

The left hand variable of the above identity —the aggregate changes in total investment— is employed here to comprehend different trends of accumulation in the manufacturing sector for a long period, say, from 1952 to 1997. Furthermore, a decomposition of the trend of total investment among sub-items like fixed assets, other investment and inventories, will help to comprehend miscellaneous responses of private investors to different situations which arose under different economic regimes that existed during the periods in question.

The change of variables on the right hand side of the above identity explains the way in which capital accumulation has been financed. Any capital accumulation may be financed either by an increase in internal savings, long term liabilities or equity capital or even by an increase in short term liabilities.

3.4. The Private Investment

The survey carried out in this section will help us to comprehend the changing patterns of private fixed assets formation in individual sectors of the economy. The study will be confined to five main broad industries, namely, plantations, manufacturing, finance, trading, and construction. It should be noted that large private firms mobilised their resources towards the service industry, specially, towards hotel and tourism since the mid-1970s. We do not include the service sector per se, but include the construction sector, which flourished as a result of the growth of tourism. A brief description of recent developments in each of these categories follows. The trend of fixed assets formation in each sector is also analysed.

3.4.1. The Plantation Sector

Sri Lanka's private sector, consisting of large firms of foreign capitalists and a few domestic ones, was engaged primarily in plantations and commercial activities since the mid-19th century. The domestic and foreign entrepreneurs invested a considerable amount of capital[11] in plantations industries. Most of the large listed Rupee companies, non-listed Rupee companies and listed Sterling companies, were owned, and managed by foreign capitalists with the assistance of agency houses.

There was a gradual decline in investments in the plantation industries since WW1 and, in particular, after independence[12]. One important determinant of the private sector's gradual shift from plantations to other sectors after independence was the unattractiveness of plantations in economic terms. The Earnings Per Share (EPS) index,[13] used by the private sector to appraise economic feasibility of investments of the plantation industry had declined over time from Rs. 4.78 per share in 1953 to Rs. 0.76 in 1970(see Figure 3.3 below and Table 3A1.4, Appendix 1).

From the British investors' point of view, a productive investment in plantations must yield an expected minimum rate of return of about 8.5 per cent after tax[14]. This included a premium of 2 per cent for the uncertainty involved in respect of nationalisation and the possible imposition of exchange controls by the state. However, the expectations of this class of investors failed to be satisfied by the plantations industry. The poor performance of the plantations thus discouraged the entrepreneurs in the plantation industry and was a disincentive to intending entrepreneurs. The number of listed companies engaging in the plantations dropped drastically by about 25%, from129 in 1956 to 96 in 1965 and to 91 in 1973.

The average investment in the plantation industry declined during this period as can be seen from the declining trend in curve 1, in Figure 3.1 (and with the data given in Table 3A1.3, Appendix 1). The overall pattern of investment in fixed capital, in real terms, took a convex shape, and flatter, signifying a trend of gradually declining enthusiasm among private entrepreneurs in plantations, especially after the 1960s (see curve 1 in Figure 3.1). According to Table 3.1, there had been a mild growth of fixed assets[15] at a rate of 0.02 in plantations discernible between 1952 and 1956. The growth of fixed assets in the plantations industry has taken a mild upward trend followed by a declining trend at a rate of -0.03.

The period after 1970 was characterised by the increase in public sector's participation in the plantation industry especially after the nationalisation of tea estates during 1974 and 1975. Since then, the private sector maintained a low profile in the industry.

3.4.2. The Construction Sector

Investment in fixed assets in the construction industry grew gradually over years. There was a moderate demand from the plantation industry for construction activities in work sites. As a result a number of construction firms were established from time to time to cater to the needs of the plantations[16]. The boom in the tourist industry after the 1960s encouraged the private sector to intensify its investments in construction[17]. There was a greater demand for construction activities after 1977 because of increased economic activities generated by the liberal economic policies of the government. Fixed assets formation in the construction sector grew at a rate of 0.11 between 1978 and 1982 manifesting a fast growth in this sector (Table 3.1). However, the construction industry after the mid-1980s experienced a serious setback (see Table 3.1). The decline in the tourist industry and the drop in foreign investments as a result of political uncertainty created by ethnic and political violence in the late 1980s may be responsible for the decline in construction activities. Overall, the industry has been maintaining an average growth rate of 0.01 in fixed investment formation over the long period between 1953 and 1997 (Table 3.1).

3.4.3. The Trade Sector:

The trade sector developed as a supportive industry for plantations. It played a vital role in the plantation network during the classical import-export economic environment in colonial days. The two wars disturbed its regular function as a supportive industry but it resumed its normal activities after the two wars. After independence, and especially with the collapse of import-export network, the trade sector faced new problems[18].

TABLE 3.1 Rates of Growth of Fixed Investment
(Real Fixed Assets as ratio of GDP)

	Plantation	*Manufacture*	*Construction*	*Trade*	*Finance*
1952–56	0.02	0.09	0.01	0.01	0.04
1957–64	-0.03	0.02	0.07	0.07	0.11
1965–70	-0.04	0.03	0.04	0.03	0.06
1971–77	*	-0.04	-0.03	-0.04	0.01
1978–83		0.043	0.11	0.20	0.14
1984–89		-0.03	0.02	-0.05	0.04
1990–93		0.01	-0.01	0.07	-0.02
1994–97		-0.03	-0.02	-0.05	0.05
1990–97		-0.01	0.02	0.03	0.03
1953–97		0.001	0.01	-0.01	0.05

*The plantations industry was not under the private sector after nationalisation.

The state imposed various import restrictions and introduced import substitution policies in the 1960s as measures to lower the import dependence of the economy. In addition, it engaged in trading activities via co-operative /state owned agencies[19]. The liberal economic policies after 1977 again revitalised private trading and the industry grew at a high rate of 0.2 (as ratio of GDP) during the period 1978-82. The industry witnessed only a moderate performance with some vicissitudes, thereafter. In all, it experienced mild declining trend equivalent to –0.01over the long period (Table 3.1).

3.4.4. The Finance Sector

The financial industry, another supportive industry with high growth potential, has flourished under the liberal market economic environment. The industry always performed hand in hand with other broad sectors of the economy serving the short and long-term financial needs of others. Before independence, the finance industry was mostly owned and controlled by the private sector[20]. However, the post-independent economic regimes favoured state-owned financial institutions thereby discouraging private financing activities[21]. On certain occasions, especially during the 1960-1965 term, the economic regime in power considered a strategy of nationalising certain financial institutions like the insurance companies and commercial banks. After 1977, the financial industry comprising private and public institutions performed as a provider of financial facilities to the growing economy in the liberal economic environment. The industry grew fast at a rate of 0.14 maintaining a high link with other sectors of the economy. It has been growing at a rate of 0.05 since independence (Table 3.1). Except for the period 1990-93, the sector continued to maintain positive rates of growth in fixed assets over the whole range.

3.4.5. The Manufacturing Sector

The gradual evolution of the manufacturing industry was discussed in detail in the previous chapter. The private sector while concentrating primarily on plantations gradually moved into certain plantation-based industries called manufactories since the last quarter of the 19th century[22]. Later, after WW 1, and especially during WW 2, the sector intensified its activities forming relatively large manufacturing and related industries. A number of relatively large private industries sprang up before WW2 and another batch of new industries came up during WW2 (see names of those industries in Table 3A1.1 and 3A1.2, Appendix 1). Most of the foreign firms, which established trading-cum-service-oriented industries in the late nineteenth century, continued to take part in manufacturing activities until independence (see Table 3A1.2, Appendix 1).

Ferguson's Directory shows the formation of about 20 large (both listed and non-listed) private firms, engaged in manufacturing activities, between 1948 and 1955. Another 45 new large firms entered the manufacturing industry between 1956 and 1965 but only 7 new large firms joined the process of industrialisation between 1965 and 1970. Only about four new large firms entered the manufacturing industry between 1970 and 1977 according to Ferguson's Directory. A relatively large number of big firms entered the manufacturing industry during the period between 1978 and 1994. These industries produced different categories of goods such as beverages, food & tobacco, consumer goods, textiles & footwear and other miscellaneous products. The establishment of new firms in the industrial sector to produce a variety of products continued even after 1994 (see Table 3.2, below).

Unlike other industries, the manufacturing industry experienced different trends of growth over time. It exhibited a negative growth in fixed assets during the economic regimes of 1971-77, 1984-89 and 1994-97 (Table 3.1). On the whole, there was a low long-term private fixed investment formation (rate of 0.001) in manufacturing since independence.

3.5. Changing Pattern of Inter-industry Accumulation

The private sector accumulation of fixed assets in different sectors of the economy underwent changes in its pattern and trends. While large new firms were entering these industries as newcomers during economically favourable periods, the old ones intensified investment activities in their own sectors. They tended to limit their investment when conditions were unfavourable.

Figure 3.1, corresponding to Table 3A1.3, Appendix 1, illustrates the pattern of private investments in various broad sectors of the economy after independence. It exhibits the fluctuating patterns of average accumulation of real fixed assets, expressed as ratio of GDP. Each curve in Figure 3.1 expresses the average willingness of firms to invest in individual sectors of the economy.

In the early 1950s, as Figure 3.1 reveals, the private sector held a large volume of fixed assets in plantations, manufacturing and trade, more or less in equal proportions. It maintained only a small volume of assets in construction and finance. This composition appeared to have changed in the course of time. Only a small volume of private capital moved into the manufacturing industry until the late 1970s and a smaller volume to the construction industry until the early 1960s. After the early 1980s, a relatively large volume of private funds moved into construction, and a volume even larger than that, went into the manufacturing industry. The construction industry began to grow much faster than manufacturing even before the liberalised economic environment commenced in 1977[23]. The two dominant industries, construction and manufacturing, attracted private capital and grew side by side continuing to remain as the sector. Accordingly, construction experienced a considerable decline while finance exhibited a moderate decline in long-term growth. Trade, having an initial negative growth until 1970s, demonstrates an upward trend of growth thereafter. Noticeably, manufacturing leading industries in the Sri Lankan economy.

FIGURE 3.1. PRIVATE FIXED ASSETS FORMATION IN DIFFERENT SECTORS OF THE ECONOMY

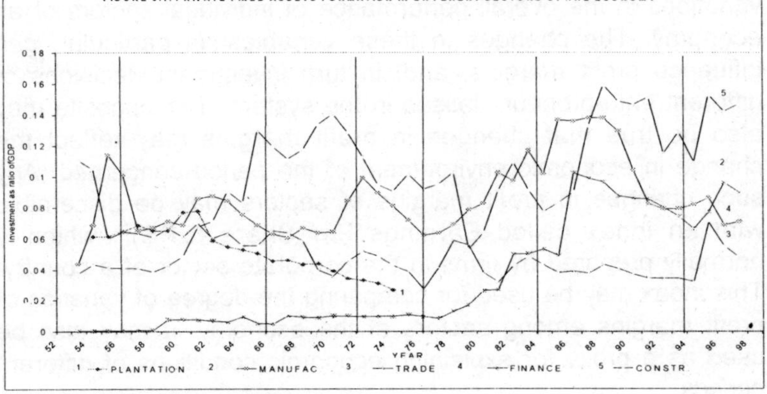

Source: Information in Table 3A1.3, Appendix 1.

holds a mild upward trend of long-term growth despite the fact that there have been cycles of growth (see the trend curve of manufacturing in fig.3.2). Altogether, investment in manufacturing experienced a consistent but slow upward mobility in the hierarchy of private investment compared with other sectors of the economy.

FIGURE 3.2 TRENDS OF GROWTH RATES OF SECTORS

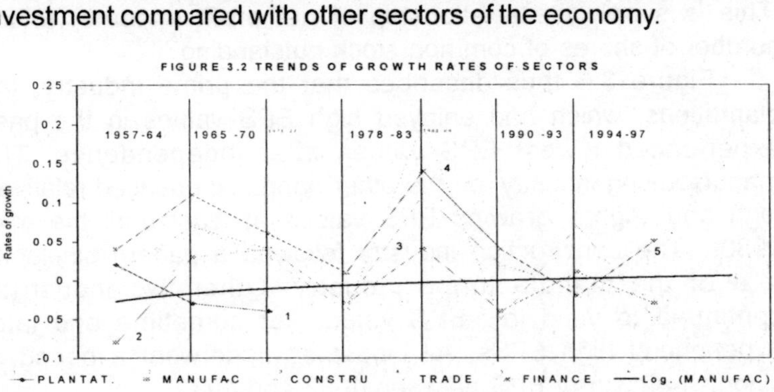

Source: Information in Table 3A1.3, Appendix 1.

Curve 6 in fig. 3.2 describes a gradual rise in rate of growth of manufacturing investment over time. The growth, however, was slow and spreads over a long phase. Figure 3.2 indirectly describes a gradual process of structural change in the Sri Lankan economy; the unproductive sectors exhibit less significance while the productive sectors, like manufacturing, grow in importance.

3.6. Economic Factors

The changes taking place in macroeconomic variables, or broadly in the economic environment, can invariably cause variations in the overall performance of individual sectors of an economy. The changes in these variables, in particular, can influence profit margins, and, in turn investment decisions of different entrepreneur classes in the system. The opposite may also be true that changes in profit margins may reflect the change in economic environment of the period concerned. Any such changes in profit margins of sectors may be discernible with an index called Earnings Per Share (EPS)[24] which is normally prepared by firms in the corporate sector of a country. This index may be used for comparing the degree of variation of profit margins among sectors of the economy. It may also be used as a proxy for explaining economic conditions of different periods[25].

Figure 3.3 explains the behaviour of EPS values and trends over time in different sectors of the economy. It is prepared using information pertaining to each industry under review. The EPS is derived by dividing the sum of net incomes of all firms in an industry by the total number of shares of the same industry[26] 'This is simply the relationship of net profit (income) to the number of shares of common stock outstanding'[27].

Figure 3.3 thus describes that the prime industry, the plantations, which had enjoyed high EPS values in the past, experienced lowest EPS values after independence. The manufacturing industry, on the other hand, experienced relatively high and slightly growing EPS values at least until the mid-1980s. The construction industry followed a pattern similar to that of the manufacturing industry. Other two industries continued to yield low EPS values for sometime and later experienced high EPSs. All industries underwent a period of sluggish growth of EPS between 1983 and 1989.

Fig. 3.3 provides a good account of the economic conditions prevailing during the periods of different economic regimes as well. The period 1952-56 witnesses a deterioration in economic conditions that prevailed in early 1950s, as profit margins were falling rapidly in all sectors. The market conditions had been quite favourable for investment in the early 1950s (due to Korean War boom effect) but these conditions changed gradually over time. Thereafter, a sluggish market economic environment prevailed in the period 1956-64. The profit margins in all industries fell gradually by the end of this period. During the period 1965-70, once again the profit margins rose in the economy signalling a favourable market economic environment for private investment except for plantations.

Figure 3.3 EPS Values in different Secors of the Economy

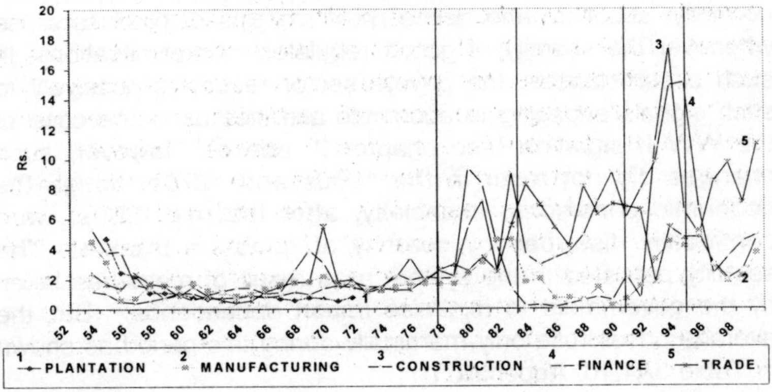

Source: Data in Table 3A1.4, Appendix 1.

The period 1970-77 exhibited an economically gloomy environment where profit margins in the industry fell once again except in the case of trade. On the contrary, the economic condition during 1977-83 proved to be highly attractive to private investment; the profit margins in all sectors rose during this period. However, the period 1985-89 was associated with a completely different economic climate where profit margins of productive sectors like manufacturing and construction felt rapidly. Trade and finance sectors were marginally attractive for some investment on speculative grounds. Again, the period after 1990 witnesses a change in the above conditions, as a result, the profit margins began to rise slightly in productive sectors.

As noted before, the behaviour of certain macroeconomic variables may have been responsible for the above changes in profit margins in different periods. Theoretically, one such variable that influences profit margins of the industry would be the change in real income of the people which would influence the buying behaviour of the people in the market. Prior to 1977, the real income of the people seems to have grown very slowly. The long-term per capita real income has grown only at a rate of 0.01 between 1952 and 1977. But it grew at a rate of 0.03 between 1977 and 1985 again at 0.02 between 1990 and 99, quite remarkably (see Regressions 3A2.1, 3.A2.2 and 3A2.3

in Appendix 2). Prior to 1977, the slow growth of per capita income and hence the low purchasing power of the people caused the demand to be sluggish in the markets. Profit margins of the firms too fell, in turn.

The price incentives that are produced by markets are important determinants of private capital formation. The prices, normally, shoot up and hence profit margins of producers rise whenever the scarcity of goods regulates market situations. In such circumstances, the private sector responds positively to such signals engaging in economic activities as in the case of the WW II situation (see chapter 2, above). However, such changes did not recur in the 1960s and 1970s though the economic conditions, especially, after the mid-1960s, were continually disturbed by scarcity of goods in markets. The scarcity persisted in the system as a result of measures taken by the government to minimise import dependence[28]. But, the average prices rose only marginally during this period as shown in Table 3A1.10, Appendix 1.

The reason for the insensitivity of prices to scarcity may be the result of governmental interference in fixing prices of many goods in the market. The distribution of goods at controlled prices was mostly effected through government institutions like the co-operatives and the Marketing Department. Thus, the private sector has lost the opportunities of reaping full benefits of the situation created by protective measures adopted in the post-1950 period. In other words, the full economic advantages of protection designed to promote private sector-led import substitution have not gone to the private sector owing to the state policy of subsidising consumers[29].

3.7. Growth of an Industrialist Class: Four Classes of Industrialists

Generally, changes in economic policies of the state cause changes in the economic and business environment of the country. The private sector taking note of these changes adopts different measures with regard to its structure of fixed assets. Many such changes took place in the overall business profile of Sri Lanka in response to changes in policies during the post-independence period.

Noticeably, certain qualitative changes took place in the configuration of the entrepreneur class, especially, after independence. In the business hierarchy, there were, altogether, four different classes of private entrepreneurs participating in the process of industrial accumulation over this period. They were, (1) the traditional industrial entrepreneur class, (2) the planning-based new industrialists that emerged in the 1960s, (3) the new industrialists who sprang up in the system after 1977, and (4) the foreign industrialists who joined the process after 1977. These groups exhibited diverse characteristics. The attitudes and practices of different business groups were highly varied. The following sub sections bring out some details about the behaviour of these different groups of industrialists.

3.7.1. The Traditional Industrial Entrepreneur Class

The majority of the entrepreneurs, who financed the manufacturing industrial base in the pre-independence era, were of foreign origin (see Table 3A1.1, Appendix 1). The traditional industrial entrepreneur class, most of whom had joined the process during World War II, concentrated mostly on trade and manufacture (Table 3A1.2 in Appendix 1). Taking from the lists of names given in Tables 3A1.1 and 3A1.2, a sample of prominent businesses commenced by domestic businessmen during this period may be listed as follows:

> Hemachandra Mills (1943), Maliban Biscuit Manufacturers Industrial Works Ltd. (1941), Richard Pieris & Co. Ltd. (1940), Don Somapala Corp. Ltd. (1939), Fransis Perera Co.Ltd. (1946), Don Carolis & Sons etc. (1895), Jinasena Ltd. (1905).

This class of entrepreneurs invested funds in manufacturing in large volumes during World War II. Due to the curtailment of imports, and the consequent rise in prices in the domestic market, both the existing as well as the potential firms were encouraged to invest funds in industry during wartime. The Earning Per Share (EPS) in the manufacturing sector was very high during the War, (about 18.4), which attracted investors into the industry (See Table 3A1.4, Appendix 1). The EPS, however, dropped to 4.49 in 1943. Except for the years 1952 and 1968 to 1978, the EPS did not rise until 1978. After 1978, the sector again enjoyed high EPS values. The manufacturing sector maintained an average EPS ratio of 1.33 during the period 1956-1964. The average EPS ratios during the periods 1965-70, 1971-

77, 1978-83, 1984 –89 and 1990 -94 were 1.79, 1.50, 3.07, 0.70 and 3.70, respectively.

The traditional industrial firms, which joined the process in the very early days, displayed a unique pattern of industrial accumulation over this long period as illustrated in Figure 3.4 and Table 3.2, below. However, the traditional industrial firm sector tended to maintain only a low annual rate of growth of fixed assets, of about 3 per cent on average, in the manufacturing industry. At times, manufacturing under this traditional class of entrepreneurs experienced higher average periodic rates of growth of fixed assets about 4, 11 and 03 percents during the periods 1965-70, 1978-83, and 1990-95 respectively, especially, in market-oriented environments.

FIGURE 3.4. PATTERN OF FIXED INVESTMENT IN MANUFACTURING BY FOUR CLASSES OF ENTREPRENEURS

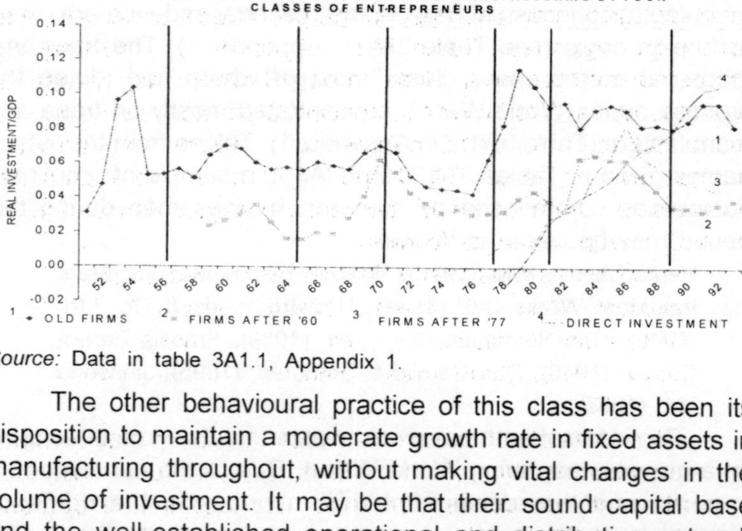

Source: Data in table 3A1.1, Appendix 1.

The other behavioural practice of this class has been its disposition to maintain a moderate growth rate in fixed assets in manufacturing throughout, without making vital changes in the volume of investment. It may be that their sound capital base and the well-established operational and distributive network allowed this class to maintain a substantially stable pattern of investment in fixed assets over a long period.

Significantly, the sector experienced negative accumulation between 1971 and 1977 and also between 1984 and 1989 (Table 3.3). Negative accumulation results when investments are less than what is required for amortisation (Robinson, 1965:39). Negative accumulation may be related to unusual developments in the political and economic atmosphere of the country during the periods concerned[30]

TABLE 3. 2. Average Annual Rate of Growth of Fixed Assets in Four Categories of Firms

Periods	*Old Firm %*	*Firm After 1960 %*	*Firm After 1977 %*	*Foreign Direct Investment %*
1956 – 64	3	8		
1965 – 70	3	12		
1971 – 77	-2	-3		
1978 – 84	12	6	14	19
1985 – 89	-12	-2.9	-5	5
1990 – 94	3	4	2	6
Whole Period	3	3	7	2

Source: Data in Table 3A1. 7, .1.

The traditional industrial entrepreneur class invested funds mostly in three broad sub-groups of industries, namely, food, beverages and tobacco (FBT), chemicals and pharmaceuticals (C&P) and miscellaneous manufacturing industries (MMI). The engineering and motors and service industries are also included in the latter group of industries (MMI). The following types of goods were manufactured under each category:

(FBT): Food, beverages, and tobacco,
(C&P): Chemicals and chemical products,
(MMI): Ready-made garments; leather, rubber, wood, paper; non-metallic Industries & metal products; construction and equipment; electrical machinery and apparatus.

Figure 3.5 below, illustrates the pattern of formation of fixed investment in each product groups by the traditional firm sector over time. This firm sector invested a relatively low volume of funds in chemicals and pharmaceuticals industries (C&P) over this long range of time. The share of investment in beverages, food, and tobacco (BFT) were high compared to the other two products until the mid-1970s. Its investment in miscellaneous manufacturing industries (MMI) follows an asymmetric trend; it has risen until 1973 followed by a decline till 1980. Capital formation in this category rose thereafter except for the period 1985–90.

Generally, the traditional industrial entrepreneur class was inclined towards a high rate of investment in all types of industries, especially, during market-oriented economic environments (1951-56, 1965-70, 1978-83, and 1990-94). The total investment (curve 4 in Figure 3.5) displays a rising trend during these periods. The distinct characteristic of this class has been its cautious business practices during uncertain periods like 1971-77 and 1984-89. Its investments have taken a downward trend during these periods as shown in curve 4 in Figure 3.5.

FIGURE 3.5 INVESTMENT IN DIFFERNENT PRODUCT GROUPS BY OLD FIRM SECTOR

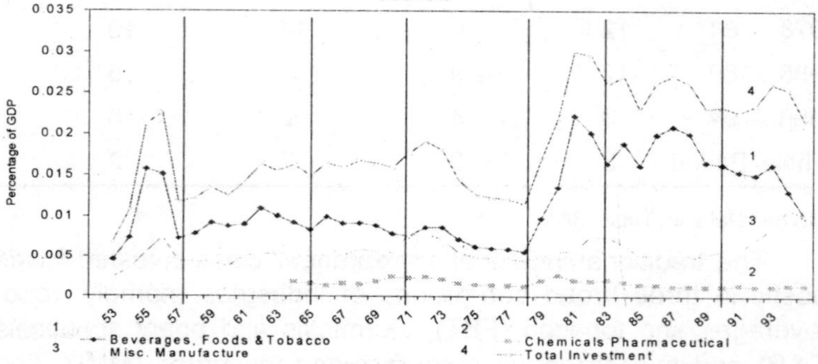

The above trends reveal that this class of investors was generally willing to invest in miscellaneous manufacturing products MMI in market-friendly atmospheres (see curve 3 in Figure 3.5 in periods 1952-56, 1965-70, 1978-85 and 1990-94). They preferred investment in food, beverages, and tobacco FBT and in other types C&P in planning-oriented economic environments. Quite unusually, these investors invested funds in large volumes in FBT during the 1978-85 period. The old firm sector has maintained a steady growth in the accumulation of fixed assets in miscellaneous manufacturing industries MMI over time.

In the past, this class of investors had enjoyed windfall opportunities, especially during uncertain environments. They earned windfall benefits in the early 1940s during World War II and in the early 1950s during the Korean Boom. However, they subsequently seemed to be indifferent or minimally involved during periods of political and economic disturbances. The planning-oriented economic policies of the post 1956 period apparently produced little stimuli to this class of entrepreneurs.

The traditional industrial entrepreneur class seemed to respond positively to the new political and economic climate after 1977. The accumulation of physical capital rose sharply after

1980 and continued to rise steadily over time as can be seen in curve 4, Figure 3.5, above. The period between 1983 and 1989 is, however, characterised by a slow down in accumulation due to political and ethnic conflicts which seriously disturbed social life.

3.7.2. Planning-based New Industrialists

In addition to the traditional industrial entrepreneur class, a group of 'new capitalists' or 'new industrialists' emerged fast in the economy. The state helped the class of new capitalists to start new businesses by providing financial assistance as well as business expertise. Simultaneously, new financial institutions were developed to assist this class of entrepreneurs with venture capital[31] In Sri Lanka, the industrial policy of the state in the late 1950s was aimed at creating a new class of capitalists and promoting import-substituting industries. These industrialists were supplied with various stimuli[32] ranging from tax holidays to other concessions[33].

The earnings per share (EPS) of these young industrial firms were high and steady compared to those of traditional industrial firms. During 1965-70, the average EPS of this sector was 2.44 compared to 1.79 of the traditional industrial firm sector. It was 1.27 compared to 1.81 of the traditional industrial firm sector in the period 1970 -77. Finally, their EPS values were as high as 5.33 compared to 4.63 in the traditional industrial firm sector during the period 1978 -94.

The post-1960-new industrialists maintained a high annual rate of growth of fixed assets equivalent to 3 per cent on average (See Table 3.2 above). The investment in fixed assets grew at rates of 8 and 12 per cent during the early periods, i.e. between 1960-1964 and 1965–70 respectively. Later, the sector experienced a moderate annual rate of growth in capital formation of 6 per cent between 1978 and 1985, and 4 per cent between 1990 and 1995.

Initially, this class of new industrialists concentrated more on miscellaneous manufacturing industries (MMI) perhaps due to the requirements laid down by the state. Later, however, they tended to enter the in beverage and food manufacturing industries perhaps because of the conditions that developed within the market system in favour of beverages and food products. The fixed investments in miscellaneous manufacturing industries (MMI) by new industrialists were rising moderately (see Figure 3.6). However, the growth of investment during uncertain periods, (e.g. the period between 1970 and 1977), took a negative trend where the fixed assets were falling at an annual rate of 3.1 per cent.

FIGURE 3.6. INVESTMENT IN DIFFERENT PRODUCT GROUPS BY FIRMS AFTER 1960

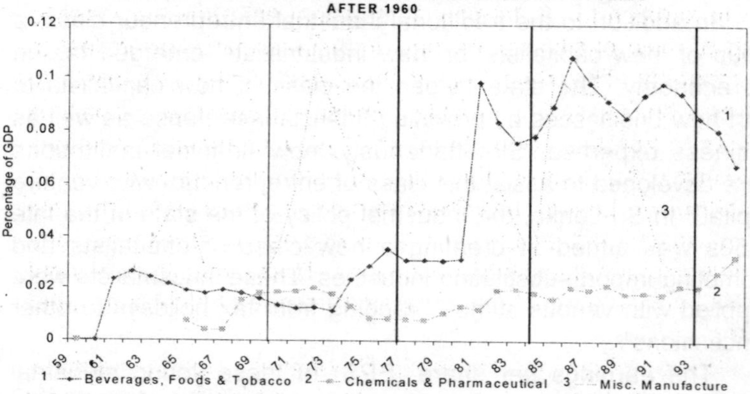

Source: Data in Table 3A1. 8, Appendix 1.

The growth of fixed investments in food, beverages, and tobacco industries FBT was rather similar to that of miscellaneous manufacturing industries MMI though of a lower magnitude. The annual rate of growth of these items was negative (-1.3 per cent) between 1971 and 1977. The annual growth rate rose to an average level of 8 percent during the market economic environment until 1991.

The new industrialists who surfaced in the 1960s maintain a relatively low average volume of capital in manufacturing *vis-à-vis* the traditional industrial entrepreneur class (Figure 3.4 and in Table 3A1.7, Appendix 1). From the very inception, these new firms recorded a rapid progress in accumulating industrial physical capital. They were able to intensify their investments in the above product lines because of the availability of internal sources of funds as revealed by financial statements of these firms.

The other behavioural feature of accumulation by new industrialists, compared to that of the former, has been their practice of curtailing investments in fixed assets excessively during unfavourable periods. Such declines in accumulation were experienced in the period between 1971 and 1977 and between 1983 and 1987. The new industrialists were averse to risk-taking because they were new to the industry and environment.

3.7.3. New Industrialists After 1977

Opportunities for the private sector increased. Opening the economy to international trade marked the policy of liberalisation in 1978. The domestic economic and political environment became supportive to the private sector's active participation in economic affairs. The relaxation of import restrictions by making easy availability of imported raw materials, the constraint faced by the sector[37], raised the utilisation capacity to high level.

The high turnover and increased profit margins, *inter alia*, promoted a bright outlook for investment in all sectors of the economy. The business infrastructure (ports, telecommunication, electronic media, road network and technical expertise etc.) was developed by the government in collaboration with the private sector. New supportive institutions like the modernised financial sector, the stock exchange and insurance firms helped to promote a favourable environment for private investment. All these led to the development of a new capitalist class comprising indigenous as well as foreign capitalists. They invested large sums of money in different areas of the economy.

The level of profits in the manufacturing sector was comparatively high (EPS was about 3.07) during the first few years until 1983 as seen in Figure 3.3 above (also in Table 3A1.4, Appendix 1). The EPS values, however, became very low (about 0.70) for the first time between 1984 and 1989. This period is characterised by political and economic instability due to the War in the North, the presence of the Indian Peacekeeping Force (IPKF) in the country, and the upheavals created by the *Janatha Vimukthi Peramuna* (JVP). The post-1990 period again witnessed a rise in EPS values of the sector (3.24 on average), perhaps due to the new industrial policies after 1989.

This class of industrialists allocated a large volume of investment funds to the production of miscellaneous manufacturing products. In addition, the foreign industrialists realised that industries like footwear and textiles were highly profitable ventures and invested a considerable amount of funds in those industries. The miscellaneous manufacturing industries MMI in this group grew at an annual rate of 12 percent during the period 1978-83 and 13 per cent during 1984–86, but this rate dropped to 1 per cent after 1989 as seen in Figure 3.8, below.

According to financial records, two factors contributed substantially to the rapid growth of fixed industrial investments of these groups of industrialists. One was the development of a modernised money market and a capital market, which supplied short term and long term financial capital to the corporate sector. The other was the internal savings, generated within the firms, which strengthened the ability to borrow and finance new projects.

The new corporate sector (including foreign firms) generated high internal savings. The generation of high earnings helped to raise 'the entrepreneurial capital base' of this sector[38]. The entrepreneurial capital base, in turn, facilitated the sector's access to the capital market to draw long-term investment funds. Kalecki postulated this process as one of the important determinants of fixed capital formation of the private sector. Figure 3.5 thus describes that the capital formation of this sector has a continuous growth except for years 1983, 1987, and 1989. The sector has been very much concerned with the political uncertainties that prevailed in the country in these years and the industrialists negatively reacted to these disturbances by curtailing capital formation.

FIGURE 3. 7. INVESTMENT IN DIFFERENT PRODUCT GROUPS BY FIRMS AFTER 1977

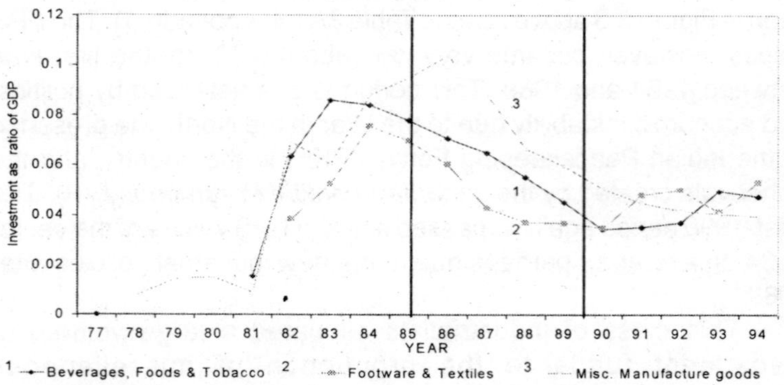

Source: Data in Table 3A1.8, Appendix 1

3.7.4. Foreign Industrialists

It was observed in chapter 2 that foreign capitalists who had invested funds in plantations and trading activities had begun to leave Sri Lanka gradually since the 1930s. This outflow speeded up during the early post-independence period with 'the continuous process of "Ceylonisation" of the country's plantations since the nineteen forties'[39] The local 'compradore capitalists' bought the plantation and trading company assets of these foreign capitalists. The Furguson's Directory provides information on the changing pattern of ownership of large plantation companies from foreign to local capitalists. Government policy since the mid-1950s was generally unfriendly to foreign direct investment. Following the above policy, the governments in the 1960s nationalised foreign-owned business undertakings like the petroleum distribution network, insurance, and commercial banks. The plantation companies were nationalised in the 1970s. These led to a rapid outflow of foreign capital from Sri Lanka.

In Central Bank reports, there are three sets of data on the inflow of funds. One refers to direct foreign investment and long-term private capital flow which are given in balance of payments accounts. The other refers to realised investment in Board of Investment (BOI) of Sri Lanka shown in the Central Bank reports under the broad heading of industry. Lastly, the Central bank publication, on "Economic Progress of Independent SRI LANKA" provides information on foreign direct investment over a period of fifty years. The last set of data is employed in this study[40].

FIGURE 3.8 TREND OF FOREIGN DIRECT INVESTMENT

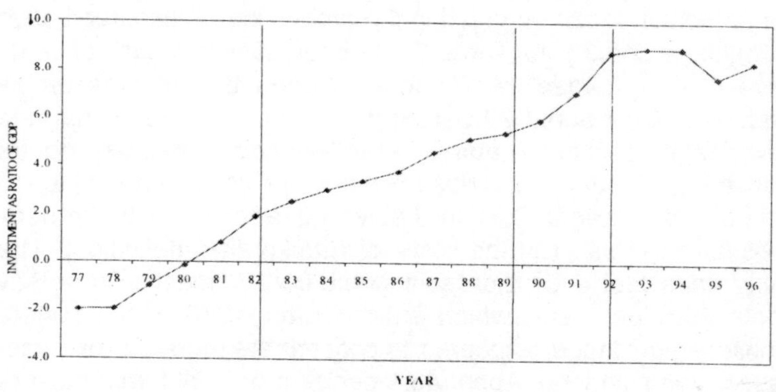

The curve in Figure 3.8 gives the average trend of foreign direct investment after 1977. The trend, however, has slightly changed after 1984 as a result of political and economic uncertainties in the system. Foreign direct investment, as can be expected, is highly sersitive to internal economic policy changes.

3.8. The Private Sector led Structural Changes

The structure and the direction of private investment may be studied with structural information provided in Table 3.3 below. The table is prepared using the same methodology used by Athukorala in his analysis of foreign direct investment in Sri Lanka (Athukorala, 1995:551). Our emphasis here is only on the role of domestic corporate investment in manufacturing. The International Standard Industry Classification (ISIC) codes are employed to classify industries into three different categories. We followed Walton's into different ISIC codes (Walton, 1987:146-63).

The classification of industries was done in accordance with four standard product groups. They are the (1) resources-based manufacturing, (2) labour-intensive consumer goods, (3) component production and assembly and (4) mature technological final products. This apparently is the 'standard practice in the literature to distinguish between different product categories'[41]. Evidently, the domestic corporate sector does not produce products in the last category, the final products with mature technology, nor does the FDI sector produce them according to Athukorala (1995).

There was a large number of firms, about 40.9 per cent, in the corporate sector engaged in the production of resource-based products according to Table 3.3. About 39.4 per cent of firms have been engaged in component production and assembly industries. Only about 20 per cent of firms, both traditional and new, have invested funds in standardised consumer goods industries (category 2). Those firms engaged in manufacturing that are in category (3) in Table 3.3 appear to be import-substitution firms[42] (on the basis of Athukorala's definition). The study finds that a considerable number of domestic firms, say about 48.6 per cent, which started after 1978 with no state monitoring/guidance, appeared to concentrate more on resource-based manufacturing. About 48.4 per cent of local firms, most of which were formed under state patronage in the 1960s, have invested funds in component products and assembling industries (See column 2 and 4, Table 3.3). None has invested funds in 'differentiated final goods' in the growing and dynamic field.

According to Athukorala, a majority of foreign firms established after 1977, about 79.4 per cent in 1982 and 61.8 per cent in 1991, concentrated on standardised consumer goods industries. Foreign firms involved in the production of resource-based products in category 1 occupy the second position, according to Athukorala[43]. It can be noticed from Figure 3.5 that that traditional industrial entrepreneur class has had a general preference towards investing funds in food, beverages and tobacco industries, throughout. However, there has been a change in their behaviour since the 1990s when this class shown an inclination to invest funds in miscellaneous manufacturing industries (MMI) as well.

Since the inception, the new industrialists who emerged during the 1960s invested funds in miscellaneous manufacturing industries (MMI) until the early 1970s (see Figure 3.6). Their capital formation in the production of these goods dropped thereafter until 1978, but rose once again until 1985. The experience after 1980 suggests that these new industrialists

TABLE 3.3 Selected Structural Information - Sectoral Distribution of (Local) Manufacturing Firms, 1993

ISIC	*Description*	*No old Firms*	*%*	*No. New Firms*	*%*	*Total No. Firms*	*%*
	Resource-Based Products		**32.3**		**48.6**		**40.9**
11	Meat, Dairy, Fish, Grain	1	3.2	1	2.9	2	3.0
12	Spices, Animal Feeds Etc			1	2.9	1	1.5
3113	Beverages	4	12.9	4	11.4	8	12.1
3131	Tobacco	1	3.2			1	1.5
3411	Pulp, Paper And Paperboard	2	6.5	2	5.7	4	6.1
3551	Rubber Products	2	6.5	3	8.6	5	7.6
3691	Cement, Lime, Plastic Etc.			3	8.6	3	4.5
3911	Diamond Cutting & Jewellery			3	8.6	3	4.5
	Standardised Consumer Goods		**19.3**		**20.0**		**19.7**

Contd.

ISIC	*Description*	*No old Firms*	*%*	*No. New Firms*	*%*	*Total No. Firms*	*%*
3211	Textiles	4	12.8	4	11.4	8	12.1
3220	Clothing	1	3.2			1	1.5
3560	Plastic Products			1	2.9	1	1.5
3240	Footwear	1	3.2	1	2.9	2	3.0
3811	Cutlery, Hand tools, Hardware			1	2.9	1	1.5
	Component Production		**48.4**		**31.4**		**39.4**
3511	Industrial Chemicals	4	12.9	1	2.9	5	7.6
3521	Other Chemical Products	6	19.4			6	9.1
3531	Petroleum Refineries			1	2.9	1	1.5
3720	Non- Ferrous Basic Metal	1	3.2	3	8.6	4	6.1
3822	Agricultural Machinery	1	3.2	2	5.7	3	4.5
3831	Electrical Machinery	3	9.7	4	11.4	7	10.6
	Total	**31**	**100**	**35**	**100**	**66**	**100**

Source: Author's Database.

tended to intensify their investment in food, beverages and tobacco manufacturing industries FBT and maintained a low profile in miscellaneous manufacturing industries MMI in the favourable economic environments as seen in Figure 3.6, above. The new industrialists who sprang up after 1977 intensified their investments more in miscellaneous manufacturing industries MMI until the late 1980s, but later moved onto food, beverage and tobacco industries as shown in Figure 3.7 above. They tended to increase their investments in footwear and textile industries in the 1990s.

The private entrepreneur class resorted to a path of slow industrial formation in the post-independence era due to two reasons. First, their aversion to risk led this class to undertake only less-risky investments in products like food, beverage, and tobacco products, which have low linkages. Some, nonetheless, were inclined to invest funds in miscellaneous manufacturing industries MMI but these were again import-substituting industries. Second, many believed that the private sector preferred to hold a merchant capital base, which discouraged the flow of investible funds towards industrial accumulation.

This, however, may be a half-truth. On the contrary, the curves in Figure 3.9 display an alternative pattern of distribution of total investible funds among the four sectors, namely, plantation, manufacturing, construction, trade cum finance, over time. Until the early 1970s, the share of fixed assets in the trade-cum-finance sector had been relatively high when compared with the manufacturing industry. The average share of trading-cum-finance was about 37.3 per cent of the total fixed investment whereas in manufacturing and construction industries it was only about 26.4 and 36.3 per cent respectively before 1980. It could therefore be argued that the private sector in Sri Lanka held a comparatively large merchant capital base until the early 1970s. After 1970s, the share of merchant capital fell to 26.9 per cent while the share of constructions rose to 45.8 per cent. The share of manufacturing rose marginally to 27.7 per cent. The construction industry has apparently grown at the expense of trade-cum-finance industries over time.

FIGURE 3.9. SECTORAL SHARES OF TOTAL PRIVATE INVESTMENTS

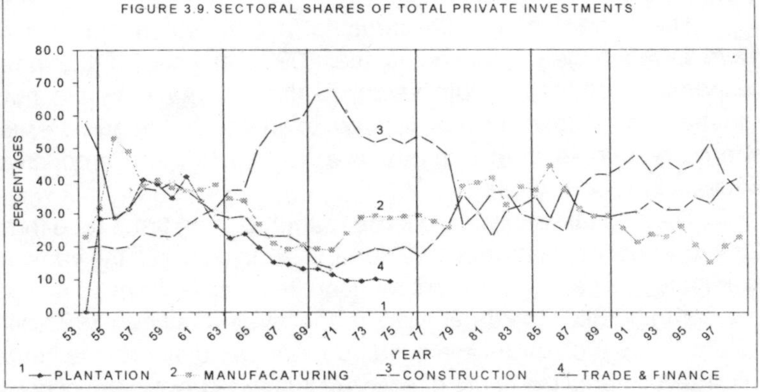

Source: Data in Table 3A1.3, Appendix 1.

Indeed, the modern production processes use heavy and expensive machinery, equipment, and buildings. The volume of fixed investment in manufacturing and construction, therefore, is expected to be high but the volume of working capital may be relatively low. On the other hand, the trade and finance industries normally demand a relatively low volume of fixed capital. It uses huge volumes of working capital depending on the nature of the business. One can, therefore, argue that the capital base of trade and finance industries could be heavy if the large magnitude of working capital is added to the fixed capital base.

Evidently, the structure of manufacturing industries of the Sri Lankan economy is changing though slowly. There has been an increase in the number of participants in industrial activities and types of products offered by the corporate sector. This can be observed in Table 3.3 above and 3A1.9, Appendix 1. Of these Tables, the former relates to experiences in 1993 and the latter in 1998. The basket of commodities produced by the corporate industrial sector in 1998 was relatively large. The sector supplied about 212 items to the market (see Table 3A1.9, Appendix 1). A large number of firms (about 182 out of 971) were involved in the production of textile and clothing. Next, about 66 firms were in the industrial chemical industry. Finally, about 120 firms were in food industry, especially in the processing of meat, fish, grains and dairy products. Apart from these major sectors, plastic industry and electrical machinery too had attracted about 98 and 97 firms, respectively. Other industries appear to be marginal in terms of size i.e., the number of corporate firms involved.

The pattern of private industrial accumulation appears to have taken a new direction in the 1990s in spite of the poor responses from the private sector to the call made by the new regime. The economy has tended to intensify the transfer of scarce resources from unproductive sectors to more productive sectors in recent years.

The capitalisation of the large manufacturing firms rose from 20.4 to 31 per cent between 1993 and 1996. In contrast, the banking & finance and services sectors reduced their capital from 35.4 to 33 per cent and 36.9 to 28 per cent, respectively, between 1993 and 1996[44]. These changes are quite important as they provide some information about the future direction of industrial development of Sri Lanka.

3.9. Summary

The pattern of private capital accumulation over a long period may be comprehended with the help of Figures 3.1 and 3.10. These may be treated as two good predictable models to explain the different practices of the private sector in different economic environments in the Sri Lankan economy. In Figure 3.10, the trend curve 1 describes the different states of preferences of the private sector in terms of investing funds in different periods. Also, the five trend curves in Figure 3.1 specify changes in the preferences of private investment in each sector within different economic environments.

In a nutshell, according to Figure 3.1, private investment in the plantations diminished sharply after the early 1960s. In trade, it rose more or less at a constant rate (with mild vicissitudes) maintaining a low profile in the investment portfolio of the private sector until the end of 1970s. Private investment in finance was comparatively low and was growing at an insignificant rate until the end of the 1970s. It rises sharply after the late 1970s. Both manufacturing and construction sectors continued to grow ever since the mid-1970s. The two main sectors of the economy, i.e. manufacturing and construction, apparently have been operating on a competitive basis after the early 1970s as is evident in Figure 3.1 above. Trade and finance operated as potential substitutes for manufacturing until the early 1970s but they appeared to perform supportive services for manufacturing and construction after the 1970s.

The private sector has been vulnerable to political uncertainty during election periods and other political upheavals. This behaviour is seen in trend curves, Figure 3.10. The average investment levels in all sectors dropped considerably during election periods 1956, 1964, 1970, 1977, 1983, 1989 and 1994. The rate of growth of investment in fixed assets dropped sharply during political upheavals in 1971, 1983 and 1987-89. The reason for the drop in fixed assets may be the deterioration of the existing capital stock 'due to lack of adequate maintenance'[46].

Also according to 3.4, the venture capital firms including foreign ones, which participated in the process of industrial accumulation in the 1960s and the late 1970s had been dynamic and resourceful compared with traditional firms joining the process during World War II. Their rate of industrial accumulation was higher than that of the traditional ones. The new firms diverted their funds to miscellaneous manufacturing industries and towards industries like footwear and textiles. They intensified their activities in areas like construction & engineering, hotels & travel, investment trusts, land & property, motor transport industries, service industries, stores & supplies and trading. The traditional firms concentrated mostly on conventional goods plus chemicals & pharmaceutical manufacturing-cum-trading industries.

The growth of a class of new industrialists and a corresponding growth of the financial market structure contributed largely to the industrial accumulation process of Sri Lanka. However, the growth of industrial products is still confined to a limited basket of commodities. Market signals had promoted mostly the production of food, beverages, and tobacco products. Sri Lankan industrial policy needs to encourage the production of component production goods and finally the 'differentiated final goods' as Athukorala points out.

Curve 1 in Figure 3.10 shows the path of industrial accumulation in Sri Lanka spreading over a long period. It exhibits a steady "take off" in the early 1980s but again experiences a slowing down in the latter part of 1980s. The path is also cyclical; there has been upward mobility in certain periods and down-ward mobility in market-hostile periods.

FIGURE 10. LONG TERM TREND OF CORPORATE FIXED INVESTMENT (Excluding Plantations)

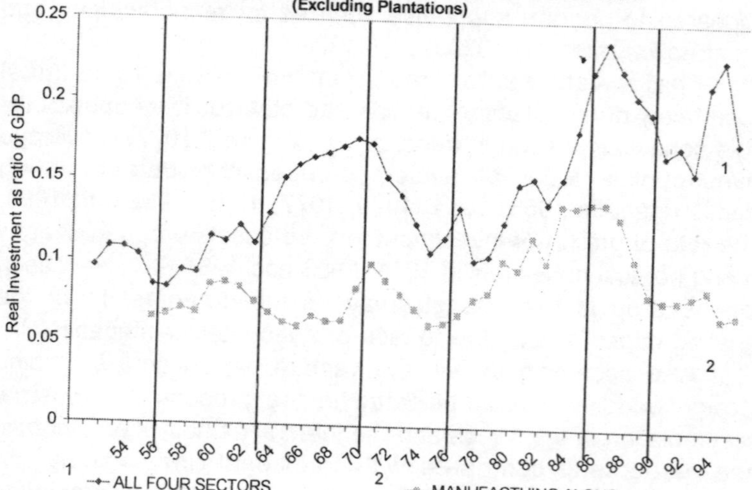

Source: Data in Figure 3.1.

An attempt will be made in the next chapter to develop a hypothesis to explain possible factors that determine the cyclical trend of industrial accumulation of the private corporate sector – the joint partner of the project of industrialisation. It will raise the issue as to whether there is dominance of non-market factors over market factors. Do non-market factors have the capacity to curb the dynamic elements of market factors? Does it have any thing to do with the slowness of capitalist industrial development in Sri Lanka?

Notes

1. For example, the Registrar of Companies and the Archives Department maintain the final accounts of all registered companies in crude form. These records are not available for public perusal and hence not of easy access to them. The Ferguson's Directory provides some information but not on a continuous basis.
2. GDFCF in Private and Public Corporations:

   (a) Planting, Replanting and Land Development which are estimated on the basis of the subsidies given to the agricultural sector and actual investment by private and public sector institution.
   (b). Building and other construction are estimated in the basis of Construction index.
   (c) Plant & Machinery and Transport equipment are estimated on the basis of imports.
   (d) Other capital goods are estimated on the basis of imports and other domestic capital goods.

   GDFCF in Government and Public Enterprises are estimated on the basis of Government Budgetary information. Source: Information collected from Statistical Department, Central bank of Sri Lanka.
3. Except for some censuses aiming at private investments conducted by Statistical Department, Central bank of Sri Lanka there was no continuity in the collection of data in detailed form. The Central Bank provides information on industrial production, number of firms, distribution of manufacturing firms, number of employees, production values, and gross domestic capital formation by private sector and public corporations. This information is not broad-based enough to extract required data for our research.
4. The listed company sector claims to have financially links with the other non-listed company sector.
5. A fraction of the Gross Domestic Capital Formation (figures are given by Central Banł annual reports)
6. For example, the total capital employed by the entire quoted company sector in years 1990 and 1993 were Rs. Mn. 34,789 and 65,328, respectively, according to information given by Hand

books of Listed Companies. The total capital employed by all public and private enterprises for the corresponding periods were Rs. Mn. 57,105 and 105,306 according to Central Bank Reports.

7. "Empirical work on investment should recognise that investment arises from many different motives, and that these apply differently in different industries . . .. Hence, it would be useful to disaggregate the investment data and develop investment functions by sector". (Bischoff, 1971:61).
8. These are currently in use by the Central Bank.
9. Even Dan Usher has noted that 'in reality, the types of capital goods are not invariant': but for the sake of simplicity in his intertemporal model he has assumed that 'the qualities remain invariant over time' (Usher, 1980: 84).
10. The methodology for the study is very similar to the one adopted in the study of 'Restructuring of Public sector enterprises in Sri Lanka ' used by the World Bank Mission in 1987 and 1988. The final accounts of companies need to be transferred to the Standard IMF format with which the data could be explained in the form of funds flow Statements showing uses and sources of funds.
11. The value of the plantation enterprise by the year 1875 was about Sterling Pounds 23,555,641 according to one rough estimate given in Ferguson's Directory, 1875. The share of the local capitalists was roughly about 3.2 percent in land cultivated. In 1925, the value of the plantation enterprise was about Sterling Pound 41,292,120 as given in Ferguson's Directory, 1925. Apparently, the plantation enterprise has doubled in size after 50 years.
12. Lakshman (1973) provides a good summary of the developments in the plantation industry over years.
13. For the application of EPS in industrial decision-making, see Peirson (1984: 111-120). Also for illustrations, see Helfert Erich. A (1972).
14. During 1954 –58 (Ramachandran, 1963: 76).
15. A semi-log regression in the following form was employed to estimate rates of growth in fixed assets. Ln F = g (t) or Ln F= a + bt where t is time. Given the function F = g (t), the rate of growth of is: $\dot{F} = \frac{dF/dt}{F}$ See Branson 1972:434-35). In the above log function the rate of growth is which is the value b.
16. For example, Brown & Company limited, 1892; Samuel, Sons & company limited, 1922, Collettes Limited, 1909, Hunter &

Company Limited, 1911.

17. A large number of new firms were formed in the area of construction and engineering and land and property development. For example, there were about 19 Listed Companies in the area of land and property developments, which were formed mostly in the 1980s. Associated Property Development limited, CT Land Development limited, Cargo Boat Development Limited, Ceylinco Housing and Real State Company Limited are some (Handbook of Listed Companies, 1994: 257-295).
18. See N.D.Samarawickreme, (1997b).
19. Like the Paddy Marketing Board, Building Materials Corporation, Milk Board, Salu-Sala, Ceylon Fisheries Corporation, Fertiliser Corporation, and Ceylon Petroleum Corporation. Lakshman cites about 16 such establishments (Lakshman, W.D, 1976).
20. The Ceylon Banking Commission in 1935 discusses the role played by the private sector in financing private investments. Accordingly, it had catered mostly for plantation-oriented investment but little for manufacturing ones.
21. Atapattu (1997:77) describes that '...the financial sector was extremely repressed and there was little room for independent and efficient financial intermediation' (quoted in Khatkhate, 1982).
22. Ferguson's Directory, 1875, gives information on such manufactories regarding their sizes, labour force involves, horsepower capacity, ownership etc.
23. This was because of the growth of the tourists industry which drew private resources to this sector since the mid-1960s.
24. This index may be used as a standard measure to compare level of profits in each sector of the economy.
25. It can be a rough index, inter alia, to describe economic conditions where the high profit margins refer to economically favourable environment and vice versa.
26. Refer to equation (1) above. In this case i in X^t_{if} is the netincomes of the fth firm in the industry. The total net income ΣX^t_{if} can be derived for the industry following equation (1).7.

    Earnings per share = $\frac{\text{Net income}}{\text{Average number of shares outstandin g}}$

    See Helfert (1972:62).
28. Measures like rationing foreign exchanges via quotas, high tariffs and complete banning of some items were implemented to effective utilisation of scarce foreign exchange and to encourage import substitutions.

29. The pressure brought by non-market forces like interest groups, the voters, and the consumer groups was stronger than that of market economic forces.
30. For example, the election and the new regime came into power in 1956 may have influenced the investment decisions. Again the elections in 1964 and 1970 led to change in regimes. The period between 1972 and 1975 was significant because of political upheaval in 1971 (armed Insurrection) followed by economic catastrophe.
31. The word 'venture capital' has derived from 'seed capital' (Woelfel, 1994:1191).
32. The argument that the state has not exerted deliberate efforts to promote import substitution industries, but even in the 1960s eventually brought about some start up of such industries is well-taken here. The state introduced some measures like quotas, tariffs and complete prohibition of some items to meet the deterioration of the balance of payment situation: they in effect became protective policies.
33. Some of the Stimuli provided by the were as follows:
    - I Tax laws were amended to provide tax relief of 5 years to government approved projects.
    - II. Development rebate of 20 % on purchase of plant and machinery, double the amount in the case of approved projects.
    - iii. Exemption from wealth taxes.
    - iv. Tariff on locally manufactured items was raised to protect the nascent local manufacturers.
    - V See Techno-Economic survey of Industrial Potential in Sri Lanka (Karunaratna, 1974). Also see the report of the Business and Industry Advisory Committee (B.I.A.C) and the White Paper on Government Policy on Private Investment', 1960.
34. For example, Glaxo Welcome Ceylon ltd., Swadeshi Industrial Works Limited, Wellawatta Spinning & Weaving Mills, Ceylon Match Co. Ltd.
35. For example, St. Anthony's Groups of Business, Upali group of businesses, and Dasa Industries are some such industries sprang up in the system.
36. For example, ACL Cable Ltd., Kandy textiles Industries, Chemical Industries Colombo ltd., and Ceylon Nutritional Food ltd. are some.
37. e.g., Hevawitharana (1986).
38. Kalecki spells out the point that higher internal savings facilitate borrowing capital in his work (1972:120).

39. For details of change in ownership see Lakshman (1973: 22-23).
40. The Director of Research, Central Bank of Sri Lanka, held the view in an interview that in the absence of detail information on direct foreign investment, the best approximation would be this information. The B.O.I investments are exempted from taxes and they are not abide by the laws applied to local companies. They are not bound to supply their financial statements to Registrar of Companies.

4

The Cyclical Behaviour of Industrial Accumulation

-Hypothesising Economic Policy Shift Effect

4.1. Introduction

The theoretical presentation in chapter 1 posits that the smooth functioning of a 'tripods structure' with a proper balance of pods — the state, private sector and foreign capital— fosters capitalist industrial development in 'new nations'. The complementary relations among the three partners, in particular, the state's role of balancing different forces in the system, may be fundamental to the achievement of an optimal path of capitalist industrial development for these countries. Empirically, certain countries among the 'new nations' have fulfilled the above basic prerequisites and achieved industrial status in a short period of time. The question is raised in this chapter as to whether the state, the private sector, and foreign investment have functioned optimally in Sri Lankan economy in a manner to fulfil the specifications suggested by the conceptual framework proposed in the first chapter.

The survey carried out in the previous two chapters reveals that the political and economic processes, which evolved, especially after WW1, hastened the initiation of a process of manufacturing accumulation in Sri Lanka. Chapter two discusses the ways in which economic environment during World War II helped to foster the process of state and private industrial accumulation. In fact, the wartime economic environment was a special case in point in respect of private investment in Sri Lanka. The private sector came forward to invest large sums of money in new manufacturing industries for the first time in history. Chapter three provides empirical evidence of two different phases, one prior to 1977 which experimented with planning-oriented policies and the other the post 1977 market economic policies. Private industrial accumulation prior to 1977 was relatively low and led only to very little structural change in the system.

The changing circumstances after independence led the state and the private sector to play their own specific roles in the 'partnership' of industrial development. Chapter three described the gradual changes in attitudes and levels of participation of the private sector over the last 45 years, especially, after 1977 resulting in the development of overall industrial capacity of the country. The overall trend of private industrial accumulation was characterised by several short and medium term fluctuations. The private sector has taken initiative to move out of unproductive sectors like finance and trade towards productive sectors like manufacturing and construction in the long run. Moreover, the net foreign direct investment (FDI) in plantations, trade and finance, though was negative before 1977 began to rise rapidly, especially, in manufacturing, after 1977, under the liberal economic environment.

In this chapter, we study the different relations that existed between the state and the private sector in their efforts to promote a 'joint project of industrialisation'. We noted earlier that the state has become the vanguard of the industrial development of the country getting involved in the formation of large and basic industries. Consequently, there were three important developments clearly discernible in the capitalist process of industrial accumulation of Sri Lanka after independence.

Firstly, there was a substantial expansion of state industrial capital at least until the mid-1970s, which to some extent, compensated for the slow private industrial formation. Secondly, though the overall private manufacturing industrial accumulation was slow in the early phases there was a satisfactory growth in it later at least until the mid-1980s. Thirdly, periodic fluctuations, associated with economic policy cycles, disturbed the process of industrial accumulation from time to time.

While the next two chapters concentrate on the first two developments, this chapter spells out the last characteristic, that is, the cyclical path of industrial accumulation. It attempts to establish a relationship between the cyclical character of the process of industrial accumulation and the changing political-economic environment —the policy shift effect. The question may be asked as to what factors contributed to different patterns of industrial accumulation in different periods. Some inferences may be drawn regarding the relations between economic policies of the state and private accumulation which determine the size of industrial accumulation in the country.

4.2. Hypothesising the Problem

The 'new nations' in Asia implemented different economic and political strategies. These naturally fostered different relations between the states and the economic structures of these nations; the latter comprised different actors of production of the economies. Some of these strategies were supportive and others hostile to fast structural changes needed for industrial development of these countries. For example, developmental states like South Korea and Taiwan collaborated with the private sector to implement developmental policies successfully and thereby achieved targeted objectives. On the other hand, the states in South Asia, most of which were politically democratic, maintained different types of relations with the private sector. In the case of India, Jenkins (1995) argues that the private sector and the state machinery worked in harmony to achieve private interests relegating national interests to a secondary position in the 'rent seeking economic structure' of the Indian polity.

We saw in the previous chapter that Sri Lanka followed a slow path of industrial accumulation like her other neighbours in the South Asian region. The relations maintained by the state of Sri Lanka with the private sector were different from that of India or even the East Asian countries. Altogether, the relations were not quite conducive for the growth of private economic activities in the system. According to Edwards (1993), '...the political structure in Sri Lanka has not been conducive to the development of an efficient manufacturing sector. The private sector was not encouraged to develop the manufacturing sector from the 1950s through to the end of the 1970s (see Kelegama and Wignaraja, 1991, 30,31), although it was encouraged in the 1980s'.

We need, therefore, to develop an alternative hypothesis for explaining the relative slowness of industrial achievements in the post-independent period. The alternative hypothesis takes the following form which is different from the conventional rent seeking hypothesis:

Disharmonous relations between the state and the private sector of Sri Lanka led to a slowing down of industrial accumulation. This was detrimental to the process of capitalist industrial development of Sri Lanka.

Using the new database on activities of the private sector, we attempt here to trace links between the private sector and state policies although 'it is a difficult task to trace the links between the industrial policies and the political structure in Sri Lanka' (Edwards, 1993:51).

4.3. The Overall Trends of Industrial Accumulation

The 'project of industrial development' formulated by the state in the post-independence era achieved varying degrees of success. The achievements of the project may be viewed from the accumulation of long-term industrial fixed assets in different periods as exhibited in figure 4.1 below. The figure points to four different types of accumulations over this period. Curve 4 describes the overall trend of fixed assets formation in the manufacturing industry. Curves 1, 2 and 3 denote the contributions of each partner in the project i.e., the state sector, the private sector and the direct foreign investment, respectively, in the process of fixed investment formation (expressed in terms of average levels of real fixed investments as a percentage of real GDP).

Curve 4 manifests the overall trend of industrial formation in Sri Lanka over a long period of 45 years. It highlights the presence of many short and long-term fluctuations in the path of industrial accumulation. The periods 1958-64, 1966-71, and 1977-84, for example, signify rising trends of fixed investments in manufacturing. Other periods, which lie in between, denote declining trends in industrial formation.

According to fig 4.1, the long-term trend of overall real industrial fixed investment (curve 4) follows a pyramidal pattern. In fact, the formation of fixed industrial investment before 1977 was low and sluggish. But, it rose rapidly thereafter until the mid-1980s followed by a downward trend. The overall growth of industrial formation in Sri Lanka reached its peak in the mid-1980s.

The three partners have contributed to industrial accumulation in different magnitudes in different periods. This is evident from Figure 4.1. The state, the main contributor, contributed immensely to the growth of industrial accumulation until the mid-1970s (see curve 1). The domestic private sector maintained a very low profile in the process while foreign capital was not a party to industrial formation prior to the mid-1970s (see curve 2 and 3 respectively).

The opposite is true with regard to the post-1977 era in industrial formation in Sri Lanka. It is evident in fig. 4.1 that state capital investment in manufacturing has been shrinking rapidly. The domestic and foreign capital takes the place of state capital after 1977. But, private participation in the sphere of industrial accumulation has not been as consistent as that of the state. Overall, the economic policies of respective regimes have influenced the behaviour of the three main parties involved in the 'project of industrialisation'.

4.3.1. Public Sector Investment

As noted earlier, the state sector played a dual role as a promoter as well as a partner in the industrial development programme since the 1930s. It functioned as the leading entrepreneur in industrial development, especially, during and after World War II. This intensified after independence, especially between 1956 and 1977. The long-term trend of public manufacturing investments over a period of 36 years is discernible in curve 1 in figure 4.1. Accordingly, the average volume of public investment in manufacturing has taken a pyramidal shape reaching an optimum in the mid-1970s. Public investment grew at average periodic rates of 20, 9 and 12 per cents during the periods 1957-64, 1965-70 and 1971-77 (Table 4.1). The interventionist policy of the state guided by socialist ideology motivated the state to involve in the economy with or without the support of other sectors (An empirical analysis of this policy will be made in chapter 5).

There was a sharp drop in public investment in manufacturing after 1977. The rate of growth of public investment dropped at different rates during different periods. For example, during the market economic policies from 1977 to 1984 public investments in manufacturing dropped at an average periodic rate of 3 per cent. But, during the period of disturbances between 1985 and 89, it dropped quite sharply at 10 per cent. With the presence of the new regime in 1994, public investment dropped in manufacturing only marginally at an average periodic rate of 2 per cent. Comparatively speaking, public investment helped to push up the overall path of industrial accumulation in the early phase of industrialisation in Sri Lanka.

FIGURE 4.1 TRENDS OF FIXED INVESTMENT IN MANUFACTURING BY THE 'ALIANCE' UNDER POLICY SHIFTS

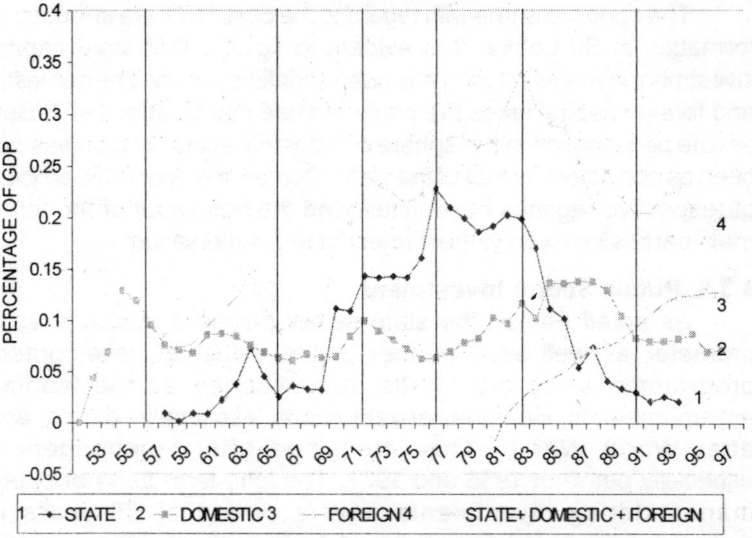

Source: Fixed Investment data, Handbooks of Listed Companies. Financial statements of State enterprises, Economic Progress of Independent Sri Lanka, the Central Bank, 1998.

4.3.2. Private Industrial Accumulation

The period before mid-1970s may be considered as the first phase and the period since then as the second phase of industrial accumulation of the private sector (curve 2, Figure 4.1). In the first phase, there were two patterns of private real investment in manufacturing. First, the private sector maintained only a low-level of investment in the manufacturing sector after independence. It continued to hold a low industrial capital base until the mid-1970s. Secondly, there were some periodic fluctuations in the volume of private fixed investments in this phase. Table 4.1 below helps to understand this cyclical behaviour of private investment in manufacturing where the rates of investment have taken negative/ positive signs in different periods. The variations in investment were associated with specific time intervals suggesting that short-term cycles of investments appeared to be policy-related.

There were two different patterns of private investment in manufacturing in the second phase. First, private industrial accumulation maintained a relatively high rate (5 percent) in the

FIGURE 4.2 CYCLICAL BEHAVIOUR OF MANUFACTURING FIXED ASSET FORMATION

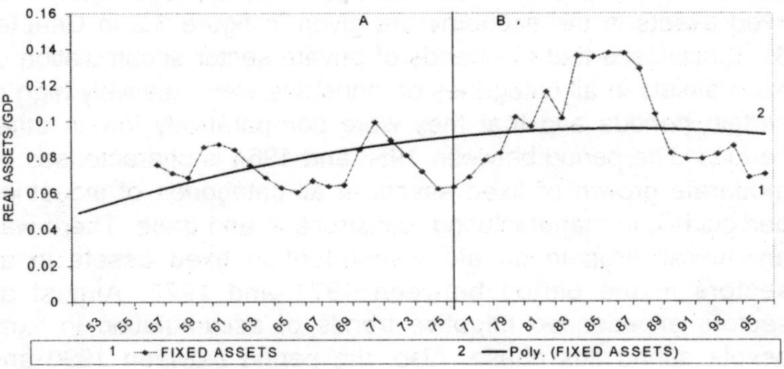

Source: Author's Database

beginning of the phase until the mid-1980s. It slowed down, thereafter. There were some picking-up processes in the 1990s but altogether the long-term trend of industrial formation seems to be one of ups and down as seen in figure 4.1. Secondly, quite similar to the first phase, there were also a few short cycles and a long cycle in the second phase of the private industrial accumulation as can be seen in figure 4.2.

Table 4.1. Average Periodic Rates of Growth of Fixed Investment

Period	*Private investment*	*Public investment*	*Foreign investment*	*Public + Private + Foreign*
1957 –64	0.02	0.21		0.06
1965 -70	0.03	0.09		0.07
1977 -77	-0.04	0.12		-0.01
1978 -84	0.05	-0.03	0.19	0.04
1985 -89	-0.04	-0.11	0.05	-0.03
1990—94	0.01	-0.05	0.06	0.02
1994 -97	-0.03	-0.02	0.005	-0.02
1990 -97	0.02		0.02	-0.01

Source: Associated with curves in Figure 4.1.

4.4. The Effects of the Shift in Economic policy

Private investment behaviour in different economic environments (associated with different economic policies) is a proxy for explaining entrepreneurs' responses to different economic regimes. The periodic patterns of accumulation of fixed assets in the economy are given in figure 3.2 in Chapter 3[1]. It discloses that the trends of private sector accumulation of fixed assets in all categories of industries were relatively high in certain periods and that they were comparatively low in other periods. The period between 1956 and 1964 is characterised by moderate growth of fixed assets in all categories of industries particularly, in manufacturing, construction and trade. There was an overall drop in private investment in fixed assets in all sectors in the period between 1971 and 1976. Almost all sectors experienced negative trends of accumulation in fixed assets during this phase. Also, the period between 1990 and 1994 marks a phase of recovery of industrial investment. In general, the private sector has successfully engaged in economic activities in all sectors of the economy in the 1965 - 70 and 1977-83 phases and marginally in 1989 -95. During the first two phases, the rates of growth of fixed capital accumulation in all sectors of the economy were significantly high.

The behaviour of private investors, in pre- and post-1977 periods, seems to suggest that private investment tended to grow in favourable market friendly economic environments and diminish in market-hostile environments. In manufacturing, the rate of growth of investment in fixed assets during the former period was relatively low (see Table 4.1). It was about 0.03 between 1965-70, which was moderately high. The rates of growth of fixed assets in finance, trade and construction were high during this period as can be seen in figure 3.2 in Chapter 3. The high rates of growth of fixed assets in these sectors may be associated with liberal market economic policies of the state. This implies that given a favourable business climate, the private sector ventures to mobilise scarce resources in productive sectors like manufacturing and semi-productive sectors like construction in the Sri Lankan economy.

Our observations appear to be, more or less, analogous with the observations of Jayasundera (1986: 43) regarding economic growth, capital expenditure, and overall productivity of investment over a long period (his table is reproduced in Table 4A1.1, Appendix 1). He finds that there was "higher economic growth in 1966 -1970 and 1976 –1985. Despite the continuous increase in the proportion of expenditure on capital accumulation [of public and private sectors] to GDP in 1956 -65 and 1971-75 periods, the average growth rates reflected a significant slow-down in the production activities in the country"(Jayasundera, 1986:68). We find that the average rate of growth of fixed assets in all sectors over the long period 1952–97 is about 0.02 (or 2 per cent. See Regression 4A2.3, Appendix 2). For Jayasundara "the Gross Domestic Product at constant factor cost prices increased approximately by 4.0 percent per annum over the 36 year period 1950 – 1985". Jayasundera (1986:68) emphasises that "... high growth rates are associated with the 1965 -1970 and 1978 -1985 periods during which acceleration of agriculture, construction and services provided a significant boost to the entire economy".

4.5. Variables Determining Investment Behaviour

The analysis of determinants of investment is an intricate task, which in the past has produced little consensus among economists (Bischoff, 1971:13). The knowledge of such determinants, however, is useful for planners to formulate growth strategies. We, therefore, make an endeavour to identify possible variables for a model of investment reviewing some work of specialists in the field of investment.

The term 'investment' is used to denote the increase in capital stock, the accumulation of capital. Its change over time may indicate the pattern of growth of productive capacity of the relevant sector. Edward J. Nell describes this accumulation of capital as a transformation of technical and productive organisation of the economy. For him '...capital must also be understood as a way of organising production and economic activity so that the accumulation of capital is the extension of the form of organisation into areas in which production, exchange and distribution were governed by other rules' (Nell, 1987:14).

In this definition, Nell brings in an institutional dimension into the concept of capital accumulation. 'Accumulation then implies the transformation of institutions as well as production'. He states that, 'the study of accumulation needs to explain both the availability of the surpluses and the *motivation* for 'ploughing it back' as a process of transformation'.

Economists have identified certain determinants of investment specific to developed countries[2]. The neo-classical investment models employed variables like 'desired level' of capital, the input prices and output prices as determinants of investment[3]. These models, however, assume that the production possibility spaces of firms are governed by Cobb-Douglas type of Production function. They are based on the conditions of profit maximisation and full employment[4]. Neo-classical economists identify market forces (e.g. the level of profits) as the fundamental determinants of investment in competitive market economic environments[5]. They used variables like internal cash flows, cost of external capital and growth of final demand as determinants of investment. However, Arthur Okun (1970:10) comments that there is a general disagreement among students of business investment regarding the relative importance of these variables.

We concentrate more on a broader environment consisting of social, political and economic variables in determining industrial accumulation of 'new nations'[6]. This is somewhat different from the neo-classical analysis of investment behaviour. We stress here Nell's notions of 'availability of surpluses' and the 'motivations for ploughing [them] back' as significant in determining the volume of investment of these nations. We consider market and non-market factors, in particular, the intensive role of the state, as determinants of the politico-economic environment of industrial accumulation of these 'new nations'.

The variables that influence the long-term expectation of private entrepreneurs would serve well in a model of investment in third world economies. These variables are associated with two complex conditions, the 'economic condition' and 'political climate' of the country. Economic and political factors are major determinants of foreign direct investment in developing countries (Schneider et. al., 1985: 161). Nevertheless, these two are broad themes. They are difficult to be quantitatively explained as these are determined by socio-political environment of the country. However, the 'level of economic activity' and the 'rate of change in the level of economic activity' might serve as approximations to 'economic situation' and 'its change' over time (Kalecki,1971:119). The political economic decisions and entrepreneurial motivational processes of regimes might determine the 'political climate' of the country. Entrepreneurial behaviours may be associated with Nell's institutional needs, 'the motivations for ploughing back effects'.

The two types of variables, economic and political (rather non-economic) are likely to determine the direction of future expectations. Their influence can produce different impacts on the magnitude of investment in different sectors of the economy. For example, the private sector may be unwilling to invest its surpluses in risky areas like manufacturing in a politically unfavourable environment but may invest in construction or commerce. Investment in construction or commerce is believed to be less volatile and less voluminous than in manufacturing. In this regard, the economic regime effects may be an explanatory variable in determining the volume of manufacturing investment of a country. The relation between investment and political environment may either be positive or negative depending upon the political regime and its relations with the investor class of the society.

A statistical relationship between change in investment and change in political regime needs to be established for developing inferences about change in attitudes of private investors because of the change in economic environment. In practice, it is difficult to find statistical information on behavioural attitudes of entrepreneurs regarding different economic regimes. Therefore, we assume that the pattern of change in the volume of investment in periods relating to certain economic policies reflects the response of entrepreneurs to such policies.

Changes in periodic private fixed investment in manufacturing and in all sectors under different economic policy conditions can be explained with figure 3.10 in chapter 3. It reveals that the volumes of private, public and foreign investment in manufacturing fixed assets are distinctively high in certain periods associated with particular economic policies and that they are clearly low in other periods.

An inference regarding the behaviour of private entrepreneurs of the manufacturing industry may thus be drawn as follows·

> "A certain degree of cyclical fluctuations in private investment in fixed assets over years may be associated with the state of mind of investors regarding economic polices of the state".

The state of mind of private investors regarding economic policies of the state may change depending upon their relations with the government. Their responses to policies of different governments have taken different forms in the past. The financial statements of the private manufacturing sector provide useful guidance regarding short-term behaviour of entrepreneurs in different environments[7]. The private entrepreneurs appeared to have adopted two alternative practices in the form of 'risk taking' and 'risk avoidance' associated with different economic policies of the state. It appears that in periods of upswings, the private entrepreneurs tended to expand their physical capital stock in main lines of production. During slump periods with uncertain conditions, they tended to intensify the compilation of inventories and engage in other kinds of short-term alternative investment activities though small in magnitudes[8].

This behaviour is noticed in practices of channelling financial resources of firms towards different types of asset formations in different periods as explained by final accounts of individual firms. Associated with certain periods, there are moves by large private firms to re-channel a part of financial resources of manufacturing towards other asset formations. This relationship is statistically identified with a regression result in Regression 4A2.2, appendix 2.This behaviour, though relatively small in magnitude, may be one of the deliberate and safe practices adopted by the private sector to evade risks or uncertainties pertaining to hostile policies of regimes in different periods. The hypothesis that firms make changes in their investment portfolios as remedial measures to avoid risks may thus be established.

4.6. Economic Policy Shift and Private Accumulation – The Statistical Relationship

The hypothesis developed earlier may be supported by a study of statistical relationships between fixed capital formation and economic policy shifts. The related variables may be the change in 'economic conditions' and 'political climate' of the country as used by Schneider and Frey (1985) in explaining economic and political determinants of foreign direct investment.

According to Kalecki, the 'level of economic activity' and the 'rate of change in the level of economic activity' conceptually represent 'economic conditions' and 'its change' in the country. He argues that there has been a correlation between favourable economic activity of the country and high internal gross savings (St) of firms. The high internal gross savings bring about high investments in fixed assets of firms. In his opinion, the 'rate of change of profits per unit of time' (Pt) would indicate the 'rate of change of the level of economic activity'.

We, additionally, assume that change in economic regimes would give rise to policy shifts which change the 'political climate' of the country. The effects of change in 'political climate' on the economy may be realised with the help of a proxy variable, a dummy (Dt) (the details of this variable are discussed in the Appendix to this chapter. In the data set, the value 1 was assigned to years between 1956 to 1964 and again from 1971 to 1977. The value 0 is given to other years e.g., from 1952 to 1955, from 1965 to 1970 and from 1978 to 1982).

Scholars often use Kalecki's basic investment model to develop investment models for different economies. For example, Hans Van Ees et al. (1997: 395-407) used the simple Kaleckian investment model to analyse 'the impact of profits on investment in the Dutch manufacturing sector, in which profits and capacity determine the level of investment'. We also use the simple structural investment model of Kalecki in this study. Kalecki's investment model is a simple but a practical one, which may easily be used for this purpose. We employ an additional dummy variable in it to explain the investment behaviour of private entrepreneurs under different 'economic policy shifts'. Based upon Kaleckian model, our regression produces the following results:

$$\mathbf{F_{t+1} = 22.81 + 0.89\, S_t + 0.28\, P_t - 27.31\, D_t}$$

S .E (7.67) (0.089) (0.053) (9.02)

$R^2 = 0.837$

$F = 43.059$

D.W = 1.47 (N =29, K = 4)

(Source: Regression 4A2.1 in Appendix 2).

Where,

Ft_{t+1} : Fixed investments in manufacturing in year $_{t+1}$.

S_t : Real internal gross savings of manufacturing firms in year t,

P_t : Rate of change in real gross profits of the economy in year t, and

Dt: Response of private entrepreneurs to economic policy shifts, the dummy variable.

S.E: Standard Error

D.W: Durbin-Watson test[9]

The outputs of the regression are statistically significant and agree with Kalecki's postulations. The variables identified by the regression tend to explain satisfactorily the behaviour of private fixed investment in manufacturing. Three important variables were identified in it:

1. The 'current internal gross savings' or the 'current level of economic activity' (St),
2. The 'rate of change in real gross profits' or 'the rate of change in the level of economic activity' $\left(\frac{\Delta Pt}{\Delta t}\right)$, and
3. The entrepreneur response to economic policy shifts, the dummy variable (Dt).

Our principal concern in this study has been to understand the attitudes and responses of the entrepreneur class to different 'economic policy shifts' of the state. We, intentionally, included the dummy variable (Dt) in the regression to measure this response quantitatively. The dummy may help to explain responses of the private sector to changes in economic policies of the state, in particular, the planning-oriented policies implemented during 1956 and 1965 and again between 1971 and 1977.

The regression coefficient of the dummy variable D_t explains this response quantitatively. The negative value refers to the adverse response of the private entrepreneur class to statist and planning-centric economic policies. Figure 4A3. 2 in appendix 3 provides an explanation to the value of this coefficient[10]. The curves 1 and 2 in it represent two levels of average fixed investments in two different business environments; one is with no interference of anti-market forces and other with interference of those forces. Curves 1 and 2 are derived using the above regression excluding and including the variable D_t in it. The coefficient of D_t thus measures the average degree of variations between the two curves.

The coefficient of 'internal gross savings' (St) —the 'current level of economic activity' —carries a positive value implying that the current level of economic activity produces some positive impact on future private investment. The coefficient of St 'indicates by how much future investments increase as a result of increments in total current savings' $[d(F_{t+1})/d(S_t)]$ described by

Kalecki (1971). The value of this coefficient is determined by many factors (Kalecki, 1971). The coefficient takes a value of 0.89 in absolute terms which is less than 1 means that the current savings tend to change future fixed investments less than proportionately (than what Kalecki had generalised: see appendix below for details). The 'internal savings' or the current level of economic activity' has had an influence on the determination of future volume of fixed investment.

Lastly, the effect of the 'change in the level of profitability of investment' or the 'rate of change in profits' (P_t) on industrial fixed investment appears to be marginal in values. It suggests that the 'rate of change in the level of economic activity', the future economic prospect, tends to stimulate the private investors only marginally.

Altogether, the 'economic policy shifts' (Dt) appeared to be an influential variable in the determination of private investment compared with the other two variables related to 'economic conditions' in the regression. It suggests that when the economy is functioning in periods dominated by anti-market forces, the 'economic policy shift' (D_t) dominantly influences the overall private investment on such occasions. When the economy operates in normal periods, the effect of D_t disappears. IIt can be asserted that the 'economic factors' dominate private investment behaviour. In such situations, both 'the current level of economic activity' (S_t) and 'the rate of change in the level of economic activity: the future prospects' (P_t) stimulate the private investor class of the country.

These imply that the strategies of 'import substitution' and the future programme of 'export promotions' could have yielded better results had those been put into practice in an environment similar to the latter. The private entrepreneurs would have responded positively to such changes in a favourable 'political environment'. The society apparently has achieved less than optimal benefits of 'economic conditions' created by the policy of 'import substitution' as a result of the 'political climate' which had been quite hostile to the private entrepreneur class. The economic regimes in periods of 1956-64 and 1971–77 implemented planning-centred economic policies. Private entrepreneurs tended to respond adversely to these policies by lowering their *desired level* of investments.

4.7. Summary

The descriptive and quantitative inquiries into different investment practices of the private and public sectors in Sri Lanka highlighted two distinctive investment behaviours under two different environments, i.e. market-oriented and market-hostile environments. The statistical findings suggest that the private sector had not been in favour of market-hostile policies of the state. In such circumstances, the private sector exercised other strategies to limit fixed assets formation in industrial activities. This behaviour of the private sector inevitably compelled the public sector to shoulder a greater share of the responsibility in implementing 'the project of industrialisation'.

Certain economic policies of the state may have discouraged private investments in industrial activities. As a result the system forfeited a large private investible fund which otherwise could have been utilised for the industrial development of the country. This, therefore, raises concern about the state of compatibility of policies of the state with the demand of the private sector in respect of achieving the objective of rapid industrialisation.

These developments suggest further research on optimal behaviour of the state and the private sector for high industrial accumulation in 'new nations'. This, in fact, requires a compromise policy mix for the state and the private sector including direct foreign investment enabling them to contribute optimum level of industrial accumulation for achieving the above objective. This implies that attention needs to be paid to the improvement of the process of policy-making of the state, the institutional framework and the mechanism of incentives provided by the state for successful implementation of 'the state project of industrialisation' of these countries. This also suggests further examination and detailed analysis of how the state and the private sector could perform effectively as engines of industrial development of these countries.

Appendix to Chapter 4

The Model of Determinants of Investment

A model of industrial fixed capital formation of the private sector may be developed with the inclusion of economic and non-economic variables to elucidate the conceptual notion of non-economic characteristics in investment functions. We are in conformity with

Kalecki's model of investment decisions and his conceptualisation of investment behaviour of the private sector.

Kalecki developing his model in the 1970s concerning the investment environment prevailing in the period introduced two main economic variables that determine investment decisions in the model. Our study refers, more or less, to the same period, from 1952 to 1983 —the period of low level market economic activities. We, however, employ an additional variable to represent possible non-economic influences on the determination of investment decisions. The dummy variable introduced in the model would help to apprehend the possible economic regime effects on private investment decisions.

The understanding of factors that determine periodic changes in private investment in manufacturing may be useful for policy decisions. The standard model of Michal Kalecki (1971:123) on determinants of investment may be helpful in understanding the determinants and the pattern of private investment in the manufacturing sector of Sri Lanka. The following is a slightly modified version of his model with a dummy variable (Dt) to represent practices of private investment in the manufacturing sector under different economic regimes.

$$F_{t+1} = c' + a'S_t + b'\frac{\Delta P_t}{\Delta t} + D_t$$

F_{t+1}: Fixed Investment in period t+1,

S_t : Past internal gross savings (in period t),

$\left(\frac{\Delta Pt}{\Delta t}\right)$: Rate of change in profits in Period t

D_t : Regime preference of private entrepreneurs (in period t).

Kalecki describes his model as "the determinants of investment in fixed capital which was reduced to past savings and to the past rate of change in profits". He defines the functions of explanatory variables as follows:

S_t on the right-hand side depends on the *level* of

economic activity at time t, while $DP_t \backslash Dt$ depends on the *rate of change* in this level. Total investment thus depends, according to our theory, on both the level of economic activity and the rate of change in this level at some earlier time (Kalecki, 1971:119-123).

The variables, internal gross savings, S_t, and rate of change in profits[11], $\Delta P_t \backslash \Delta t$, can be assumed to be determined outside the firm level. The determinants of internal gross savings like depreciation, undistributed profits, personal savings are assumed to be influenced by external factors like the state of technology, market dividend rate etc. Kalecki has stated that high internal gross savings tend to enhance investment in fixed assets of the firm:

> ...the rate of capital accumulation (of the private sector), F, is an increasing function of total gross savings, S (Kalecki, 1971:111).

Like Kalecki, we too included depreciation, undistributed profits and 'personal savings' (the additions to the shareholders' equity funds and investment in other companies) in internal gross savings of the private sector.

Market conditions and competitiveness[12], *inter alia*, influence the expected profits $\left(\frac{\Delta Pt}{\Delta t}\right)$, which subsequently lead to changes in fixed assets. "The operation of this factor involves a kind of accelerator mechanism" as described by K.Laski (Laski: 14: 1987). Kalecki used the change of profits per unit of time and interpreted it as the level of change of economic activity.

> When the profitability of new investment projects is being weighed, expected profits are considered in relation to the value of the new capital equipment. Thus, profits may be taken in relation to the current prices of investment goods (Kalecki, 1971:112).

Kalecki argues that 'the effect of change of profits per unit of time is of decisive importance in determining the character of cyclical fluctuation'. Hence, 'the rate of investment (decision) is an increasing function of $(\Delta P/\Delta t)$'.

The gross internal saving is also an important determinant of investment in fixed assets in manufacturing. Laski interpreting

Kalecki's explanatory variable, the gross internal savings of a firm (St), argues that 'the increase of business savings influences investment decisions positively because it provides finance for investment, gives the firm a larger access to the capital market and allows for 'increasing risk' involved' (Laski, 1987:10).

Additionally, we include a dummy variable as a proxy to explain the attitudes of the private sector to different market economic environments and its impact on the private investment process. The dummy variable (Dt) describes the degree of sensitivity of private investment to change in entrepreneurial attitudes in respect of economic regimes in power.

Kalecki had his reservations regarding the magnitude of the coefficient of (St), which to him would take different values under different conditions. He states that " the conflicting factors leave us still uncertain about whether the coefficient 'b' will be greater or less than 1 "(Kalecki, 1971:120).

> ...the increment in the 'internal' savings of the firms which is relevant for investment decisions is smaller than the increment in total savings. This factor in itself would tend to make 'b' less than 1. ... An increment in internal savings that enables the firm to absorb outside funds at a higher rate if investment is considered desirable. This factor tends to increase investment decisions by more than the increment in 'internal' savings (Kalecki, 1971:120).

Notes

1. The periods were chosen according the types of economic policies implemented in the economy. The following specification can be found in each period as identified in section 3.3 above;
   1952 - 55 active-market economic policies,
   1956 - 64 More planning- oriented economic policies,
   1965 - 70 Active-market economic policies,
   1971 - 77 Inactive-market economic policies
   1978 - 85 Liberalised market economic policies
   1984 – 90 Period of political and economic instability due to the ethnic problems and JVP insurrection, and, 1990 - 90 The period of new industrial policies.
2. Bischoff briefly touches on certain neoclassical investment models such as the cash flow model, General Accelerator model,

the Security value model, the Standard Neoclassical model and the Federal Reserve-MIT- Pennsylvania econometric model.

3. For example, Jorgenson et al. (1968) assumes that firms adjust their capital stocks towards a 'desired' stock of capital. The desired stock is assumed to be dependent upon planned output and 'the ratio of output price to the implicit rental price of the services of capital goods' (Bischoff, 1971:21).
4. See in Bischoff (1971:21,60) for details.
5. The existing literature was surveyed by Jorgenson (1971: 1111 – 47).
6. We attempt here to explain the cyclical behaviour of investment and to discuss the institutional process that facilitates accumulation. Kalecki type equation may be best suitable for explaining the determination of private capital stock in Sri Lanka. In developing investment models, Amit Bhaduri and Marglin have benefited greatly from the work of Kalecki See. Pp. 983-991, *The New Palgrave A Dictionary of Economics*, E to J series (1991).
7. The series of Handbooks of Listed Companies from 1942 to 1999 were used to find information.
8. The entries in balance sheets in Listed Companies during such periods, for example, between 1970 and 1877, refer to various OTHER types of investments such as fixed deposits, deposits in convertible Rupee accounts, Tax reserve certificates, on-site Insurance claim deposits, tax reduction certificates and investments in subsidiaries.
9. Null hypothesis is developed stating that successive disturbances are negatively correlated. This test was carried out and the null hypothesis is accepted as $d > d_U$ ($d=1.47$, $d_U = 1.40$) at the 1 per cent significant level. (See, Theil, 1971:199 –203).
10. For understanding the usefulness of dummy variables in regressions and interpreting the coefficient of the dummy variable, see Thomas H. Wonnacott and Ronald J.Wonnacott, 1969, *Introductory Statistics,* John Wiley & Sons, Inc,: 269-73.
11. Mayer et al., (1957), argue that the investment depends on the level of profits.
12. Mayer, J. and Kuh, E (1957).

5

The Slow Growth in Industrial Investment up to 1977 : The Disparate Forces

5.1. Introduction

The main factors that influence the overall industrial accumulation process have been statistically identified in the previous chapter. The analysis of data reveals that the conflict between 'market forces' and 'forces hostile-to-markets' in the process of private industrial accumulation has lowered the pace of industrial growth of the country. The findings are useful for understanding the causes for low industrial accumulation of the country.

It is equally important to have an inquiry into econo-political historical events to identify the nature, causes and effects of conflicts in the system under the heading of 'historical institutionalism' suggested by Steinmo et al. (1992). It might reinforce the significance of our statistical findings in the previous chapter. The sources of disturbances on capitalist industrial development require to be identified for understanding different types of conflicts in different periods. In effect, the state-based hindrances on private economic activities that took place in early decades need to be distinguished from hindrances that errupted in socio-political fronts in the post-1977 period. We will discuss the former in this chapter and postpone the latter to the next chapter.

Most East Asian countries, in particular, Korea, Taiwan and Singapore were successful in employing domestic private, foreign and state capital in industrial development under state-guided markets or a market guided planning framework (Fernando, 1997:104). Such frameworks enabled these countries to achieve fast industrial accumulation. South Asian countries, like Sri Lanka and India, employed domestic private, foreign and state capital to mobilise resources towards industrial accumulation more on a 'plan-centred' economic framework. The latter countries apparently experienced a slower process of industrial accumulation and generated less than optimal benefits to society. Then, the question arises as to what factors impeded the growth momentum of the latter groups of countries. What were the causes that delayed the economic forces overcoming hostility to markets in these countries thereby preventing rapid industrial accumulation?

The writings on various measures adopted by successive governments in the past to promote industrial accumulation and the shortcomings of those measures are many and varied (Snodgrass, 1966, 1974, 1988; Lakshman, 1997; Athukorala 1997; Attapatu, 1997: Abeyratna, 1997). Yet, the question inadequately answered is what hindered Sri Lanka's progress along with the capitalist industrial path while her neighbours in Southeast Asia were able to accumulate capital. Has the state as the promoter been unsuccessful in developing necessary relations with the other two parties, the domestic private capital and foreign capital, for sustainable capitalist industrial development in Sri Lanka?

The present chapter endeavours to identify the behavioural factors that determine the policy cycles. There were two main policy regimes or 'coalitions', which were in operation in alternate cycles. The two 'coalitions' believed in policies and ideologies of pro-market capitalism and pro-interventionist mixed economy. The chapter examines causes for and effects of interventionist policies and the impact of forces hostile to markets on general growth of industrial accumulation in Sri Lanka.

5.2. Policy Shifts on Industrial Investment

'New nations' effected various institutional changes in both political and economic spheres with a view to revitalising economic forces for fast and compressed (capitalist) industrial accumulation. These changes have taken place in the form of promoting private industrial activities, encouraging foreign investment, introducing market approaches favouring capital accumulation in industry, improving supportive services and welfare programmes. The degree of success of these changes, however, varied from country to country, depending upon many things, importantly, the competence of the state – in decision-makings and implementation.

It is normal for countries like Sri Lanka and India with democratic governance to experience frequent changes in the socio-economic and political climate. Yet, most newly industrialised countries (NICs), which practised authoritarian rules, were able to maintain relatively stable political and economic processes. The longevity of policy regimes in countries apparently was an important contributor to development. Sobhan's (1999:53) comment on the longevity of regimes is interesting. 'In these countries, policy continuity tends to be weak and there is a lack of capacity to make bold and decisive policy decisions'. He, however, believes that 'regime continuity remains a necessary but far from an essential condition for development process'.

In Sri Lanka, there were several phases of intermittent shifts in economic policies from planning to liberal market policies. A fairly short phase of liberal market policies on industrial development commenced during World War II and continued until 1955. The second phase based upon planning principles continued for a long period. It started a little latter than 1956 and was carried on until about 1977. The third phase proceeded steadily for about seventeen years from 1977 (Rajapatirana, 1988). The recent one commenced in 1994.

There were underlying economic objectives behind these 'policy shifts'. The primary objective was the structural change in favour of industrial development relegating plantation development to a secondary position. The other was the institutional change favourable for the alternative economic strategy, the industrial development. The latter was, nevertheless, complementary to the former. The 'plantation accumulation strategy' of colonial capitalists, of course, 'reached its expansionary limits' with independence. '[A] further expansion of capitalism would, even at the time of independence, have required moves towards altering the industrial base' (Uyangoda 1992:181). Therefore, the State was compelled to adopt an alternative modus operandi, the structural change under 'the industrial accumulation strategy'.

5.2.1. Phase I (1948 –55): Liberal Market Ideology on Industrial Accumulation

Snodgrass (1998:11-12) titled the period between 1948-56 as one of "Economic populism with an open economy". He characterised the political regime of the United National Party (UNP) as one which '... was happy to provide welfare benefits as a way to attract voter support' while implementing liberal market policies. The state was under tremendous pressure from many social, political and economic forces at work. An excellent example of which is the *hartal* in 1953. The government decided to raise subsidised retail price of rice when the 'cost of the welfare provisions was breaking the bank' but failed to implement it because of the intense pressure that came from different groups (Snodgrass, 1998: 12). There were different social groups behind the 'liberal coalition'. The groups involved were the Westernised-elite, the private sector investors, and the personnel in administrative and professional posts who emerged from the land-owning and merchant classes (Wilson, 1975:19; Warnapala, 1992:148). The others were the (i) small and medium planters and landowners, (ii) agrarian landlords, and (iii) merchants.

The upper middle (capitalist) class element, which was behind this regime, was politically strong compared to either the lower middle class or the working class. Myrdal describes the elite class as a small well-to-do upper class 'whose economic interests had become closely allied with those of the British and who had a personal and professional interest in playing the game of politics' (Myrdal, 1968). This group exerted pressure on the 'liberal coalition' to implement liberal economic policies. The state thus promoted institutions like free internal markets to strengthen the broad economic policy of 'micro-level laissez-faireism' (Uyangoda, 1992:184).

The position of the 'liberal coalition' of the UNP on industrial development as a strategy of restructuring was not clear; it is vaguely mentioned in its two Six-Year development programmes announced after independence[1]. The 'coalition' viewed industrial development in Sri Lanka as a natural and gradual process and expected that the industrial process would continue over a long period for the country to reap its full benefits. The regime had 'an optimistic belief in Sri Lanka's slow but eventual entry to the path of industrial growth' (Uyangoda, 1992:181-2). Its main emphasis was to develop agriculture during the first six-year period relegating industrial development to a secondary position. Consequently, the allocation of funds to industry was nominal in the first programme when compared with the allocation of funds to agriculture. In Snodgrass's words 'the emphasis on industrialisation was deliberately scorned' (Snodgrass, 1966:110). Even the second Six-Year Plan of the coalition provided only a little support for industrial development. Ponnambalam says 'the government policy in respect of industrialisation was virtually non-existent'. Its vision was to achieve industrial development 'through the private sector' (Ponnambalam, 1980:29).

Karunaratne (1999:239) holds the view that the regime even 'pursued a policy of de-industrialisation and closed down some of the factories that had been established to meet World War II contingencies' following advice from the World Bank (1953). The state owned about seven industries during this period[2]. Most of these factories, however, were running at a loss and, consequently, were closed by 1953[3]. The losses in some factories (e.g., the Plywoods factory) were due to poor management, lack of co-ordination and under-utilisation of capacities[4]. The only 'important industrial ventures [which commenced during the period 1948-55] were the cement factory in Kankesanturai and the hydro-electric power station at Luxapana' (Ponnambalam, 1980:23). The UNP in its last few years in office contemplated the transfer of the remaining state industrial undertakings to the private sector first converting them into public corporations and then to public companies as joint ventures[5].

The private sector did not work towards industrial accumulation during this phase with as great enthusiasm as during the Wartime. For example, the overall surplus generated by the private sector and invested in new share capital of private firms was about Rs. 360.0 million during the period 1941 -53[6]. Much of these, about 70.4 percent, were invested in shares of private limited companies and only 29.6 percent was invested in large public firms[7]. These firms engaged in various sectors of the economy like agriculture, manufacturing, construction, finance & insurance, services and trade. The surplus that went into the manufacturing industry during 1940 and 1953 was only about Rs. 60.5 million, or 17 percent of the above surplus fund. The balance 83 percent moved into quick yielding sectors like finance, services, and trade[8].

The number of public and private limited companies rose at

an alarming rate of 140 percent from 454 to 1090 between 1940 and 1947. However, these have risen only at a moderate rate of 48.3 percent from 1179 to 1742[9] during 1948–53. The 'Bulletin' of the Central Bank of Ceylon in 1954, comments that 'the flow of new capital has been predominantly in three groups (tea-cum-rubber, manufacturing and trade)'. New companies were 'formed to take-over businesses owned by foreigners and companies incorporated abroad.'

Ferguson's Directory provides names of 20 private manufacturing firms which were set up during the period 1948-55. Most of these were relatively small private firms; some of which disappeared from production processes after some time[10]. The records in Ferguson show that large firms, particularly the public companies, established during this period were engaged mostly in the plantations, the motor trade, trade and the manufacture of beverages and pharmaceutical products[11].

The liberal regime provided only little support to develop a private industrial sector to serve as an engine of growth. The liberal economic policy of the regime tended to discourage the provision of necessary stimuli, micro and macro, for private industrial development. The main concern of the state was to promote institutions favourable for a competitive market environment in line with the liberal import policy of the regime[12]. As a result, the private sector, the co-partner of any project of industrialisation, showed no enthusiasm in undertaking industrial investment[13]. The liberal regime, nevertheless, offered attractive concessions to the private sector in 1955 (The Budget Speech, 1955-56). But the private sector did not respond favourably to this last moment call.

The state failed to attract foreign investment for the industrial development programme of the country. The Government offered an attractive package of incentives to foreign capitalists in 1954 (The Budget Speech, 1954-55: 13). But, 'there was no marked inflow of private foreign capital into the country' (Das Gupta, 1954: 16). The threat[14] of nationalisation of foreign assets and the low returns on industrial investments may have discouraged them from investing funds in industry.

The conservative political elite[15] and a variety of pressure groups[15] intervened in the determination of the 'political agenda' of this 'liberal coalition' during 1948-56. Their main interests centred on plantation agriculture and only marginally on industrial development[17]. Consequently, 'planning strategy was clearly centred around agricultural development' and the private sector was considered the engine of implementing these policies (Moore, 1985:19).

Ponnambalam tends to deduce that the main reason for state not providing direct support to industrial development may be its obligation to satisfy the aspirations of interest groups that supported it at the election. He argues that it may have shaped state policy so as not to entertain any import substitution industrial package which may have been thought to affect the interests of party supporters adversely[18]. The state's priority thus was to satisfy the consumers in the system making available the imported consumer goods in the market (Ponnambalam, 1980: 12).

Snodgrass is critical of the inadequacy of the state's 'public policy' which caused 'the disappointing performance of the private industrialists'. Disappointment arose when the state failed to provide a protected economic environment and necessary institutional structure (resembling a situation that prevailed during the War periods or similar to that which prevailed after 1958) for the private sector to engage in industrial accumulation. On the contrary, it brought down import duties on a large group of consumer goods to create a competitive market atmosphere.

This policy led to a decline in attracting private capital to manufacturing industry. The rates of profit earned by six leading manufacturing corporations during 1948 and 1956 evidently follow a downward trend as described by Ramachandran[19]. The policy, however, contributed to the rise in levels of profitability of other economic pursuits like trade, plantations, and real estate. The earnings per share in trade, plantations and construction sectors were substantially higher than that of manufacturing during this period. As a result, resources were reallocated in favour of trade which yielded quick returns.

Snodgrass (1966:172) presumes that a proper 'public policy' would have helped the entrepreneurs to 'accumulate industrial experience' and to 'direct them away from their traditional fields of operation in agriculture, trade and real estates'. The contemporary governments, which did not have any industrial vision, thus, favoured agriculture on an *ad hoc* basis under liberal market economic principles[20].

The private sector also suffered from certain deficiencies as an engine of industrial development. The Minister of Finance in his 1955 budget speech highlighted 'various factors, which were hampering economic development in the private sector'. He pointed out the following constraints faced by the private sector in the task of industrial formation:

1. Scarcity of investible funds.
2. Lack of technical knowledge and personnel.
3. Smallness of markets.
4. Foreign competition.
5. Scarcity of basic raw materials.
6. Lack of adequately developed social-overheads.

Some of these shortcomings appeared to be fundamental and required the assistance and co-operation of the state to overcome them in the long run. The capacity and the prospects of the private sector thus, were limited; it served only as a sluggish partner in the industrial projects of the fifties.

The 'liberal market economic strategy' as a policy failed to establish the necessary 'industrial investment climate' to generate private industrial surpluses and to mobilise them towards industrial development. Karunaratna (1999:239) says that 'the UNP missed an opportunity to grasp the industrialisation imperative and to restructure the dualistic economy', 'despite the prevalence of favourable initial conditions and macroeconomic fundamentals'.

5.2.2. Phase II (1956-64): Shift towards a Planning-oriented Industrial Policy

Snodgrass (1998:12) characterises the second regime as 'economic populism with economic controls'. This regime brought in controls and interventionist policies into the system under a populist and socialist framework. Pereira (1993) in his thesis on logic of growth cycles of the state highlights that these types of changes in ideology are natural in 'new nations'. He justifies possible intervention of the state at the early stage of any process of late industrialisation and describes the ways in which the intervention of the state could correct market failures. Such direct interventions may take place in the form of direct participation in economic activities by forming state-owned enterprises, particularly in the initial stage of industrialisation[21].

The purpose of state intervention in early stages of

industrial processes of 'late comers' is to lay the initial foundation for economic development of those countries. Some suggest that the governments in less developed countries must 'engage and finance 'big push' programmes to take-off their economies in a short period'[22]. The common consensus of critique has been that these countries must achieve their industrial development 'as rapid as possible' (Roy, 1974).

The second phase commenced in 1956 under the patronage of the 'lower middle class'[23]. This process of transition from the first phase to the second phase is well-documented (Ponnambalam, 1980; Moore, 1985; Uyangoda, 1992, Warnapala, 1992). An early understanding of the regime, its objectives, vision, and its peer groups, may help in explaining the role of the state and its relevance to the fulfilment of the vision of the 'new nation'.

5.2.2.1. The Composition

Different writers have described the political change in 1956 in different ways. Wilson commented that the failure of the UNP to attract rural masses and the underprivileged urban classes dispite the fact that 'the party stood not at the extreme Right in politics but to the Right of Centre' caused bad election defeat of 1956 (Wilson, 1975: 9). Wriggins (1960) says that the new coalition 'came to power after mobilizing engulfing waves of accumulated political, cultural and economic grievances' in the election campaign. Warnapala (1992:156) describes the victory of the 'coalition' as '...the mass movement led by the new leadership, rooted in the traditions and culture of the village in Sinhalese society, was able to take governmental power away from the English-speaking elite. ...It was a political alliance formed to defeat the UNP on the basis of a common programme'.

Warnapala's characterisation appears to be quite consistent with the description provided by our model in chap. 1. Some influential pressure groups in the system became politically powerful and interacted with the elite class. The 'coalition' of '...layers of Sinhalese society whose interests were not adequately aggregated in the rather conservative socio-economic programme of the UNP' appeared to have got together as a dynamic movement led by the Sri Lanka Freedom Party (SLFP) (Uyangoda, 1992: 184). Other elite including elite in the

LSSP and the CP, and the working class in the plantations, trade, services and manufacturing industries backed it. The strength of the state grew steadily over a period of 20 years as a phase under this 'coalition'.

The 'coalition' underwent many periodic changes in its configuration in the course of its existence. These changes came about because of its flexibility. It had not been 'bound together by strong ideological bonds' (Fernando, 1961:173). It rather adopted an adaptable economic ideology - the mixed economy - along with its political ideology - the social democracy (Uyangoda, 1992:187). Wilson (1975: 22) says that the '[g]overnment policies did not necessarily follow a defined and predictable path. Instead, they were largely formulated on an ad hoc basis mainly on pragmatic consideration'.

This flexibility allowed the 'coalition' to integrate distinctive groups and classes with different values and practices into the movement at different points of time[24]. Different class factions began to penetrate the coalition from its beginning itself (Fernando, 1961: 175). Later in the 1960s and 1970s, the socialist parties strengthened their relations with the 'coalition' in different capacities (Uyangoda, 1995: 185).

In effect, the dominant factions within the 'coalition' exerted their influence in the process of decision-making and implementation. These factionalist interventions, in a way, contributed to the shifting of original objectives of the 'coalition' to correspond with the changing environment. The other built-in character of the 'coalition' was the dominance of the bureaucrats and the coalition's own trade unions in the process of decision-making and the machinery of implementation (Wilson, 1975: 23-5).

5.2.2.2. The Planning-Orientation

We noticed earlier that even with the provision of micro-level stimuli, the domestic private and foreign capital did not come forward to shoulder the process of industrial development of Sri Lanka during previous liberal economic environment. Therefore, the modality of how the policy of industrialisation was to be shaped to effect long over due structural changes on the economic front had been discussed extensively in Parliament after 1956 (Ceylon Hansard, 1956:260). The consensus of members of Parliament was that the state was to participate actively in industrial accumulation in a situation where private industrial accumulation was not forthcoming[25]. Foreign·

participation was marginal during this period with 'a considerable drain of the resources of the country both from the point of view of dividends and repatriation of capital' (Ceylon Hansard, 1957: 684)[26]. The Minister of Industries after reviewing the situation and the level of cooperation of the private sector suggested that the state should develop a comprehensive plan and step-in to mobilise resources towards industry with the assistance of the private sector (Ceylon Hansard, 1956: 993).

The 'contemporary regime perceived industrialisation as the only remedy for the ills of the old system and agitated for early industrial development'. It 'advocated direct statist-socio-economic policies' for achieving this objective (Uyangoda, 1992:184). One reason for the implementation of statist policies was the poor state of development of the private sector. It was deficient in capital, dynamism in entrepreneurship and motivation. Among international experts invited to examine the low level of private capital formation in Sri Lanka, Joan Robinson commented that the conditions necessary for 'the capitalists to employ the available labour force have not been forthcoming'[27]. The smallness of the capital base in Ceylon was reflected in the small size of the share market. Even the foreigners who had invested funds in plantations in the past were reluctant to invest in industry, despite many government incentives provided (Wijesinghe, 1975: 19).

Sri Lanka's new economic strategy came into being under the umbrella of 'state interventionism' (some call 'state capitalism'). This was the common strategy in many post-colonial countries, and practised widely during this period (Uyangoda, 1992). Deepak Lal (1980: 212) holds that 'countries that consider private entrepreneurs to be unwilling or unable to take a lead in industrialisation turn to public enterprises for an essentially promotional role'. In fact, the 'state capitalist industrial policy' in an industrially primitive economy may be viewed as a stepping stone for the promotion of future industrial activity of the country. The state was believed to have a dual role to play in this new set up. The state had to perform as a provider of 'primary' and 'secondary contributions' to the industrial accumulation process. Primarily, it had to become the lead sector, the 'large entrepreneur' of the economy at least until the industrial private sector begins to play its part in the system. Secondarily, the sector needs to provide both micro-level and macro-level stimuli, proper guidance and direction to the weak private sector.

The basic features of the new industrial policy of the state may be traced from the Manifesto of the Sri Lanka Freedom Party (the main partner of the Coalition). It says, "all key industries must be run by the state. Small industries such as cottage industries can be in the hands of private enterprises"[28]. The state allocated funds to establish state enterprises from annual government budgets. The state also received assistance from friendly countries in the form of plant and machinery, factories, and equipment to increase the existing industrial capacity of the country (Karunaratna, 1974, Lakshman, 1976; Karunatilake, 1987, Hewavitharena, 1989). In addition, the government nationalised certain private industries, services and manufacturing enterprises, and added them into the list of state enterprises[29].

The new policies of the state produced multifarious effects on the economy. They had both short and long term implications. These can be viewed from two different directions: (1) the contributions of the state to the capitalist industrial development process and (2) the response of the private sector to new policies. In effect, the state as an entrepreneur added a new dimension into the industrial accumulation process of the country. At the same time, the new policy tended to discourage the traditional private sector which, as a result, played an insignificant role in the process of accumulation. The role of the state and that of the private sector will be discussed below.

'State capitalism' as an alternative force provided a new direction to the process of industrial accumulation in Sri Lanka[30]. Uyangoda views that 'the initial record of the state's capacity to laying the groundwork for public sector industry was impressive, as testified by the rapid expansion of this sector in the five years from 1958 to 1963'. He, however, was pessimistic about the progress of 'state capitalism' as a source of industrial accumulation in the capitalist development process of Sri Lanka[31]. Such remarks about 'state capitalism' are quite convincing, when viewed from a long-term growth perspective. But, from a short-term macro perspective, 'state capitalism' has obviously produced high growth impulses rendering multiple effects on the future industrial accumulative process of the industrially weak economy.

The 'coalition' has provided an impetus to industrial capitalist development in four directions.

1. The formation of state industrial enterprises with state funds, and the provision of some 'secondary benefits' through public enterprises to the economic base.
2. The provision of infra-structural facilities.
3. The upgrading of a 'new entrepreneur class' since 1960.
4. The change in the course of social development[32].

The Sri Lankan State formed its own 'enterprise sector' with about 77 large manufacturing enterprises by 1974[33]. This helped substantially to broaden the 'industrial base' of the country. Figure 4.1 in chapter 4 provides a good account of accumulation of industrial capital by the public sector as the 'big state entrepreneur' and by the private sector as the 'small industrial private entrepreneur' (including foreign investment).

The state enterprises produced a 'wide range of consumer durables and intermediate goods' in a protective environment (Ponnambalam, 1980: 123). The foreign counterpart provided the necessary capital and technology for these enterprises[34]. The private sector manufactured 'exclusively consumer goods, largely semi-essential and luxury items' for the captive market for manufactured goods[35]. It, at times, joined with foreign enterprises in establishing 'joint ventures' to manufacture these items. Karunatilake (1987:92-100) provides a detailed account on the areas of investment, types of products, number of firms, domestic and foreign, the incentives provided by the state, utilisation of technology etc.

The state industrial performance was far ahead of private industrial achievements in terms of average volume of industrial accumulation as explained by figure 4.1 in Chapter 4. The technology employed in public sector industries facilitated the use of local raw materials like timber, limestone, clay, ilmenite, kaolin, straw, and rubber in production processes. The processes converted these raw materials into finished products. 'As a result, in industries such as plywood, cement, paper, ceramics and tyres the local entrepreneurs absorbed a major portion of the process technologies involved' (Marga, 1978:16).

The state enterprises provided secondary benefits to the system. By 'secondary benefits' we mean 'benefits other than the very establishment of the activity in question, and may be either temporary or permanent' generated by the economic activity (Ramanadham, 1963:31). For example, the provision of intermediate inputs at subsidised prices may provide financial surpluses to the input users in the system. The secondary benefits may be of different kinds but we are concerned here only with the kind of benefits 'that a basic industrial structure of a country gives rise to the establishment of several subsidiary activities which benefit from the former's operation' (Ramanadham, 1963:33).

5.2.2.3. The secondary benefits generated by state enterprises

The degree of complementary relationships among state enterprises themselves and between state enterprises and private industries is considerably high in Sri Lanka's industrial structure. One striking feature of Sri Lanka's 'state enterprise base' is the dominance of intermediate goods industries in the structure (See Table 5A1.3, Appendix 1). The composition of intermediate goods producing or processing industries was about 67 percent of the total number of state enterprises established after independence. These enterprises produced backward and forward linkage benefits to the system providing domestically produced or processed intermediate inputs to public as well as private industries.

The prices set by certain corporations producing intermediate inputs like steel, fertiliser, cement etc., were consistently subject to government ceiling[36]. The state enterprises produce utilities like electricity at fixed prices on a "no-profit, no-loss" basis in many occasions because the majority of the public utilise these inputs. The prices were normally set on a "cost-plus" basis to maintain a low relationship of prices to the costs of those products where the government was the major consumer (Ramanadhan, 1963: 91-93).

The non-market orientation of pricing policy of state enterprises would lead to a practice of indirect subsidisation of the entire sector which produce or process intermediate inputs. That is when one state enterprise utilises low-priced intermediate inputs manufactured by another to manufacture its own intermediate goods, the former's costs of production of goods may fall. This practice continues within the system; each firm sells its outputs at a subsidised price to the other and so on. Theoretically, this enables all firms in the system to enjoy the benefits produced by subsidised pricing and to bring down the cost of production in the entire sector. The extent of low-cost advantage earned by the system, however, depends upon the degree of backward linkages produced by the system and, most importantly, the efficient utilisation of resources in production.

When the private sector utilises these subsidised inputs to manufacture intermediate and final goods, its cost of production too would remain low. Unlike in state enterprises, these subsidy benefits would flow into the pool of profits of the private sector. For this reason, it can be argued that the subsidised pricing policy of the state enterprise sector has enhanced the generation of surpluses of the private sector. This may be regarded as an indirect flow of profits of the state enterprise sector to the private sector which could otherwise have been retained by the former. These unintended transfers may be socially undesirable in situations where the state enterprises incur losses partly due to the subsidised pricing policy. A part of the annual transfers from the government budget to settle such losses of state enterprises may indirectly add up to profits of the private sector. These, however, do not go into the hands of the final consumers.

The consumer and producer classes in the system (the latter consisting of the state sector and the private sector) may jointly enjoy these secondary benefits. Roughly speaking, the magnitude of subsidies gained by the firm sector (both private and public) is roughly equivalent to the difference of expenditure incurred by the firm sector on these inputs valued respectively at subsidised and market prices[37]. The experience in the early 1970s suggests that about 15% of total costs of each state enterprise was made use for purchasing intermediate inputs from other state enterprises (Samarawickreme, 1997a).

The opposite of this argument is the notion of over-pricing of products. Certain state enterprises like the Petroleum Corporation enjoy monopoly powers due to 'non-economic political objectives' of the state. These would charge high prices for their products causing the entire cost structure of the system to escalate. The cost of production of enterprises which employ the above inputs, may go up. Every one suffers including the private sector and final consumers as a result of such monopoly benefits of public corporations. The total magnitude of the social undesirability of over-pricing, however, depends on the degree of forward linkages produced by monopoly enterprises.

Numerically, the approximate value of total secondary benefits generated by the state enterprise sector in the year 1974was about Rs. 1041.0 million or 32.2 per cent of total value of production of the sector. The private manufacturing sector and final consumers earned 479.1 million and Rs. 561.9 million worth of secondary benefits, respectively[38].

5.2.2.4. The Private Industrial Entrepreneur Development

The state fostered a class of entrepreneurs —a new class of industrialists— under the project of 'state capitalist development'. It initiated a programme to build up a new class of 'industrial entrepreneurs' supplementary to the state industrial sector to ease the dearth of 'private industrial entrepreneurs' of the economy. This class of entrepreneurs was provided with financial assistance, guidance, and direction to establish new enterprises.

The state provided many stimuli, mostly micro level stimuli, to this new class of entrepreneurs (Karunatilake, 1971). Its policy towards the industrial private sector was stated in its 'Investors' Guide' in 1960[39]. About eight forms of schemes were announced to encourage private entrepreneurs who intended to take part in industrial development[40]. The state introduced heavy tariff and import bans to reduce import-dependence which produced a highly protected 'investment environment' for local industries[41]. 'The emergent industries were offered protection from the competition coming from imports'[42] (Karunaratne, 1999). It lowered duties on capital equipment and industrial raw materials to stimulate private sector investment in manufacture. The state has also increased investment in infra-structural facilities such as power, transport and technical education and established institutions to promote industrial investment facilities for future industrial growth (Karunaratne, 1999).

Thus, Athukorala's point of view that the participation of the private sector in industrial activities 'was an outcome of stringent import restrictions rather than of conscious policy' of the government is only partially true[43]. Indeed, there were two types of entrepreneurs, who sprang up in the new environment after 1960s according to a statement of the Minister of Finance in the Budget Speech (1976:4). They were:

(1) Merchants whose business was subject to import restriction, integrating backwards into producing domestically the sort of things which they previously used to import, and

(2) A new brand of indigenous home-grown entrepreneurs from humble beginnings but with the capacity of taking risks and putting in hard work.

The latter type of industrial entrepreneurs who benefited from the advantageous economic and political environment in the country extended its response to the offers made by the 'coalition' in the 1960s.

The entrepreneurship development process of the 'coalition' should not therefore be overlooked. The stimuli provided to the new 'venture industrialist class' by the 'coalition' helped them to secure high Earnings Per Share (EPS) —a favourable economic environment. The rising trend of EPS of industrial products manufactured by private industrialists under the new market environment with 'stringent import restrictions' can be observed with figure 3.3 in chapter 3. The EPS values of manufacturing industries were rising along with those of trade, finance, and construction industries, especially, after the 1960s. This class of entrepreneurs was provided with inputs at concessionary prices. The closed economic structure with little competition from imports facilitated the firms to enjoy high economic profits. Karunatilake (1971:217) mentions that certain products like plastic, metal products, electrical goods earned very high profit margins 'as much as 200 per cent'[44]. 'The price controls, in certain cases, resulted only in reducing the profit margin from 200 to 100 per cent' (Karunatilake, 1971:217).

The producer-oriented protected business climate after 1960 favoured the growth of an indigenous private 'venture industrial capital'[45]. The pattern of investment of these firms (listed companies) is described by curve 2, figure 3.4 in chapter 3, which exhibits a clear take-off during 1960-71. A large number of indigenous medium and large industrial firms were registered in 1961. The ministry of industries approved about 115 firms with a total capital of Rs.78.5 million. Another 272 small-scale firms with a capital base of Rs. 17.6 million were approved (Central Bank Annual Reports, 1960-67).

In 1962, of the 714 applications received for registration, 370 applications had been approved. The number of firms, which were solely Ceylonese, was about 351 and the number of firms with foreign capital participation was about 18 according to the then Minister of industries (Ceylon Hanzard, 1962: 297) see also (Ceylon Hanzard, 1962: 547–567). The majority of these firms later became large listed or unlisted limited companies.

These companies have concentrated mostly in miscellaneous manufacturing industries[46]. Specific feature of the investment behaviour of the new entrepreneur class has been that most of their new projects covered manufacturing industries like the production of textiles, metal products, miscellaneous chemical products and electrical appliance (see Table 5A1.1, Appendix 1). Out of the total of 115 medium and large industries approved in 1961, about 74 industrial projects covered industries in the above types.

The old firm sector, which was dominated mostly by foreigners, later responded favourably to the new economic environment; the sector reallocated its resources from other investment activities towards the manufacturing industry[47]. Their behaviour was a direct result of the state policy of import restrictions on industrial goods. 'Marga' (1978) states that the trading community 'found that one of the answers to the import restrictions was to produce the things locally'[48]. The rates of industrial accumulation of the trading community (see curve 1, figure 3.4 in chapter 3) were steadier and comparatively higher than those of venture industrialists. The steady accumulation behaviour of the former may have been due to the strong capital base and the business maturity of this class.

5.2.3. Phase III (1965 –70): Market-Oriented Economic Forces

The 'coalition government' formed by the UNP with the support of the Federal Party (FP) and the Ceylon Workers Congress (CWC) came into power in 1965. It was a liberal government committed to democratic principles under Prime Minister Dudley Senanayake (Wilson, 1975:32; Snodgrass, 1998:13). Senanayake government was against the policy of state interventionism but it was in favour of a mixed economic system with the active support of the private sector. Its economic vision was to ensure a healthy functioning of the private sector under a national plan. The national government, as this was called, believed in individual freedom and democratic traditions[49]. Wilson states that the government invited the private sector to run 'a few of the nationalised industries' and '...took vigorous measures to attract foreign private capital' (Wilson, 1975:33).

The government maintained a "softer attitude" towards

foreign capital. It 'proceeded to compensate the foreign petroleum companies (mostly owned by U.S companies) whose businesses had been nationalised by Mrs. Bandaranaike's Government during 1962-4' (Wilson, 1975:33). The government relaxed the tight trade and exchange controls and introduced a multiple exchange rate system in 1967[50]. All these resulted in the local and foreign capital to respond favourably to new economic policies of the government. 'This rightward political shift brought renewed foreign help through an aid consortium in which the United States participated, an IMF standby agreement, short-term credits from Western banks'[51] (Snodgrass, 1998: 13). This regime introduced limited liberalisation policies but it made no move to disband or curtail public enterprises established by the previous regime. '[I]ts 1965-70 term in office proved to be the period of fastest economic growth in Sri Lankan history' in terms of real GDP per capita[52] (Snodgrass, 1998:14). Wilson (1975) noted that '[t]here was a phenomenal increase in investment expenditure, the highest on record and evidence of the confidence that the Government had inspired'. However, this regime was able to implement quasi-liberal policies only for a short period.

5.2.4. Phase IV (1970-77): Intensification of State Intervention

The change in the government in 1970 was a reflection of loss of confidence of people in market oriented system which failed to provide societal objectives[53]. The new government was a representation of 'the people's desire for a socialist transition' (Uyangoda, 1992:193). It consisted of moderate democrats and radical Marxists; the latter group held a few important Cabinet portfolios including the Ministry of Finance.

From the very inception, the government faced a major social challenge with the outbreak of an armed insurrection in 1971. The unprecedented oil price hike inspired by OPEC in 1973 and the World food crisis of 1973-74 disturbed its planning targets which compelled the regime to bring in new economic measures like food rationing, exchange controls and establishment of new institutions to handle the new situation[54]. 'This marked the beginning of a period of governing the country under state of emergency'[55]. Many drastic reforms were implemented on economic and political fronts under the influence of socialist planning including changes in the constitution[56].

The so-called 'people's Government' implemented socialist-oriented policies with the expectation that the system would gradually 'move further to the Left' (Wilson, 1975:39). The economic policies adopted after the insurrection in 1971 were quite radical. 'The seven years of the United Front regime was thus the highest point of statism that originated in the mid-fifties' (Uyangoda, 1992: 193). The quasi-market-oriented system, which hitherto prevailed, was transformed into a controlled economic system based on principles of national planning. The Five-Year plan of the 1972 envisaged that 'the necessary corollary of the country's commitment to the building of a socialist society is the expansion of the public sector of economic activity'.

There were crises growing in both domestic and external environments, the government approached them 'moving further in the direction of redistribution and public ownership' (Gunatilake, 1999:199). Uyangoda provides a good account of changes that were effected in different institutions of the economy between 1970 and 1977. The nationalisation of the foreign-owned plantation was a big step in these changes (Gunatilake, 1999:199). The service sector expanded adding a few trading corporations into the existing set. About twenty-four private business enterprises were nationalised under the Business Undertakings (Acquisitions) act of 1971. The Act authorised the Minister of Finance to nationalise any firm if he deemed such an action to be in the national interest.

The socialist regime faced an acute shortage of foreign exchange as a result of the oil crisis and food shortage in the external front. By way of remedial action, it adopted several strict measures to minimise import-dependence of the economy. One was the restriction of imports through high tariffs and in some cases, import bans. The imports were brought down 'in 1973-74 to forty-one percent of the 1970-72 level' (Snodgrass, 1998). The other was the encouragement of import substituting industrial development through 'high tariff and incentives with emphasis on public sector and local ownership'. Consequently, certain import substituting industries thrived under heavy protection during this period. 'Manufacturing grew during this period, partly to substitute for unavailable or unaffordable imports' (Snodgrass, 1998). The socialist regime was later compelled to lean towards Foreign Direct Investment changing its previous anti-FDI policy. '...[T]he policy was changed later (1972 to 1975) to encourage foreign investment in collaboration with local investment, with local investors holding the majority share'[57]

The public was not content with the outcomes of policies of this regime. It lost the election held in 1977, with the liberal group — the UNP— gaining a landslide victory winning 140 seats out of 168.

5.3. Pro-market and Anti- Market Effects of ISI Policies

The government of Sri Lanka via ISI policies intended to create a favourable environment for production of industrial goods in the economy. Evidently, the industrialists were able to determine prices of their products 'quite independently of costs', in the absence of a competition from imports. The prices of certain products were very high in the local market. For example, the prices of products like plastic, metal products, electrical goods had been very high as much as 200 per cent (Karunatilake 1971:217). These helped the producers to raise profit margins.

The government provided various incentives to the class of new entrepreneurs under the infant industry argument (discussed earlier). It established different institutions to facilitate transfer of technology to the system (Wijesekara, 1998:403). It formed NDB and DFCC to supply with 'venture capital' for new entrepreneurs. The government also helped the promotion of managerial and entrepreneurial skills of people by forming different institutes of technology and gearing Universities to offer business management degrees. The Academy of Administrative studies undertook training of public sector personnel. The new industries that were set up in this protected environment also trained personnel in advanced technology and in different skills. 'Several management and technology firms have sprung up in the private sector to give advice and evaluate projects' (Karunatilake, 1971:220). The government took measures to improve infrastructural facilities like transport, communication, power generation etc. required for industrial development.

However, the certain measures of the government had produced disincentives, and strengthen 'forces hostile- to-market' in the system. Some measures produced direct disincentives and others indirect disincentives on the system. For example, the measures taken by bureaucrats to minimise social inconveniences created by the 'policy of import substitution' caused the drop in price advantages and hence profits margins of producers. These measures were meant to minimise unfavourable effects of rising prices on the consumer class. Measures like 'control pricing' in lieu of 'market pricing' were introduced in certain transactions. Control prices helped the buyer to purchase the same quantity at a lower price which pushed down profit margins of producers. Karunatilake (1971:217) says that price controls have resulted in the reduction of profit margin, in certain cases, 'from 200 to 100 per cent'. The other was the 'rationing'. The quantities available for sales in certain scarce commodities were rationed. This was implemented through issuing 'rationing coupons' to individual consumers.

Most items in the basket of goods of an average consumer during the period prior to 1977 were either rationed or price-controlled items. The state machinery carried out the supervisory function of these two schemes. However, these measures were only partially successful because of bureaucratic inefficiencies, 'rent-seeking practices' of the state officials and 'directly unproductive lobbying activities' (Karunaratne, 1999:241). Consequently, there was a grown-black market for most of items in markets. The industrial producers and the class of speculators apparently shared the benefits of 'market protection' under the 'import substitution policy' of the state. All these resulted in the lowering of EPS of manufacturing firms operated in the protected environment before 1977 as elucidated in Fig, 3.3, Chap. 3.

Another strong measure that resulted in producing disincentives was the policy of nationalisation. In fact, the intention of nationalisation, in most cases, was to improve the internal political economic environment (the market distortions created by the colonial rulers). But, this very measure, in most cases, became counterproductive to the development of 'market forces' in the system. One good example was the nationalisation of distribution of petroleum products of foreign companies in the early 1960s. These companies had earned huge surpluses from the distribution of petroleum and a large potion of which was sent abroad without reinvesting them locally. The political decision to nationalise these foreign assets without paying compensation created further political confusion in the system. Internally, the nationalisation of private assets discouraged the private sector, both domestic and foreign, to reinvest funds in the industry. Foreign capital began to leave Sri Lanka because of the threat of impending nationalisation. Externally, foreign countries reacted strongly to this move in the forms of interrupting markets abroad for Sri Lankan products and blocking financial assistance of Western financial agencies. As mentioned earlier, Senanayake government in 1967 had to rectify this decision and to pay compensation prior to receiving foreign assistance.

The land reform programme of the government produced mixed results. The domestic economy in the early 1970s suffered considerably from the remittance of large sum of foreign exchange in the form of interests and dividends by the plantations Agency Houses, which resulted in the depletion of already meagre foreign reserves of the country[58]. The nationalisation of plantation industry, therefore, was partly meant to minimise the above costs on the economy and partly to introduce a land reform programme. The land reforms, what some other 'new nations' implemented[59], were meant to reduce pressures coming from traditional land-owning capitalist class against industrial development (discussed elsewhere) and to divert scarce resources towards the manufacturing industry. However, there was a backlash of this policy on the domestic front. It compelled the foreign plantation investors to take their capital away and to restart plantation in African countries. This was a serious blow to Sri Lanka's tea market abroad.

The other ventures like passenger transport, port and harbour, insurance and banking[60], plus large segments of import and wholesales trade and foreign owned port cargo operations were also subject to nationalisation in the 1950s and 1960s. A large number of business undertakings were nationalised under the Business Undertakings (Acquisitions) act of 1971. The nationalisation of some institutions of the above list tended to produce unfavourable repercussions on the financial market of the country[61]. For example, the share market that previously prospered with private capital coming from the above sources hardly survived thereafter (Wijesinghe, 1975). The private sector then had to depend largely upon the money market for long-term capital investments. The money market of Sri Lanka, mainly comprised state banks, was oligopolistic and resorted to various forms of red tapes in lending funds to the private sector (Karunatilake, 1971). On the other hand, the state savings institutions like NSB, Insurance, SMIB extracted the surpluses generated in the economy in the absence of the private banking sector. The majority of these surpluses were channelled to finance government expenses, which produced 'crowding out' effects upon private investment (Attapatu, 1997).

The cost of nationalisation, therefore, was quite high; it antagonised foreign capital, the most important 'pod' in capitalist industrial accumulation, from the industrial development process of Sri Lanka. Foreign capital did not respond favourably to the calls made by pro-market regimes for investment in manufacturing. For example, the UNP government (1965-70) offered various stimuli and also gave the assurance of not nationalising foreign assets in a White Paper in 1967. The response to this call, however, was quite mild (Karunatilake, 1971:213-4). The type of asset redistribution through nationalisation, therefore, has 'increased the country risk, and triggered capital flight and cut off foreign aid' (Karunaratne, 1999:240).

One other source of disincentive was the state policy of taxation. The state levied heavy taxes on the corporate sector and a wealth tax on the wealthy people of the society. The Finance Minister in 1974 identified about forty such families as wealthiest business families in Sri Lanka[62]. Part of the incomes withdrawn from private savings through taxes thus was diverted to government consumption (Hewavitharena, 1989). Atapattu (1997) gives a detailed account of government income and expenditure, and comments that '[P]ublic expenditure, tending to favour social welfare items, pushed up public consumption expenditure'. This resulted in a heavy 'crowding out effect' on private investment in industry. For Atapattu, '...the overall policy package [of the state prior to 1977] contained inconsistencies in this regard thus preventing the emergence of a favourable atmosphere for private investment' (1997: 73).

Some forms of rent seeking[63] practices grew in the system along with the allocation[64] of public sector resources among potential industrialists during the 1960s and 1970s (Moore, 1985; 1991). Information on some can be gathered from various sources. One source, for example, was the election manifesto of the United Left Front in 1977 which criticised the acts of the previous regime 'a small group of favoured *mudalalis* have been helped to develop big capital enterprises, which exercised great influence on the government policy'. Moore also (1990:21) commented on this state favouritism. For him '[a]t all levels, opportunities for commercial profits were seen to depend on good political connections'. The Minister of Finance in his budget speech in 1977 referred to some names of big businessmen who were favoured by the previous regimes prior to 1977. However, these situations have not developed into a large scale 'rent seeking practice' in Sri Lanka. The main reason for this may be that the industrial private sector as an institution was not developed adequately to influence the bureaucratic class of the system. Similarly, the latter itself was not developed as a powerful institution in Sri Lanka to influence the industrial private sector. The competitive political structure in Sri Lanka was also an obstacle to 'rent seeking practices'.

The political ideology and the pressure group politics were not in favour of the 'coalitions' to develop friendly partnerships with the private sector for a joint project of industrial development (Gunatilake, 1999:194). The private firms received little attention in initiating, formulating and undertaking investment, 'it had been left to manage its own affair for a long period' (Karunatilake, 1971:270). Only the liberal regime in 1965 came forward to assist the private sector which started a separate division of private sector affairs for promoting private business activities. This regime offered various incentives, tax concessions, and 100 per cent rebate of custom duty on imported raw material used for exported commodities. The White Paper offered various benefits to foreign investors. The private sector responded in some way, establishing firms for assembly and progression manufacture of motor cars, spinning and weaving of cotton & synthetic textiles, making of galvanised sheets and electrical components, pharmaceutical products etc. (Karunatilake, 1971:214).

The worsening industrial relations at firm levels, especially after 1956, produced an unfavourable impact on the investment climate of the country. A strong trade union movement grew in the structure under the socialist economic foundation, which developed links with the 'coalitions' and even backed the 'coalitions' in general elections (Uyangoda, 1992: 199). The industrial relations and the labour policy were strongly biased in favour of the workers during this period (Gunatilake, 1999). Therefore, the trade unions under the socialist regime were able to enjoy 'special privileges' (Tilakaratna, 1990:84). The period between 1956 and 1970 was quite significant for worsening industrial relations. Trade union movements carried out frequent work stoppages as can be seen in figure 5A3.1 in Appendix 3. This makes it evident that the plantation and the industrial sectors suffered huge losses in man-days of work because of strikes. Frequent work stoppages were costly to the private firm sector. These have created industrial disharmony at firm levels reducing profit margins and undermining entrepreneurial expectations.

Above all, the political instability iunder different regimes ever since independence created a disincentive to private investment. Large scale political instability after the assassination of the Prime Minister in the late 1950s extended as far as the 1960s followed by the insurrection of Janatha Vimukthi Peramuna JVP in 1971 critically disturbing the investment environment of the country.

5.4. The Slow Industrial Growth

The findings in Chapter 4 disclosed two forces, market forces (the joint effect of $\mathbf{P}_t$ and $\mathbf{S}_t$) and market-hostile-forces ($\mathbf{D}_t$) (see equation (1) in Chap. 4), which determined the process of industrial accumulation of Sri Lanka. The empirical analysis in the above section also disclosed that both the market friendly forces and forces-hostile-to-market were active in the system prior to 1977. It can, now, be asked as to what pressures have these forces exerted in the determination of industrial accumulation of Sri Lanka.

Capitalist accumulation practices require a self-generating growth process for sustainable industrial development of the country. The self-generating growth process requires two types of stimuli, namely, micro-level and macro-level, in establishing an 'investment climate' favourable for industrial entrepreneurs. The entrepreneurs would then generate surpluses and accumulate them in the industry. The market forces can provide incentives for industrialists to achieve high level of productivity through efficient allocation of resources which in turn help 'high rates of surpluses and re-investment'[65].

Sri Lanka's process of industrial accumulation under ISI policies apparently was short of self-growth-generating characteristics required for a 'compressed and fast' industrial development. Critics argue that industrial structure was largely dominated by state capital. This sector had failed to generate necessary surpluses for self-growth[66] and therefore depended heavily upon the state budget for expansions (Hewavitharena, 1989; Atapattu, 1997; Lakshman, 1979). The main problem inherent in the industrial structure of Sri Lanka prior to the mid-1977 was the weak generation and accumulation of surpluses within the structure. " ...[T]hat in ISI, the profit-surplus conditions of self generating growth and productivity growth and that the reinvestment condition remain unfulfilled because of market inducement was not there" (Hewavitharena, 1989:36).

Had the private sector, the counterpart, possessed the capacity to generate surpluses for a sustainable industrial development in Sri Lanka? The enquiry into this hypothesis requires a great deal of information on the generation of surpluses by private and state industrial enterprises. These should be provided by the national databases. The yearly profits earned by these enterprises may be considered as reasonably good approximations for surpluses although these entail a certain amount of underestimation. The indices of 'returns to capital employed' may also be good proxies for assessing the competence of these enterprises to generate surpluses required for industrial development.

The existing databases of the Central Bank or the Census and Statistical Department are very limited in terms of comprehensiveness of coverage. Information provided on the generation and accumulation of surpluses of the above two sectors is limited. The major shortcoming is that the data are not segregated according to industries, like construction, trade, finance and manufacturing. The database provides only the aggregate values of the above industries in the economy. Our database, on the other hand, provides a substantive sectoral segregation of profits and other variables helpful for a study of this nature. We used here, what is called the *economic approach,* as the method of measuring surpluses in each of the above industries of the economy[67]

Table 5.1 below, gives information on pattern of manufacturing surpluses generated by two largest sectors, the state and private, of the economy. It should be noted that this data set refers to the most successful period of industrial accumulation of the state. The data in table 5.1 describe that average surpluses of public manufacturing enterprises were far below the levels of that of the private sector. The surpluses of the public enterprise sector were low partly because of relatively low prices fixed by the state, and partly because of low productivity of resources of the sector (Hewavitharena, 1989:34; Jayasinghe, 1979:171).

Table 5.1 signifies two features associated with the planning-oriented industrial strategy. First, under the planned industrial development, the industrial sector, comprising private and public sectors, generated a relatively low volume of surpluses required for the expansion of industrial activities of the country. Furthermore,

Table 5.1. Average Level of Surpluses Generated By Privateand State Sectors [68] (Percentage of GDP)

	State Industrial Enterprises %	Private Industrial Enterprises %	Total %
1965	0.2	3.0	3.2
1966	0.1	2.3	2.5
1967	0.0	8.7	8.7
1968	0.6	4.0	4.6
1969	0.9	4.2	5.1
1970	0.8	5.3	6.1
1971	0.8	5.7	6.5
1972	0.7	6.3	7.0
1973	0.8	6.5	7.3
1974	1.7	1.6	3.3
1975	1.0	4.8	5.8
1976	0.7	2.9	3.6

Source : Equation in footnote 67 was used for private surplus estimations. The profit levels were used for estimating state industrial surplus. (All are in real values).

there were fluctuations in the generation of surpluses (column 3, Table 5.1). Two, the table implies that the state was compelled to provide financial capital through budgetary means to finance industrial development when foreign savings were not forthcoming through FDI.

The distribution of sectoral surpluses over time is given in Figure 5.1 below in real terms. The Figure highlights that the generation of surpluses in each sector during the period of planned industrial development was relatively low. It displays that there had been declining trends of private surpluses in all broad sectors of the economy. Manufacturing and finance were the two significant sectors that generated at least moderate surpluses; other two sectors produced only meagre surpluses. The generation of surplus in periods 1960 -63 and again 1967-71 were relatively high but it was quite low in the period 1971-77.

In addition, Figure 5.2 describes the behaviour of two macroeconomic variables — surpluses and taxes—of the economy. There have been periodic fluctuations in surplus generation and payment of corporate taxes (difference between

FIGURE 5.1 SECTORAL GENERATION OF SURPLUSES (Including TAX fund)

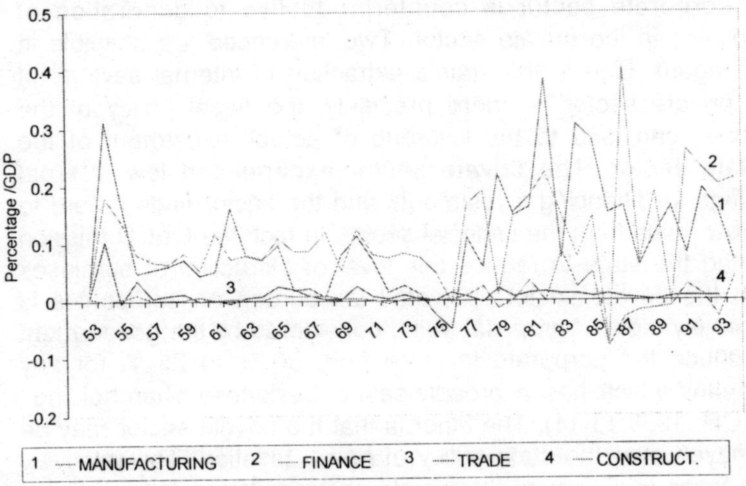

Source: Data in Table 5A1.4, Appendix 1.

two curves in the region A) in the economy. The long-term trend of generation of surpluses in the private sector witnesses a sharp drop in the late 1950s which continued until the mid-1970s. Similarly, the payment of taxes on corporate surpluses was rising until the mid-1960s thereafter remained at a moderate level. These results are in conformity with the findings of Business and Industry Advisory Committee (B.I.A.C), of OECD (1969:13-14), which indicates the high rate of corporate taxes, amounting approximately to 50 per cent in the 1960s.

FIGURE 5.2 TAX EFFECTS ON SURPLUS GENERATION OF THE LARGE FIRM SECTOR

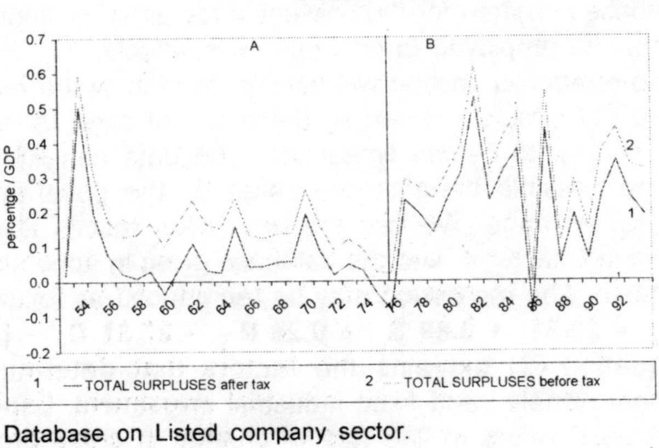

Source: Database on Listed company sector.

The extraction of private surpluses levying high taxes on the corporate sector is counterproductive to generation of surpluses in the private sector. Two inferences are possible in this regard. One is the state's extraction of internal savings of the private sector — more precisely, the fiscal policy of the state—, can lead to the lowering of actual investment of the private sector. The private sector experienced low internal savings for financing investments and the sector finds it hard to borrow funds from the financial sector. In fact, the OECD mission wanted the state to reduce this level of extraction of surpluses from the private sector. '[O]verall tax burden on companies is extremely high. ... proposal being considered by the government to reduce the corporate tax rate from 50 % to 25 % for any company which has a broadly-based Ceylonese shareholding.' (OECD, 1969:13-14). The other is that the private sector may be dismayed over the state policy of heavy taxation. The relatively high taxes might cause the private sector to lower its investment as a response to the antagonistic attitude of the state towards the private sector[69]

The loss of confidence of the private sector resulting from unfavourable fiscal policy of the state can produce adverse effects on industrial accumulation. This requires further attention. The adverse effects may be low if the state uses these resources more efficiently in growth-increasing activities than does the private sector, and vice versa. However, the assessment of these effects, more precisely the 'crowding out effects', is quite difficult because of insufficient information on different activities available in common databases. Nevertheless, the database prepared for the present study provides information which may be employed to estimate such effects.

The remaining section will attempt to identify the extent of 'crowding out effects' created by the policy of state taxation, of course, subject to certain limitations. The data can limit us in identifying possible benefits generated by the government in utilising these funds. We use the regression results that were estimated in Chapter 4, and the database given in appendix 1 for this purpose. The regression may be reproduced as follows:

$$\mathbf{F_{t+1} = 22.81 + 0.89\, S_t + 0.28\, P_t - 27.31\, D_t} \qquad \mathbf{(2)}$$

Equation (2) explains the factors that determine the 'investment climate', and fixed industrial investment. Especially, the variable P_t refers to 'the rate of change in gross profits' in manufacturing industry. The Kalecki's meaning is the **'rate of change in the level of economic activity'**. The change in prices, therefore, profit levels in the system may reflect change in the level of economic activity of the country.

Let us assume that the government wishes to lower the corporate taxes so as to provide some stimuli to the entrepreneur class of the system[70]. This decision will undoubtedly result in the increase in gross profit margins of the industrial sector. High profit margins will help the entrepreneurs to develop positive expectations about the future 'investment climate'. The tax incentive would, thereby, stimulate private entrepreneurs to make investments in manufacturing fixed assets.

Quantitatively, the above effects on industrial fixed investment could be measured using equation (2) above. First, the amount of tax withdrawn by the state can be added back to each year's gross profits. Then the new 'rate of change in gross profits' (Pt) may be recalculated. Substituting these new data in

FIGURE 5.3 CUMULATIVE EFFECTS OF HIGH TAXES AND POOR INVESTMENT CLIMATE ON FIXED MANUFACTURING INVESTMENT

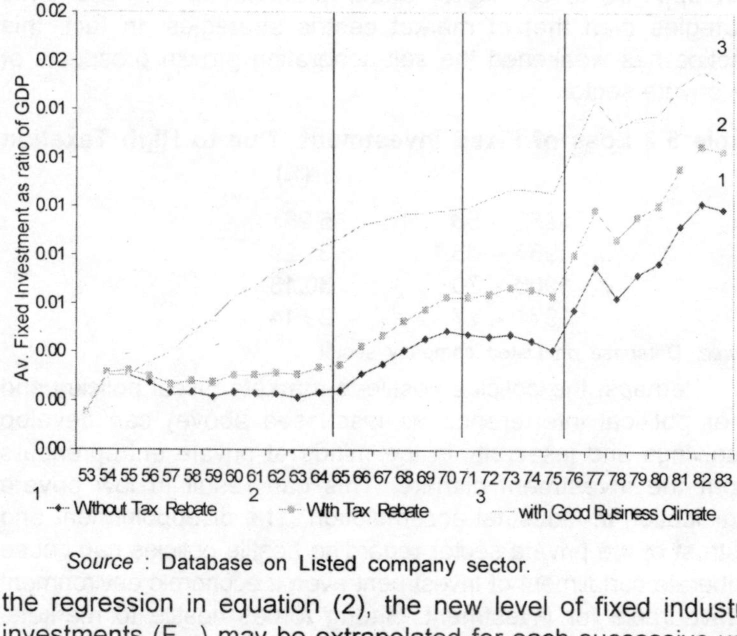

Source : Database on Listed company sector.

the regression in equation (2), the new level of fixed industrial investments (F_{t+1}) may be extrapolated for each successive year from 1953 to 1983. Let us assume supposing the regime prior to 1977 had brought down the tax rate from 50 percent to 25 percent as recommended by OECD Mission in 1969! After adding these values to each year's gross profits, the new 'rate of change in gross profits' can be recalculated. The resultant cumulative values of (F_{t+1}) (with tax rebate) are shown in curve 2 in figure 5.3 below. The curve 1 describes the cumulative values of fixed investment without any tax rebate.

The differences between curves 1 and 2 are increasing. It suggests that the cumulative losses of manufacturing fixed assets as a result of the drain out of private surpluses in the form of corporate tax are significant in the Sri Lankan economy. The losses of private fixed investment in manufacturing produce cumulative effects, which have been widening over time. The magnitude of this gap under different economic regimes is measured in percentage terms and given in Table 5.2, below. The costs or 'crowding out effects' of the drain in private surpluses appear to be high. But, the actual opportunity cost of this fund, indeed, can vary depending upon the benefits, otherwise, reaped by its alternative use in the state sector. This cost appears to be higher under planning-centric economic strategies than that of market centric strategies. In fact, this practice has weakened the self-generating growth prospects of the private sector.

Table 5.2 Loss of Fixed Investment Due to High Taxation

	(%)
1952 – 56	5.26
1957 – 65	31.29
1966 – 70	30.13
1971 – 77	39.14

Source: Database on Listed company sector

Perhaps, the policies hostile-to-markets (fiscal policies and other political interference as discussed above) can develop misgivings and insecurity in the minds of private entrepreneurs about the investment climate. This can result in low private participation in industrial accumulation. The disappointment and mistrust of the private sector regarding hostile policies can cause deliberate curtailment of investment even if economic environment is favourable for investment. Strong forces hostile to markets, such as nationalisation threats, taxation policies, bureaucratic red tape, trade union activities and pressure group politics (death to capitalist slogans!) could disturb private confidence in investment even if certain economic stimuli that were favourable for private investment. Therefore, the private sector would respond cautiously even to favourable policies of the state.

The magnitude of low-level participation of the private sector in the industrial accumulation process in Sri Lanka can be visualised with curve 1 in figure 5.3 above. We saw that the manufacturing industry was growing only at an average long-term rate of 2 percent over this period (see Regression 5A2 .4 Appendix 2). The low-level investment and the cyclical trends characterise low growth prospects of the manufacturing industry. The curve 2 stipulates the rising trend of industrial accumulation under favourable taxation policies of the state. Good fiscal policies would improve the accumulation process at a long-term average rate of 3 per cent (see Regression 5A2.3 Appendix 2). The curve 3 characterises a viable industrial accumulation process with an average long-term steady growth rate of 4 per cent (see Regression 5A2.2). The figure 5.3, thus, provides policy options for decision-makers. First, it warns about the growing cumulative effect of any short-sighted policy on long term behaviour of investment (gap between curve 1 and 3). It also highlights the importance of neutralisation of forces hostile-to-market in the system enabling the economy to enter a viable and self-generating growth path. The curve 3 was drawn on the assumption that forces hostile to markets would play a neutral role while allowing the market forces to be active in the system (Giving 0 values to all Di values in each year).

5.5. Summary

The interference of forces hostile to markets in economic policy decisions, apparently, is a general characteristic in most economies of 'new nations'. In Sri Lanka, the state as the 'big entrepreneur' contributed to the industrial formation in three ways. First, it directly enrolled in industrial accumulation *via* its network of public enterprises. Secondly, The State promoted a new class of private entrepreneurs providing them with different stimuli and finally, it promoted an investment climate for the private sector to earn economic rents. Though the industrial accumulation under this regime was substantial, the traditional capitalists have not supported much to the new order.

The long-term consequences of the state intervention in the economy were threefold. There was an over-expansion of the state-manufacturing sector in the economy. Secondly, it was seen that the private sector participated only marginally in manufacturing activities. Lastly, the FDI involved itself scarcely in industrial activities, apart from the assistance provided by socialist countries. The state, apparently, was increasingly biased towards the development of the state-manufacturing sector ignoring the capacity of the private sector as an industrial investor[71]. This policy has resulted in a high level of public industrial accumulation and a moderate participation of private sector in the economy.

This policy has led to a high accumulation of industrial capital in a relatively short period. However, from the long-term point of view, this industrial growth was found unsustainable because the state industrial sector was found deficient in generating surpluses for further accumulation[72]. The public sector industrial formation is said to be a low self-growth generating industrial process which to be supported intermittently by budgetary transfers. Contrary to the public sector, the private industrial accumulation process is normally endowed with self-growth-generating characteristics. However, the self-growth generating ability of the private sector in Sri Lanka had been weakened by the interference of forces-hostile-to-markets in the economy.

Our database suggests that the private sector with its self-growth generating features could have instituted a sustainable industrial growth path in the economy after 1956, had the policy of the state encouraged private industrial accumulation and neutralised market hostile elements in the system. The possible consequences of the poor policy of the state can be visualised using our standard database. The curve (3), figure 5.3 witnesses the magnitude of the industrial accumulation otherwise could have been achieved, had the state made necessary adjustments in the industrial policy to accommodate private industrial accumulation effectively. Such adjustments would have helped the industrial sector to improve its cost efficiency and competitiveness for a successful export-orientation.

The new phase of economic development with the dominance of market forces in resource allocation commenced after 1977. The liberal policy of the state paved the way for the private sector to participate effectively in industrial accumulation. All groups, the traditional, new venture industrialists, and the foreign direct investment engaged in industrial accumulation process after 1977. The next chapter will study the new economic environment, role of the state and the private sector in such an environment, in detail.

Notes

1. The first one was a scrappy listing of a series of projects the government was hoping to undertake and the other guided by World Bank advice was a programme covering merely government expenditure.
2. Minister of Industries, G.G. Ponnambalam (Ceylon Hanzard, 1952/53:2558).
3. Acting Finance Minister, Mr. M.D.H.Jayawardena answering questions divulged that 'Glass, ceramic, Acetic Acid, and drug factories have been closed down. The coir factory at Katunayake has been handed over to a Co-operative Union' (Ceylon Hanzard, 1953/54).
4. (Ceylon Hanzards, 1951-53: 618).
5. The Budget Speech, 1954 -55.
6. Based on the information provided in "New Issues of Joint Stock Companies- 1940 -1953" (The Bulletin, 1955).
7. The public firms are the large firms selling shares to the public.
8. The information in the Bulletin (1955), "New Issues of Joint Stock Companies 1940- 1953" was used.
9. The Central Bank of Ceylon, "New Issues of Joint Stock Companies- 1940 -53".
10. Some of those early names do not appear in Ferguson's records later.
11. See Table 5A1.2, Appendix 1. Also the Survey of Private Investment in 1954 conducted by the Department of Census and Statistics gives the pattern of distribution of private investment among different sectors and industries.
12. The import duties on a large group of consumer goods were brought down to 1947 levels in 1950 51 (Budget Speech, 1952 –53).
13. The private industrialists had experienced good times during World War II. They enjoyed economic advantages from a favourable environment characterised by rising prices, shortages of imported commodities, less competitive market conditions

owing to the curtailment of imports and, more importantly, few capital-labour conflicts. The War environment of inflation and scarcity stimulated private industrialists.

14. Due to the powerful influence of left politics.
15. Myrdal (1968:345) identifies these political elite in the late forties as 'conservatives' who had no ambitious program of economic and social reform'.
16. United National Party 'is the organ of the wealthy landowning upper class financed and supported by the established vested interests and the new rich. The party's electoral support hinges around the landowning families in the Sinhalese low-country areas who through their hold over the rural peasantry are able to influence their voting' (Ponnambalam, 1980: 19).
17. The members of the Cabinet of Ministers were elites of the 'Comprodore Bourgeoisie class' mostly the landlords or trading capitalists whose interests were largely private profits. Mick Moore Identifies D.S.Senanayake, the Prime Minister of the 1947 Government, as 'a member of the wealthiest Sri Lankan plantation-owning family...' His son Dudley, who was to succeed him as Prime Minister, followed his example (Moore, 1985:45).
18. Manufacturing goods 'would have caused dislocation to the trade of the former and discomfort to the consumption of the latter' (Ponnambalam, 1980: 23).
19. For example, after tax return on these large manufacturing enterprises fell from 5.6 % in 1948 -50 to 5.5 % in 1951 -53 to 5.1 in 1954-56. pp. 10 -15, M.Ramachandran, Central Bank Bulletin, 1963.
20. The Taxation Commission too saw this slow progress as one of State's negligent attitude to industrial development commented on the liberal economic policy. The programme in respect of industrial development was a simple list of projects with estimated costs and the possible date of completion '. Report of the Taxation Commission (Ceylon Sessional Papers, 1955: 3).
21. 'In the initial stage of the cycle regulatory policies will be successful in coordinating the economy, correcting market failures. Usually they will (a) stimulate national production through an increase of State expenditures and modernization of given industries though several types of subsidies and tax exemptions (b) distribute income through taxation and welfare expenditures (c) limit abuses through many forms of regulation' (Pereira, 1993:1344).

22. Roy G. D. puts forward this idea in writing a forward to Ghosh's book on '*The changing Profile of India's Industrial Economy*' (Ghosh, 1974: 1).
23. Wilson (1975: 21) describes the nature of the political Coalition, 'the MEP: comprising SLFP, the Marxist-oriented LSSP of Philip Gunawardena, *Sinhala Bhasa Peramuna* (Sinhalese Languge front) of W.Dahanayaka, Electoral pacts with LSSP and CP'. Ponnambalam (1980:16) also talks of this coalition.
24. "... it was bound to experience conflict, and serious differences of opinion arose in connection with the implementation of its manifesto' (Warnapala, 1992: 156).
25. Minister of Industries, P.H.W.de Silva, Parliamentary debates (The Budget Speech, 1956-57).
26. Dr. N.M.Perera (The Budget Speech, 1957).
27. Papers by Visiting Economists, p.71.
28. Ceylon Daily News, February 6, 1958. P.8.
29. The government decided to nationalise all cargo handling operation of the port Colombo in 1958 under the Port (Cargo) Corporation due to bad labour discipline. It decided to nationalise the entire bus transport system due to the concentration of private monopoly power. In the early 1960s, the Bank of Ceylon and Life Insurance were nationalised. This decision was said to be with government's policy of socialism and the need for the direction of banks towards country's economic development. (Hansard 1961/2, Vol. 43, p.931.). Foreign firms held the Insurance business. "The main argument for nationalisation was that the remittances of premia, profits and dividends by the foreign firms were an undue strain on the balance of payments" (Jayawardena, p. 42). "Perhaps the most controversial and interesting of nationalization acts of the 1960-65 Government was the take-over of the Petroleum import and distribution companies - SHELL, ESSO and CALTEX" (Jayawardena, 1978: 44).
30. '... the impulse for industrialisation in post-independence Sri Lanka originated with a pessimism about, and even a hostility towards, the expansion of private capital in industry' (Uyangoda, 1992).
31. "[Q]uantitative and institutional expansion of State industrial ventures only concealed the inherent limitations of `State capitalism' in Sri Lanka" (Uyangoda, 1992).
32. I do not intend to elaborate on this as it is beyond the purview of this research. See (Uyangoda, 1992) and (Hettige, 1999) on the subject among others.

33. Lakshman (1979) gives a detailed account of state enterprises, objectives, form of establishment, market structure etc. in Appendix B.
34. The diplomatic relations with the Communist bloc of East Europe gave rise those countries to provide 'capital equipment and technology for several projects including tyre, steel, hardware, textiles, plywoods, and roofing tiles' (Gunatilake, 1999:193).
35. Ponnambalam (1980:124) gives a list of items produced by these private enterprises e.g. food, cigarettes, pharmaceutical, talc powder, toothbrushes, torch batteries, ink, electric bulbs, textiles, galvanized sheets, sewing machines, footwear etc. Also refer to chapter 2 for further information regarding the names of such producers.
36. Jayasinghe et al. (1979) gives detailed account of markets of public enterprises, degree of monopoly enjoy by certain enterprises, the pricing policy and factor influence the determination of prices by individual enterprises.
37. These market prices are determined by the levels of protections given to industries under the import substitution policy.
38. The former is about 30 percent and the latter is about 35.2 percent of total profits of State enterprise sector of the year (Samarawickreme, 1997a).
39. Bulletin 1, Series 1 issued by the Development Division of the Ministry of Industries.
40. Some of them were as follows:
    Excessive protections were provided to the industrial structure. There was a list of stimuli which were even proposed in the mid- 1950s. They were as follows: Exemption of profits from tax either partially or wholly, 2. Development rebates by which investments are exempted from income tax up to a percentage of the expenditure incurred. 3. Depreciation allowance. 4. Concessionary rates of duties on equipment and raw materials 5. Government's participation along with private capital in the establishment of small consumer industries 6. Loans to industrial ventures. Technical assistance through the CISIR 7. Protection of domestic manufacture through import control, tariff adjustment, industrial products (regulation) act. 8. Government purchases (Annual Report, Central Bank, 1961:112).
41. These industries produced consumer goods such as confectionery, biscuits, aerated water, and the assembly of refrigerators and air-conditioners using imported components (Karunaratna, 1999:240).

42. Also (Annual Report, Central Bank, 1961:112).
43. Uyangoda claims that 'private capital began to take part in industrial investment only in the early sixties' (Uyangoda, 1992: 187).
44. 'The industries were able to determine prices quite independently of costs, because they became monopolists no sooner import restrictions became operative' (Karunatilake, 1987:95)
45. Similar emergence of a private sector in industry was experienced even during the World War II.
46. According to Table 5A. 1, in Appendix, about 61.3 % of old firms were manufacturing firms and about 68.6 of new firms were manufacturing firms.
47. The large firms were owned by mostly by foreigners. Some of them are Wellawatta Spring & Weaving; Liver Brothers who produce detergents, Margarine, toothpaste; BCC who produce coconut oil and Soap; CTC produces Cigarettes; Swedeshi Match Company; Tile Factory; Bicycle Factory; the major engineering firms like Walkers, Browns, Colombo Commercials (Marga, 1978:17).
48. Nature and the volume of these foreign subsidiaries and joint ventures are discussed in the editorial note (Marga, 1978:17-19).
49. The Budget Speech of the Minister of Finance, August 3rd, 1965.
50. Information is provided in *Economic Progress of Independent Sri Lanka,* p.19, The Central Bank, (1998).
51. Aid consortium consisting of Australia, Canada, Japan, the UK and the US was set up to assist Sri Lanka It was later joined by the Germany. The reform helped to receive US $ 30mn from IMF (Economic Progress of Independent Sri Lanka, 1998:19).
52. For comparison, see his table 1 in page 3.
53. Hettige (1999:43) talks on the unfulfilled expectations of the society by 1970 and its growth towards a crisis.
54. State corporations for import-export trades, Co-operative Wholesale Establishment (CWE) for internal trade, Business Acquisition Act in 1971to take-over private sector businesses, restrictions were to control Agency houses (Economic Progress of Independent Sri Lanka, 1998:20).
55. The summary form of detail information on all regimes (Economic Progress of Independent Sri Lanka, 1998:19).
56. (Economic Progress of Independent Sri Lanka, 1998:19).
57. (Economic Progress of Independent Sri Lanka, 1998:20).

58. Report of the Commission of Inquiry on Agency Houses and Brokering Firms" (Sessional Papers, 1974).
59 For example, China, Japan, Taiwan, South Korea 'all went through major transformative land reforms, which virtually eliminated a feudal, rent-seeking class in their respective societies' (Sobhan, 1999:55).
60. In Sri Lanka, the banks and insurance provided little financial assistance to domestic entrepreneur class. The foreign banks accessed to the resources of these banks (Carl Iverson, 1956:10). Japan and S.Korea have nationalised these types of industries on the same ground which helped the State to become more industrial biased.
61. Godfry Gunatilake (1999:191) discusses the causes and effects of these nationalisations in detail.
62. The socialists looked prejudicially at the business community.
63. Jenkins (1995:4) defines rent-seeking hypothesis as "...most powerful economic groups in a controlled economy derives their rents from the existence of highly regulated markets, they have as little incentive as political elites to favour reform even if reform might enrich the economy generally,"
64. Karunaratna (1974) gives examples of procedures adopted by bureaucrats to distribute the fund.
65. Hewavitharena (1989:34) discusses in detail the deficiencies in the process of self-generating growth in the period prior to 1977.
66. Lakshman has estimated 'the direct contribution of public enterprises to the government revenue in 1974 amounts to about 6.6 per cent of their employed capital'. The lending rate of state institutions were in the range between 5.0 13.0 per cent. Thus the surplus generations were very low in state enterprises (Lakshman, 1979:172). Figure DA.5 describes that profit/capital employed is very low when compared with lending rates given in Lakshman's.
67. Henderson et al., (1984:116) refers to T. A. Lee's work on *Income and value Measurement*, Nelson, Walton –on-Thames, 1980, p.6. We adopt the criteria of measuring profits expressed sym bolically by Henderson in the following form:

II

$$\Pi = K_o - K_1 + D - A$$

Where,

Π = Business profits for a year;

K_1 = business wealth or capital at the end of the period;

K_0 = business wealth or capital at the beginning of the period;

D = dividends paid during the period;

A = capital contribution during a period receiving from other sources.

The data on K, D and A were compiled using our database, and are given in nominal values in Table 5A1.4 in Appendix 1. We included all surpluses, including the tax component paid to the government which were generated by each industry.

68. All manufacturing industries in the large database and all state manufacturing enterprises were used for the purpose.

69. Mr. Wijesinhge (1976), the Chairman, the Chamber of Commerce, was very much concerned with the excessive tax burden on the private sector prior to 1977.

70. President Ronald Reagan applied this policy of tax cut in US in the early 1980s.

71. Walton has found that the "some public manufacturing enterprises currently receive well above average levels of effective protection". "There is little inherent economic justification of treating the private and public sectors dissimilarly" (Walton N. Geoffrey, 1987:104).

72. 'The economic efficiency and productivity were undermined by policies which were guided by consideration of equity. Examples were the pricing policies of the public enterprise sector...' (Gunatilake, 1999:197).

6

Industrial Accumulation and Market Forces

6.1. Introduction

As discussed in the foregoing chapter, the process of industrial accumulation in post-independent Sri Lanka commenced in a small way in the mid-1950s with a limited number of industrial ventures. This process grew after 1956 with the active participation of the state in industrial activities. The participation of the state brought about two patterns of accumulation. First, it helped the accumulation of state capital in the manufacturing industry. Secondly, it encouraged private industrial accumulation; a new venture capitalist class emerged in the system intensifying capital accumulation in the manufacturing industry. The old industrialists maintained a low profile in the process of industrial development.

The volume of state capital that went into industrial formation over this long period 1956-77 was quite high. One adverse outcome of this practice was the over-dependence of the public manufacturing sector on the state. This sector failed to generate sufficient surpluses internally to establish a self-generating growth process, and therefore, relied very much upon the state budget for its advancement. The private sector operated in an unfavourable 'investment climate' as certain policies of the state were counterproductive to the activities of the sector. The private sector responded cautiously to such policies making only limited capital investments. Foreign capital played an insignificant role in the industrial accumulation process of this period.

In its last few years, the interventionist state realised the limitations and ineffectiveness of its extreme interventionist policies on industrial development. The public enterprise sector as the leading sector had reached its limits of expansion and growth capacity by the 1970s, causing the state to explore alternative strategies for economic development of the country. The state gradually leaned towards liberal economic policies after 1975, especially after the Marxist fraction left the coalition government. The change of political environment favouring a capitalist state in 1977 opened up prospects for an alternative accumulation strategy associated with domestic, foreign as well as state capital in industrial development.

This chapter examines the causes which led to the adoption of alternative industrial strategies. After 1977, we see the response of domestic and foreign capital to policy changes based upon neoliberal economics. There are two arguments. Some critics argue that the industrial achievement in Sri Lanka since the mid-1970s is quite satisfactory. Others hold that it is only a dismal achievement. Therefore, the question needs to be raised, in the end, as to the adequacy of industrial formation under the market-oriented system for a high and sustainable industrial growth. The post 1977 period will be divided into two phases. The first phase until 1983 was the period in which the market forces were active and the private sector responded favourably to market signals. The second phase was the period after 1983 in which the institutional forces hostile to markets were dominant in economic activities. The industrial formation varied in accordance with the above phases.

6.2 Changes in the External Environment

The international economy was undergoing a process of rapid change in the 1970s generating multifarious effects upon developed as well as developing nations. It confronted with oil price shocks in 1973 and again in 1979. There was a move for change in economic policies of developed as well as developing nations since the mid- 1970s. The developed nations began to cast doubts upon the relevance of the 'so-called neo-economic policies of Keynes' economics' to face new challenges. 'There was a restatement of monetary theory of Friedman's economics of the classical school, which gradually became the mainstream of current economic thought' (Wou, 1997:130).

The 'privatisation of state institutions', a by-product of the above policy shift, focused upon strengthening market forces in economies. This new move was to 'make markets to work and achieve higher productivity growth' in economic systems[1]. Privatisation gained momentum as a strategy to overcome problems of inefficiency and to promote competitiveness at firm-levels. By the same token, the developed nations began to implement new strategies like deregulation of economic activities and adaptation of new technologies under the influence of GATT and later World Trade Organisation, WTO, as measures to raise productivity and to promote competitiveness in the international economic order.

The changing process of the international economic order continues with other developments like 'globalisation of production', 'technological changes' and 'reductions in transport and communications costs', especially, in the 1990s. The 'progressive globalisation of the production process'[2] was hastened by the 'competitive pressures ...[which] have encouraged firms to seek new markets and increase efficiency' (World Bank, 1997). These changes resulted in a large-scale outflow of financial resources towards developing countries as foreign direct investment (FDI) (samarawickreme, 1991). The FDI flows sought environments 'that offer macroeconomic stability, supportive regulatory frameworks, well-developed infrastructure (transport and telecommunications), low costs in relation to productivity of the labor force, and more open trade regimes' (World Bank, 1997:92).

The challenges faced by 'new nations' which emanated from the above changes on the external front were high. These nations were to respond to them quite positively. It is interesting, therefore, to understand how these nations were adjusting themselves to changes taking place in the international economy. The above changes produced two types of outcomes favourable for these nations. One was the opening up of new prospects for developing nations to market their products in markets of developed nations. The other was the prospect of borrowing productive resources and technology, and employing them in production processes of 'new nations'.

Some 'new nations' responded favourably to the changes in the international order. For example, the NICs and the emerging markets in South East Asia greatly benefited from the new economic policy of President Reagan (Yoo, 1997;Wou, 1997;

Rao, 1997; Onchan, 1997; Sivalingam, 1997). South Korean experience was a case in point to explain the way some 'new nation' responded to new economic policies of the West. South Korea responded positively and promptly to the policy changes in America and expanded trade with America (Yoo, 1999:118).

At the same time, the new nations' invited FDI for bridging the investment-savings gaps and for modernising production processes of their economies. These countries competitively offered various stimuli and favourable 'investment environments' to the suppliers of FDI. The counties in East Asian bloc –the NICs and other newly emerging markets like Thailand, Malaysia, Indonesia, Vietnam, the Philippines and China- have successfully accommodated FDI in their economies satisfying the above requisites on competitive basis.

These changes have helped these countries to form 'alliances' with domestic private, foreign and state capital —the 'tripod structure'—for the early industrial take off in a relatively short period of time as prescribed by Gerschenkron (1962). The 'tripod structure' brought about new process of industrial accumulation to 'new nations' (Akira, 1989; Evans, 1979; Evans et. al., 1985; Chan, 1996; Wade, 1990). Most importantly, it opened up a new route for advanced countries to transfer technology to these countries for a 'fast and compressed' industrial development. The NICs, first borrowed technology to develop their internal productive capacity, later underwent a 'learning process' and finally began to invent their own technologies. They began to export technology to developing countries (Hobday, 1995).

6.3. Changes in Internal Environment of Sri Lanka

The main components of the polity of Sri Lanka were the state, working class, political elite group and the private sector (see Figure 1.1 in chapter 1). The interactions among the components of the above structure determine the 'internal environment' of the economy. The socialist ideology of the state was to underpin and coordinate the relationships among the above components of the 'internal environment' until 1977. The socialist state aligned satisfactorily with the above components of the polity (except with the private sector) to develop strategies for achieving national objectives. The state–business sector relations required for capitalist industrial formation did not prosper in this 'internal environment'.

The period of the early 1970s was the turning point towards capitalist industrial path in Sri Lanka. Especially, the oil crisis and the world food shortages produced shocks which worsened the balance of payment problem of the country were hard to bear. Under the planning centric approach and the regime of fixed exchange rate, there was hardly any policy element other than the curtailment and ban of imports to arrest the deterioration of balance of payment conditions. In fact, the government was compelled to implement pro-market policies including the provision of various stimuli to the private sector to promote industrial exports[3]. The government, in its budget proposals in 1976, went to the extent of reversing certain policy decisions made by the previous socialist Minister of Finance. This was done with the intention of improving relations with the private sector and developing a favourable investment climate[4]. The 'socialist coalition' went ahead even to invite FDI, to take part in export industrial development. The White Paper on Foreign Investment, which was presented to the Parliament in 1972, offered lavish and 'most extravagant' concessions to foreign investors[5] (Hansards, 1977: 2236). In 1974, the National Planning Council[6] prepared a report on the establishment of a free trade zone in Sri Lanka. The FDI, however, did not respond satisfactorily to the call made by the interventionist regime (Vidanpathirana, 1986:180). 'After the White Paper of 1972, 16 ventures were established with foreign capital participation amounting to Rs. 23 million' (Hansards, 1977:2237).

Conflicts sprang up in the internal environment when the government began to respond to the challenges coming from the external environment. The measures adopted by the state were painful to the public, especially, to the working class. There was 'severe unemployment, galloping inflation and food shortages' in the economy (Fernando, 1984, 9). The working class, the pressure group of the 'coalition government', resisted the policies of the state. They felt that '[they] were moved by an illusion'[7] of the socialist state. They even organised trade union action against the regime in 1976 and 1977.

A new political culture was growing in the above polity with the penetration of new participants into the structure. The UNP, the regime which came to power in 1977, was 'having its main base among the more wealthy, and generally favouring private enterprise' (Moore, 1990:22). While in opposition, the UNP leadership was able to reorganise the party and combine all its forces into a 'more populist, centralised and professional machine'[8]. As our model in Fig.1.1 describes, the state consisted of a political party with a new ideology —the market economic ideology— after the General Election in 1977. Warnapala describes the transfer of power in 1977 as an outcome of the dominance of this capitalist class, which strengthened its power over the lower middle class in the system.

> The massive election victory of the UNP in 1977 gave an opportunity to the classes it represented to restore their strength through the use of political power. The capitalist class, the urban and rural middle class and the section of the working class rallying round the UNP, which, through a new system of government and a new style of leadership, was determined to restore the old order. 'The general election decimated the traditional left...' (Warnapala, 1992: 166).

The new regime was different from the previous 'liberal coalitions' of 1948-56 and 1965-70 in many ways. The pressure groups behind this regime were substantially different from those of previous ones. They were mostly the wealthy businesspersons, technocrats and industrialists (resident and non-resident). The colonial-minded feudal groups who supported the former liberal regimes were not any more powerful in politics. The attitudes of the political elite class were also quite different to those of the previous ones. The key personnel in the ruling class were technocrats[9] and 'new politicians' who were elected to Parliament in 1977. The ruling class and its close peer groups relied very much on market economic principles to 'break free of its cycle of economic retardation, poverty and bureaucratic lethargy' (De Silva, 1994:368).

The working class structure also changed during this period. The workers who previously supported the socialist policies of the centre left government lost confidence in them by the mid- 1970s. 'There were clear indications by 1977 that broad sections of the working class had moved away from left political parties towards the UNP'. 'Many of them became politically aligned with the UNP at the elections, and thereafter, most of them joined the UNP unions' (Fernando, 1984:10). The working class unified under the *Jathika Sevaka Sangamaya* (JSS) —the- UNP trade union—which became 'the largest trade union outside the plantation sector by 1977. The purpose of the JSS was 'to deny an important element of backing and militancy to the left'.

The overwhelming change that took place in the Sri Lankan economy in 1977 was the transformation from 'controlled economic' or 'regulatory economic policies' to 'liberalised economic policies'. There were queries about this transition. Some were related to the nature of the transition and others the delay in the transition. The main query was as to whether the change was inevitable, or was it an outcome of a natural process of capitalist economic development of 'new nations'. Long before this, in 1966, Prof. B. R. Shenoy, an Indian scholar, made a critical evaluation of the Sri Lankan economic structure[10]. He proposed to the then government to link market economic forces with the prevailing accumulation cycle for a sustainable growth of the economy. His suggestions were based on the policies of the new Monetarist school[11], which advocated governments to implement pro-market policies in the economic structure to reallocate resources according to market signals. The Cabinet, however, turned down these extreme pro-market policies of Shenoy for the reason that it was politically inexpedient to implement them at the time. The economic package set in motion by the new government in 1977 was very similar to what was proposed by Shenoy in 1966. According to De Silva, 'the reforms Shenoy had recommended, except the balanced budget, were introduced by J. R. Jayewardene's new government as essential features of his economic reforms' (De Silva et al., 1994:334).

Then the question arises as to why such suggestions, based upon market oriented policies, sprang up intermittently but were not implemented in the Sri Lankan economy until 1977. More over, what caused Shenoy type of recommendations, which had not been accommodated previously, to gain recognition in the post 1977 period? It may be that the pressures that developed within the Sri Lankan polity, resulting from factors originating in internal and external environments were behind these changes, as proposed by our model in Figure 1.1, Chapter 1.

Internally, the change of dominance from the lower middle class to the capitalist class in political and economic spheres is inevitable in systems of 'new nations' according to political economists. Michal Kalecki observed that conflicts developed within market forces and 'forces hostile to markets' in systems of capitalist development in 'new nations'. He noticed a "repetition of the well-known historical pattern" —the final submission of the lower middle class to the interests of big business— (Kalecki, 1972: 162-3).

The new government in 1977 began to make a gradual transition of the polity from its socialist foundations to a capitalist one, minimising possible conflicts in the internal structure. In the transition, the state came up with a new policy mix, a combination of growth and welfare objectives, in its political agenda (Budget Speech, 1981:2). The popular Mahaweli and housing projects were the welfare generating ones, the main package offered at the election campaign. A large volume of resources was allocated to these projects. De Silva et. al. (1994) highlight the special attention given to the Mahaweli project by the President and the Minister of Irrigation in their discussions about this project. However, Moore was quite critical about the political objectives behind this policy. He argued that these two programmes helped the government to assist its party supporters, providing them with government contracts in the construction sector (Moore, 1990:21).

Industrial development was the growth-generating project of the UNP government. However, its policy on industry looked more or less the same as was in the early 1950s. It was a liberal industrial policy compared to the policy of the previous regime. The latter had placed high priority and commitment on industrial development of the country. The new regime kept faith in the private sector and treated it as the main engine of industrial growth of the country. Such a strategy may have been meant to minimise possible conflicts in the transition to a capitalist foundation from a socialist base[12]. The implicit strategy of transforming the economic structure to a capitalist one was well expressed in the statement made by the Prime Minister J. R. Jayawardena (before he became the President) who said in Parliament:

> Except for the small enclave that wants to create –it has been called a Free Trade Zone; ...in the rest of Sri Lanka we do not encourage big capital ventures to thrive. We will encourage small and medium scale industries. (National State Assembly Debates, 1977:337).

When Mr. Jayawardena was making the policy statement of the government in 1977, as President, he reiterated the same viewpoint, 'the establishment of labour intensive, local raw material-based, small- and medium-scale industries will be encouraged by straightforward fiscal and other incentives'. He gave only minor importance to the industrial development in the overall speech but paid some attention to a balanced development programme emphasising banking, services, trade, and construction.

Industrial development was not a lead project of the government at the start. The government provided certain necessary stimuli –both micro and macro, but, treated it as a project of the private sector. Its initial objective, in fact, was to transform Sri Lankan economy to an 'off-shore banking Centre' and furthermore to 'an international financial centre in this region'. The Finance Minister in his Budget Speech emphasised these objectives. He said that '[f]oreign banks of the highest international repute have opened branches in Sri Lanka. Tourism has flourished. Construction and manufacture have shown remarkable progress' (Budget Speech, 1981:2).

The industrial accumulation process under the initiative of the private sector thus commenced in a small way with some stimuli provided by the government. The government's role was only to provide 'stimuli' to create a favourable 'investment climate' for the private industrialists.

6.4 Transition to Market-oriented Industrialisation - The Stimuli-

Contrary to previous practices, the two principal 'pods', foreign direct capital, FDI, and domestic private capital took the lead in the process of industrial accumulation in the post 1977 period. On its part, the government carried out certain reforms in economic and political spheres and offered a number of stimuli to the above two groups. The important stimuli offered to FDI were largely the micro stimuli like tax benefits, lump-sum depreciation and development rebates etc. (National Assembly Debates, 1977: 2236-38).

Some of the micro stimuli[13] offered by the state to promote 'investment environment' were as follows. International trade was partially liberalised. Partial reforms in the exchange rate were introduced to reflect the true opportunity cost of foreign exchange. Certain barriers against foreign investments were removed. Some other measures like the reduction of the level of protection were also introduced. An institution called, Presidential Tariff Commission, (PTC), was established to monitor the tariff levels and to determine effective protection rates for various products[14].

The public manufacturing enterprises, PMEs, were subject to reforms with a view to restructuring enterprises making them commercially viable. The PMEs were suffering from two main deficiencies in the existing market environment. They were able to produce only low commercial surpluses. Most state enterprises were either making losses or operating with low profit margins. Fixed assets and current assets of PMEs were declining over time. Table 6.1 based on observations on the performance of a sample of fifteen large PMEs during 1978- 1987 describes this behaviour[15]. The operating profits or the surpluses dropped at a rate of 8 per cent while fixed and current assets declined at rates of 2 and 1 per cent, respectively.

Table 6.1. Public Sector Performance After 1977
(A semi-log regression)

	Operating Profits	*Fixed Assets*	*Current Assets*
Rate of growth	-0.08	-0.02	-0.01
Std. Err.	0.03	0.002	0.004
R Squared	0.63	0.90	0.57

Source : 10 Year Performance 1978 –1987,15 Selected Manufacturing Corporations by Ministry of Finance and Planning.

The majority of state enterprises relied heavily upon the state budget for recurrent and capital expenditure. The industrial policy committee appointed by the Cabinet in 1987 to look into the affairs of the public manufacturing enterprises was concerned about the excessive budgetary subsidies demanded by some of the large PMEs. For example, the budgetary transfers to government corporations and institutions were as high as 49.1 per cent of government revenue in 1986[16]. The Committee recommended the introduction of certain reforms in PMEs with a view to improving the overall efficiency of the PME sector. It recommended, inter alia, the following reforms:

1. Reducing tariff protection and other privileges simultaneously with changes in PME management practices, and eventually closing PMEs that could not withstand increased competitive pressure on their own, and

2. Divesting PMEs (totally or partially) unless they had to remain under government's ownership for specific reasons.

One other new institution, free trade zones, FTZ, favourable for the capitalist industrial development was introduced. Among other types of stimuli provided to the capitalist class, the significant ones were the reduction of corporate taxes and the wealth tax previously charged from the capitalist class. The wealth tax was abolished in 1990. The tax concessions were streamlined to encourage potential investors to form listed companies in the company structure (Budget Speech, 1981:20). Various tax concessions were announced encouraging foreign share capital to invest funds in the local capital market and to take part in long-term direct investments[17].

Some measures that were brought in to reorient the political and economic spheres tended to improve the investment climate of the country. These included the major changes made in the Constitution[18] and economic policies[19] that were required for the capitalist industrial development. Certain institutional changes were also introduced over time. The capital market which, hitherto, was virtually non-existent, was revitalised under the Security Exchange Commission[20] (SEC). Certain institutions were revived including supportive services like insurance, money markets[21], media freedom, advertising and political stability to instil confidence in the private entrepreneurial class. Operational machinery to implement the programme of privatisation of public enterprises was set in motion in the late 1980s. The state invested funds in physical infra-structural facilities to expand the road network, communications system and power generation in the economy.

The government adopted policies to boost the business confidence of the private entrepreneurs. It returned some of the enterprises, which were taken over by the previous regime under the Business Undertakings (Acquisitions) Act of 1971, to the private sector. Secondly, it gradually liberalised certain sectors of the economy facilitating the private sector to enter them and to compete with the state sector. Industries like banking, insurance, transport and garment manufacture were liberalised. Thirdly, certain sectors like state banks were commercialised allowing the managerial functions to be more liberal and commercially oriented for these to generate their own surpluses. Fourthly, it later proceeded with a policy of privatisation / peoplisation of certain identified state enterprises, especially after 1989[22]. The plantations industry, the

Table 6.2 Sectoral Share of Capital Employed In Listed Firm Sector (Real Values)

	1979		1984		1993		1997
	No. Firms	**Fixed Capital Rs. Mn*	*No. Firm*	**Fixed Capital Rs. Mn*	*No. Firms*	**Fixed Capital Rs. Mn*	**Fixed Capital*
Manufacture and Related ***	34 (30.6)#	440 (17.4)	53 (33.1)	5094 (34.3)	62 (32.6)	12970 (21.2)	(31.0)
Construction and Engineering	4 (3.6)	88 (3.5)	5 (3.1)	368 (2.5)	4 (2.1)	2224 (3.6)	(2.0)
Services	56 (50.5)	1402 (55.5)	82 (51.3)	7219 (48.6)	90 (47.4)	23474 (38.4)	(28.0)
Trading	9 (8.1)	139 (5.5)	9 (5.6)	297 (2.0)	14 (7.4)	2464 (3.9)	(5.0)
Bank, Finance and Insurance	8 (7.2)	458 (18.1)	11 (6.9)	1863 (12.6)	20 (10.5)	22508 (35.4)	(33.0)
TOTAL	111	2527	160	14841	190	63640	

\# Numbers in brackets are percentages.

* Figures were estimated from sector-wise Fixed Capital formation.

** Extracted from Handbook of Listed Companies, 1996.

*** All Manufacture, Beverages, Food & Tobacco, Footwear and Textiles, Chemicals & Pharmaceutical sectors

Sources: Handbook of Listed Companies, 1979, 1984, 1993 and 1996.

biggest state enterprise, thus was subject to the process of privatisation.

6.5 Industrial Changes under Neoliberal Economic Policies

6.5.1 The Phase I

Private industrial accumulation accelerated after 1977 as is evident in figure 4.1, chapter 4. Two broad patterns of change in industrial accumulation were noticed under market economic policies of the state. One was the relatively high rate of capital accumulation during the period 1977-83. New investments moved towards manufacturing, banking and finance and services in different magnitudes over this period. The other broad pattern was the low-level capital accumulation in all areas after 1983. Evidently, the former trend of accumulation was an example of successful performance of capitalist industrial development in Sri Lanka under the neoliberal economic policy.

There were three types of domestic firms that participated actively in the process of economic development in Sri Lanka after 1977. They were the listed companies, non-listed large companies and small and medium scale enterprises, SMI; these grew under the new market-oriented environment. Table 6.2 summarises the changes that took place in the listed company sector over the long period. The columns of the table referring to the number of firms suggest that a considerable number of listed firms joined in manufacturing and services in three different periods. There were 34 and 56 listed firms in manufacturing and service-related sectors, respectively, in 1979. The number of firms has apparently doubled in 1993 in both sectors to bring it to 62 and 90, respectively. The number of banking and finance firms was only 8 in 1979 but grew up to 20 by 1993.

The inter-sectoral distribution of private capital was quite different from the above pattern of distribution of firms (see Figure 3.9, chapter 3). Table 6.2 describes that there was an absolute increase in the volume of private capital in all sectors over the period between 1979 and 1997. There was a huge increase in real fixed investment in all sectors. Manufacturing, services and banking and finance experienced intensive capital formation. Of the total volume of capital in the listed firm sector, manufacturing has attracted 17.4 and 34.1 per cent in 1979 and 1983, respectively. It has dropped to 21.2 per cent in 1993 but again risen to 31.0 per cent in 1997. On the other hand, the share of banking and finance was 18.1 per cent in 1979. It dropped to 12.6 in 1983 but has risen dramatically to 35.4 per cent in 1993. There was a slight drop in it to 33.0 per cent in 1997. The service

Table 6.3 Type of Products, Nature of Ownership and Number Of Firms in the Non-Listed Firm Sector

	Sections & Types of Products	*Proprietorships No. firms*	*Partnerships No. firms*	*Family-based Cos. No. firms*	*Private ltd. Cos. No. firms*	*TOTAL No. firms*
1	Food, Beverages And Tobacco	1(5.9)*	4 (23.5)	8(47.1)	4 (23.5	17(100)
2	Textiles, Weaving Apparels and Made-up Garments	3(6.4)	1(2.1)	39(83.0)	4(8.5)	47(100)
3	Manufacture of Chemicals and Chemical Products		1(3.8)	12(46.2)	13(50.0)	26(100)
4	Manufacture of Leather, Rubber, Wood and Paper	2(6.9)	1(3.4)	18(62.1)	8(27.6)	29(100)
5	Base Metal Industries – Manufacture of Metal Products	1(8.3)		7(58.3)	4(33.3)	12(100)

(Contd.)

(*Contd.*)

	Types of Products	Proprietorships No. firms	Partnerships No. firms	Family-based Cos. No. firms	Private ltd. Cos. No. firms	Total No. firms
6	Manufacture of Machinery (Except Electrical Machinery) Manufacture of Transport of Equipment	1(14.3)		2(28.6)	4(57.1)	7(100)
7	Manufacture of Electrical Machinery Apparatus and Appliance		4(22.2)	11(61.1)	3(16.7)	18(100)
8	Miscellaneous Manufacturing Industries	2(4.2)	8(16.7)	23(47.9)	15(31.3)	48(100)
	Total	10(4.9)	19(9.3)	120(58.8)	55(27.0)	204(100)

* Percentage of firms in each section is given in parenthesis.

Source: Ferguson's Directories.

sector, which was based mostly on tourist industry, experienced a fall in the share of private capital all along though it held a high share in 1979. These figures suggest that different patterns of private accumulation in different sectors of the Sri Lankan economy have taken place under the market economic environment.

Table 6.3 provides the pattern of participation of the non-listed large firm sector in industrial accumulation. This information is collected from the database on non-listed firms in the Ferguson's Directory (see for detailed information on this sample firms Table 6A1.1, Appendix 1). The Directory provides information on names of firms, years of establishment, nature of the ownership and type of products produced by these firms. The interesting characteristic of the non-listed company sector has been the dominance of family-based and large private limited companies[23] in the structure of manufacturing.

The non-listed large firms manufactured products like textiles, weaving apparel and made-up garments; leather, rubber, wood and paper products and chemicals and chemical products. (Ferguson's Directory provides details of products manufactured by each firm in the sample). Family-based firms concentrated more on the production of textiles, weaving apparels and made-up garments. Large private company sector specialised in the manufacture of chemicals and chemical products. (The industrial accumulation by the SMI sector is not discussed here).

Past experience suggests that there has been some disproportionate distribution of private resources among different sectors of the economy. These productive resources have accumulated largely in non-manufacturing activities under the open market economic policies of the government (see Table 6.2). According to some critics, the reason for this was 'the public sector investment boom' under open market policies which propelled the growth performance of non-tradable sectors -construction, transport, utilities, trade and other services sectors (Athukorala et. al., 1998).

Some tend to believe that there wasn't a large flow of FDI towards manufacturing in Sri Lanka. Kelegama, (1999:61), for example, finds that '...it attracted only $0.8 billion in the 8 years 1990 –97'. In particular, advanced and high tech industries like electronic industries with heavy capital bases —the industries that can cater to the growing international industrial product market— have not sprung up in Sri Lanka's industrial structure (See Table 3.3, chapter 3). Such industries are 'highly sensitive to the risk of production disruption'. Athukorala refers to two such FDI multinationals, The Motorolla and Harris Corporation, which had planned to set-up industries but had later left Sri Lanka without doing so. The simple and light manufacturing activities involving low financial commitments have mostly thrived in the 'investment environment' of Sri Lanka. These were the safest and low-risk industries, which are like garments, footwear, food and beverages, which involved relatively low capital requirements.

6.5.1.1 The 'Tripod Structure'

The outstanding feature of the process of capitalist industrial development under neoliberal economic policy is the involvement of all classes of investors in the process of industrial accumulation. These involved capitalist classes, including state capital, which can contribute in different magnitudes to the industrial accumulation process of the country. The above three types of capital, state, private domestic and foreign, have contributed enormously to the processes of capitalist industrial formation in other 'new nations'[24] . However, the level of participation of the above three types in industrial development process in Sri Lanka was low and subject to fluctuations.

Figure 4.1 (chap.4) provides the long-term trend of industrial capital formation by the owners of the above three forms of capital. The industrial formation during interventionist regime prior to 1977, as discussed in chap. 5, was predominantly state-dependent. Private capital had contributed only marginally which foreign capital had scarcely participated in the process. This pattern changed after 1977. The contribution of state capital in industrial capital formation has gradually declined under the market-oriented policies of the UNP government (see the declining trend of curve 1, fig. 4.1, chapter 4). The new policies instead have encouraged the private sector to participate in industrial accumulation. The private entrepreneurs mobilised their resources towards manufacturing as a result of profitable opportunities that sprang up in the economy under liberal economic policies. Consequently, private capital of both domestic and foreign origin actively took part in industrial formation. This change can be noticed when we refer to regions E, F and G in figure 4.1 in chap. 4. The dominance of state capital in industrial accumulation has changed in region E where domestic capital and foreign capital have replaced state capital in the industrial accumulation process. The rates of accumulation of domestic and foreign capital have risen to 5 and 19 per cents, respectively, during 1978-83. State capital experienced a negative rate of growth of –4 per cent (See Table 6.4 below).

The participation of foreign capital in economic activities of Sri Lanka has a long history (See chapter 2). This fel to a very low level after independence because of 'political radicalism and instability in this country' (Moore, 1990). The governments after independence invited FDI for industrial development on several occasions but FDI did not respond favourably to such calls because of poor 'investment climate' in the country. The government after 1977 adopted a series of urgent measures to create a 'FDI friendly investment climate' for private investment. Some of those measures took in the following form (Moore, 1990; Wignaraja, 1998).

1. The development of physical infrastructure for an export processing zone,
2. Handing over a large proportion of Sri Lanka's national textile quotas in industrial country markets to quota-hopping entrepreneurs from East and Southeast Asia, and
3. Provision of credit facilities from domestic banks at extremely low rates.

There was some inflow of FDI during 1977-1985 (see fig. 4.1). Vidanapathirana (1986:188) gives information on foreign investments approved by Greater Colombo Economic Commission (GCEC) and foreign Investment Advisory Committee (FIAC) during this period. These FDI flows helped Sri Lanka to make headway towards capitalist industrial accumulation after 1977 (see Figure 4.1).

State capital reduced its direct participation in industrial activities but engaged in infrastructural development. The region B in fig. 6.1 elaborates this new pattern where curve 2 describes a negative trend of investment in manufacturing enterprises. The curve 1 describes the fast increase in investment in infrastructure. The investment in infrastructure under interventionist policies, in region A remained at a level of 6 –7 per cent of GDP. It rose to about 16-17 per cent of GDP in region B, fig. 6.1 during 1977-83. The state spent money on the transport network and services such as communication and mass media, energy, irrigation facilities, internal trade, tourism and financial services.[25]

Industrial development after1977 followed a self-generating growth process. This can be found in figure 5.1 in chapter 5. It provides a comparison between two different patterns of growth of industrial surpluses under planning and market-oriented economic strategies. Figure 5.1 shows the generation of huge surpluses in all sectors—

FIGURE 6.1 DISTRIBUTION OF STATE INVESTMENT FUND

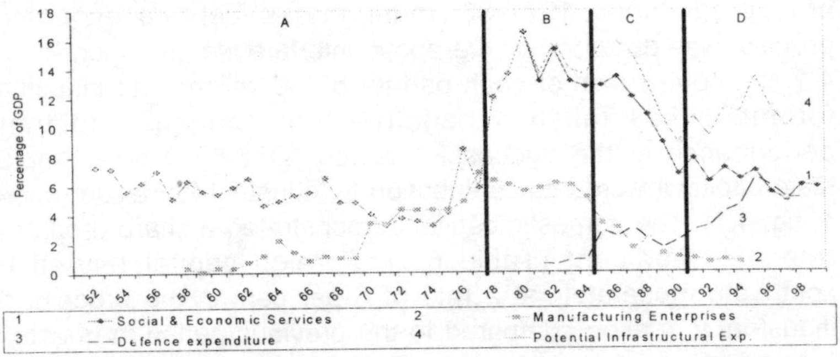

Source: Annual Report, Central Bank of Sri Lanka, 1998, and our database

manufacturing, finance, trade and construction— after 1977 as compared to the previous period. The surplus in manufacturing alone, which had been very low in the previous period, rose steadily between 1977 and 1985, according to figure 5.1. The manufacturing accumulation demonstrates a simultaneous growth with surplus generation during this period. All three partners of the 'alliance' were in action as predicted in the development theory. This trend of industrial formation continued until ethnic violence started in 1983.

6.5.2 Phase II

The post 1983 period witnesses an era of instability in both political and economic environment of the country. Many have written about the uncertain environment and the 'poor investment climate' that prevailed after 1983 (Moore, 1992: 69-80; Athukorala, 1995:547; Snodgrass, 1998:29). Political instability, ethnic problems, the JVP insurrection of 1988 -89 and finally worker unrest in the 1990s disturbed the 'investment climate' of the country (These will be discussed in detail, later). Figure 4.1 indicates the sluggish growth in fixed industrial investment after 1983.

Table 6.4 Annual Rates of Growth of Manufactureing Capital

Periods	*State Capital*	*Domestic Capital*	*Foreign Capital*
1978-84	-0.04	0.05	0.19
1985 –89	-0.11	-0.04	0.05
1990 –94	-0.05	0.01	0.06
1994 –97		-0.03	-0.02
1990 –97		-0.01	0.02

Source : The database.

The 'alliance' of domestic, foreign and state capital that prospered during 1977-83 under market-centred economic policies, was disturbed by the above interference. In region F, fig. 4.1, the contribution of each partner of the 'alliance' to industrial formation has taken a negative turn compared to their performance in the successful period 1977-83. For example, state capital lowered its contribution to industrial formation (curve 1, fig. 4.1). The domestic capital demonstrated a sharp drop at a rate of 4 per cent (Table 6.4). Foreign capital tended to contribute moderately at a rate of 5 per cent in the process of industrial formation compared to the previous period in question (curve 3, figure 4.1).

The state reduced expenditure on infrastructural facilities as well as industrial fixed investment during this period as depicted in region C of fig. 6.1 and region F in fig. 4.1. Defence expenditure rose rapidly after 1983 (curve 3 in fig. 6.1). It has risen from 0.8 per cent of GDP in 1983 to about 5.0 per cent of GDP in the latter part of 1990s. There was an overall drop in average total industrial fixed investment at the end of the 1990s which was nearly equal to the pre-1977 level (see curve 4 in fig. 4.1).

6.6. Dilemmas under Market Orientation

The unusual slowness of industrial accumulation under neoliberal economic policies requires further explanation. It was noticed in fig 4.1 that industrial growth under the liberalised economic environment after 1977 continued with some success only for a limited period. Growth, however, slowed down even under the 'second-wave' of liberalisation after 1990 with a high degree of privatisation and further liberalisation[26]. There were two possible reasons for this behaviour of industrial accumulation in Sri Lanka. One may be related to relevance and potency of the neoliberal approach to the industrial development of Sri Lanka. The other may be related to the adaptability of neo-liberal policies to the internal 'investment environment' effectively in Sri Lanka's political and economic structure.

The neoliberal economic policy presupposes a stylised pattern of participation of the 'tripod structure' in the economy. Accordingly, domestic and private foreign capital is to serve as the principal source of capital supply in the economy contributing to 'fast and compressed' industrial development. State capital helps to improve infrastructural facilities of the system at least in the early phases of development[27]. But, Sri Lanka's experience exhibits that the 'tripod structure' has performed quite differently to the above neoliberal stipulations. Two broad factors influenced the working of the 'tripod structure' in the industrial accumulation process. One important variable was the influence of economic factors on industrial behaviour. The other was the effect of non-economic factors (rather 'institutional forces hostile to markets'). The combined effects of these determined the process of industrial accumulation. Thus, **economic** and **non-economic factors** have influenced the determination of the 'internal environment' of the polity.

6.6.1 The economic Factors

The unusual experience under conditions of the quasi-neoliberal economic policy after 1977 suggests that unlike in the previous regime, productive resources have moved more towards other sectors than manufacturing (Budget Speech, 1981:4). One explanation may be the low margin of profits in manufacturing as compared to other sectors like trade, finance, services and construction. This was the reason for low private investment in the manufacturing sector. Figure 3.3 in chapter 3 supports the assertion that manufacturing earns relatively low EPS values compared to other sectors of the Sri Lankan economy. After 1983, the EPS values tended to be very low in manufacturing and construction as compared to finance and trade. Construction activities, on the other, began to enjoy relatively high margins of profits which manufacturing received only low margins even after 1990.

What caused manufacturing to earn relatively low profit margins as compared to other sectors of the economy? This was largely associated with market and relatively high cost of production of manufactured goods in the economy. In fact, both were determined mainly by policies of the state. The neoliberal state after 1977 was able to revive **external** and **internal markets** for domestically produced industrial goods. Price signals and profit margins, generated in these two markets helped to determine how the 'tripod structure' worked to promote industrial formation. The degree of performance of domestic and foreign industrialists in these two markets can be analysed using Fig. 6.2 below.

6.6.1.1 The External Market for Industrial Products

The policy of trade liberalisation can be viewed as a strategy adopted by the government after 1977 to promote industrial exports for strengthening of the country's balance of payments. The liberal economic policies provided necessary incentive machinery for export-oriented industrial development, eliminating economic sluggishness of the import substituting industrial policy of the preceding regime. Under the new policy, the economy was expected to undergo certain structural changes producing competitive economic advantages favourable for foreign trade. The liberal reforms provided the necessary guidelines for restructuring the economy to create a competitive industrial economic structure.

The neoliberal policy presupposed the country to go along with certain reforms in macroeconomic management of external[28] and internal sectors. The reforms themselves were quite painful since these required a firm commitment in the political and economic spheres of the country for successful implementation. The reforms under the active guidance of the state helped certain countries in East Asia to achieve export-oriented industrial status in relatively a short period of time. Their experiences suggest that the successful transformation towards industrial development was a direct outcome of effective participation of two main 'pods', the private sector and the state, in the economy. For example, the 'hard'[4] and 'developmental states'[5], like S. Korea and Taiwan were able to implement the reforms, even unpopular ones, successfully in achieving that status (Wade, 1990). One prerequisite, therefore, may be relatively 'hard' character of the state for implementing reforms required for capitalist industrial accumulation. Rowen (1998:10) suggested the concept of 'effective governance' as an approach for government to go about in implementing these reforms.[31]

Did the state and the private sector in Sri Lanka adhere to conditions specified by quasi-neoliberal policies? It appears that domestic and foreign capital have responded cautiously to the liberal economic policies of the state. The foreign firms, the firms under the Board of Investment, have performed with some success in export of industrial products compared to domestic ones. According to curve 1 in Figure 6.2, real export earnings of BOI firms evidently have grown rapidly since the 1980s. The firms were very much cost-conscious at the firm level and were competitive at the market level[32]. The sector employed some new technology[33], professional management skills[34], know-how, cheap off-shore capital and, above all, the protected environment in the FTZ, (exempted from labour disputes) to become cost-effective and competitive in the external markets.

The BOI firms have effected 'ongoing pattern of commodity diversification' in product combinations depending upon circumstances (Athukorala, 2000:128). This can be noticed in changes in sources of export earnings over this long period. The earnings of BOI firms from textiles, apparels and leather product were about 97 per cent of its total manufacturing exports in 1980. This has dropped[35] to 63 per cent in 1997 (see Table 6A1.1 Appendix 1). The export earnings from chemicals, petroleum, rubber, and plastic products have risen to 11 percent in 1997 from 3 per cent in 1979[36]. The BOI firms knew that textiles and garment industries would be facing marketing problems once the quota provisions under the Multi-fibre Arrangement (MFA) are abolished by Western nations by about 2005. Moreover, they know that comparative advantages of the garment industry in Sri Lanka were diminishing gradually as nominal wages have been observed to be rising over this period[37]. It is natural, therefore, for FDI to make changes in their investment portfolios moving towards capital intensive industries[38].

Domestic industrialists have not been as dynamic as BOI firms in export diversification and promotions. This can be seen with their poor export earning behaviour as shown by curve 2 in Figure 6.2, indicating the trend of long-term (real) export earnings of domestic private industrialists. It explains that the export volume remained almost constant over the whole period.

What caused the real export earnings of domestic private industrialists to be almost constant throughout this long period? There appears to have been certain structural impediments which weakened the performance of these firms in foreign trade. One obvious reason is the slow modernisation of production processes of this sector in terms of technology and management[39]. The government in 1989 identified this deficiency and proposed certain remedial measures for improving technology, managerial functions and entrepreneurial skills in its medium term policy framework (Budget Speech, 1988: 51). But, in practice, there had been no effective transfers of technology and managerial talents to this sector (Athukorala, 1997).

The domestic private industrialists have concentrated more and more on textiles, apparel and leather products in contrast to their foreign counterparts (see Table 6A1.2, Appendix 1). The real export earnings from textiles, apparels and leather products of domestic industrialists were about 20 per cent of their total export revenue in 1979. This grew up to 72 per cent in 1997. On the other hand, the share of chemicals, petroleum, rubber and plastic products in total export earnings was about 63 per cent in 1979. It dropped to almost 4 per cent in 1997. Domestic industrialists have intensified industrial activities in labour intensive 'diffused technology industries' (Athukorala, 1997;Lall[40], 1998; Wignaraja, 1998).

FIGURE 6.8 (REAL) EARNINGS FROM INDUSTRIAL PRODUCTIONS BY LOCAL AND FOREIGN FIRMS

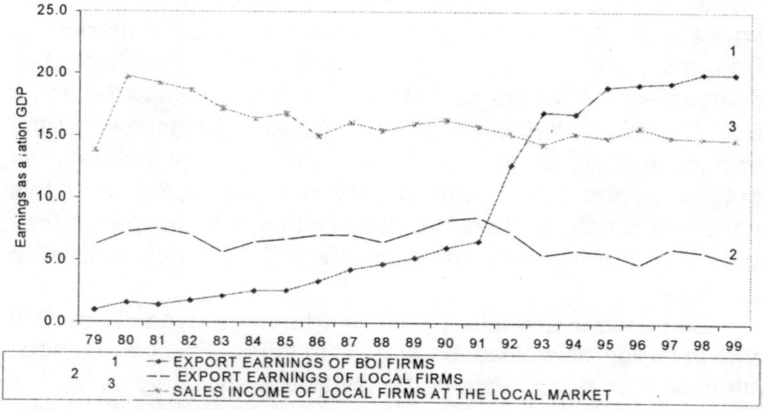

Source : The Central Bank Reports[41].

The unfavourable 'investment environment' in the country may have impeded the prospects for industrial exports of domestic industrialists. One good example was the labour market condition. The domestic industrialists hired labour from the competitive and unprotected labour market. Labour, therefore, was relatively expensive for domestic industrialists[42]. Their foreign counterparts hired labour from a protected labour market in Free Trade Zones. The imported inputs that locally owned enterprises used in production processes were not exempted from custom duties. But, the imported inputs used by BOI firms had been exempted from customs duties. Another was that domestic industrialists were denied the opportunity to access foreign capital markets for borrowing for their investment needs. They borrowed funds at a high rate of interest from the domestic financial market. The capital, therefore, was relatively dear for domestic industrialists[43]. In contrast, the BOI firms borrowed funds at relatively low interest from offshore capital markets. One other factor was the macroeconomic instability, especially after 1983, which resulted in domestic industrial products becoming internationally less competitive (Budget Speech, 1988). The government's failure to implement macroeconomic policies lowered the competitiveness of private industrial goods abroad (Rajapatirana, 1986)[44]. Wignaraja, (1998:153) describes all this as 'the lack of systematic approach to protect infant industries to encourage the acquisition of technical capabilities and the attainment of international competitiveness'.

Again, the 1990s brought in new challenges to the industrial development process of the country. The threat of 'globalisation' and the change in political climate brought about new challenges to both parties from both ends, imports and exports. From the direction of exports, both domestic and FDI firms earned lower real earnings from exports compared with previous periods. This is revealed in Figure 6.2. The (real) industrial export earnings of FDI have risen at a huge rate from 1990 to 1993 followed by a low rate (see curve 1). Real foreign earnings of domestic industrialists have shown a negative trend throughout the 1990s. Real earnings fell probably due to the drop in volumes of exports. The reduction in the volume of exports, on the other hand, may be the result of either drop in production or problems of marketing in foreign markets. The former is more probable as the political economic environment was not conducive to private investment in Sri Lanka especially after 1993. (No other database is found to describe the drop, especially, in the production of industrial products of the domestic private sector. However, our database evidences the drop in industrial capital of the private domestic company sector which can be a good proxy to the above).

The industrial infrastructure of Sri Lanka was not sufficiently developed to face challenges from the highly competitive world market. Sri Lanka's underdeveloped infrastructural conditions resulting in relatively high transport costs worked as a disincentive for export development. These included the physical infrastructure like transport, communication, power, technology etc. and 'human and intellectual development as a carrier of technology complementary to that embodied in physical capital' (Naseem, 1999:218). Wignaraja (1998) highlights the limited application of technology in the industrial development of Sri Lanka. Wijesekara et al. (1998) draw attention to the deficiencies in the promotional process of science and technology, S&T, in upgrading technological capacity of the country. They blame the public sector institutions for ignoring the development of the technological base required for the process of industrial accumulation in Sri Lanka. '[E]ven with an impressive network of scientific institutions, scientific research failed to grow the direction needed' (Wijesekara et. al., 1998: 404). The private sector in Sri Lanka also spent only little in R&D for this purpose.

6.6.1.2 The Domestic Market for Industrial Products

The domestic market prospered after 1977 no sooner the restrictions were lifted and foreign goods were permitted to enter the market. The effects of these policy actions were considerable and, one important outcome was that, '[t]he nation was flooded with consumer goods as well as luxury goods' (Dissanayaka, 2000:665). In general, this policy affected the functioning of the local market at least in two ways. Firstly, the free supply of intermediate and investment goods helped domestic firms to increase capacity utilisation of plants[45] and to increase supply of consumer goods to the local market in the medium term. Secondly, the trade sector simultaneously was able to increase the supply of imported consumer goods to the local market under the liberal trade policy[46]. The traders or the importers supplied goods at world market prices and obtained quick returns. Domestic producers, operating at local costs of production made relatively low margins of profit. In this process, the direct importers were able to earn a relatively high share of profits generated in the 'shortage-ridden suppliers' market' as soon as markets were opened for foreign competition.

Trade liberalisation was, thus, counter-productive to the production activities of domestic industrialists. The rent-seeking oligopolists who thrived[47] during the previous regulatory economic environment faced the risk of losing their market shares due to the overflow of foreign goods in the local market. The abundance of imported goods in the market thus lowered profit margins of domestic industries manufacturing fabricated metal products, chemicals, bicycles and tyres, printing papers and dairy products (Kelegama 1999). The liberalisation of trade and 'allowing the domestic market to be flooded with cheap imports had tended to undermine domestic agriculture and industry' (Kelegama, 1999:61). This policy of liberal trade and the opening of markets for foreign competition appeared to be counter-productive for domestic industries 'in a majority of developing countries that are struggling to build their new industries' (Kelegama 1999: 62).

It appears that the state policy of trade liberalisation was directly aimed at providing welfare to the classes of consumers and businessmen iin the system. Apparently, the powerful classes of consumers and importers, who suffered greatly during 1970-77, brought pressure on the government to liberalise trade.

In fact, trade liberalisation was one of the major items in the political agenda of the UNP and was the main slogan in the election campaign. Moore's (1990) comment provides an insight into the motive of the state behind trade liberalisation after 1977[48]. He says that the '[p]rivate businessmen certainly wanted a reversion to much freer access to foreign exchange in order to meet consumer demand' (Moore, 1990:21). He added that the policy of liberalisation after 1977 was primarily to put 'an end to controls, queues and shortages' rather than to implement rigorous neoclassical economic policies. This was exactly the case in post-WW II era and again during 1948-56 under liberal economic policies. The state favoured the interests of pressure groups and allowed imported consumer goods to flood local market ignoring its adverse impact on the producer class on both occasions (see chapter 5).

Did the domestic market produce favourable signals and, in turn, the domestic industrialists respond favourably to them? We saw earlier that the domestic market produced only weak profit signals because of foreign competition in local markets. The three classes of domestic industrialists, the listed companies, non-listed companies and small and medium sized firms, responded to these signals differently. The response of the listed company sector was quite low. The real earnings of this class from trading industrial products in the local market was falling after 1982. This behaviour is depicted in curve 3, figure 6.2. Accordingly, the sector has responded positively to favourable signals produced by the local market until 1981 but thereafter with no clear direction.

The effects of 'globalisation' that transpired on the local market after 1990 were unfavourable to domestic industrialists. The imported goods began to flood the local markets under the 'second wave' of liberalisation in 1989. The market was flooded with foreign products like garments, footwear, chemical products etc., that were relatively low in prices. These products, which were produced in countries like China and India, were competitive in terms of price, and were good substitutes for local products. There was also competition from products of Transnational Corporations[49] (Kelegama, 1999:62). Consequently, the large firms faced the threat of being deprived of their market share for the products at the local market[50].

The signals produced by the market after 1977 were not

strong enough to stimulate the non-listed company sector —the breeding ground of listed companies of the economy. Table 6.5 provides some data regarding this sector based on information provided by Ferguson's directory. The companies covered by Ferguson's directory provide a good sample of non-listed companies in Sri Lanka. Two outstanding features of this sector can be noticed. First, the firms in this sector were slow in moving upward to a higher strata in the business hierarchy. The other is that the majority of companies were family-based. About 56.7 per cent (110 out of 194) of firms were family-based companies and about 24.2 per cent (47 of 194) were private limited companies.

The non-listed company sector displayed a slow upward mobility in the business ladder. Table 6.5 describes that the firms, which started either as family-based companies or partnerships, have continued to hold the same status for long without switching over to the next strata of the firm hierarchy. For example, there were about 62 family-based firms that started prior to 1977 which continue to remain as family based companies even in the late 1990s. About 34 firms were formed as family-based ones in the period 1977-85. These remain still as family-based companies. Similarly, there were about 24 private limited companies that were formed before 1977; these remain as private limited companies without moving to the listed-company status. This suggests that the non-listed company sector in Sri Lanka –the largest sector—has been quite static and that it has not shown much enthusiasm in climbing in the business ladder for growth. But, the business dynamics has been that growth-oriented firms move fast in the business ladder and reach listed company status in a relatively short period.

The main weakness of this firm structure apparently has been its sluggishness in effecting changes. This may be because family-based firms were not open to inter-firm competition. The capital base and skilled manpower were confined to a few internal sources like family members, relatives and friends without depending much upon markets for labour and capital. This behaviour can be noticed with information given in the Ferguson's directory where most managerial and directorial personnel have been holding their positions in same firms for quite long periods. The closure of firms to outside competition limited the inflow of new management inputs, cost effective methods and better technology into the firm sector. More seriously, the limitations of equity capital set limits for expansion. In turn, the limited equity base set further limits to borrowing loan capital as existing equity base determined the size of the asset structure of these firms on which loans were granted.

Why did the non-listed company sector, the large sector and the breeding ground of listed-companies, follow a conservative policy over this long period? The main reason may be that strong incentives have not been produced by the market system to encourage new and old firms to engage

Table 6.5 The Structure of the Large Company Sector

Type of ownership prevailing	*No. of Companies operating to-date that were established:*				*Total*
	Before	*1977–85*	*1985-89*	*1990-97*	
Proprietorships	3	3	2		8
	(2.8)	(5.0)	(11.1)		
Partnerships	11	4	1	1	17
	(10.1)	(6.7)	(5.6)	(14.3)	
Family-Based Cos.	62	34	8	6	110
	(56.9)	(56.7)	(44.4)	(85.7)	
Private Cos.	24	18	5		47
	(22.0)	(30.0)	(27.8)		
Listed Cos.	9	1	2		12
	(8.3)	(1.7)	(11.1)		
Total	109	60	18	7	194
	(100)	(100)	(100)	(100)	

Source : Ferguson's Directory, 1997.

in industrial activities. The limited stimuli and profit margins produced little challenge for firms to change their present status to a higher level in the company ladder. The economic environment produced little incentives for the sector to rise[51].

6.6.2. Forces Hostile to Markets

The question as to why quasi-neoliberal policies have been unsuccessful in delivering the expected results after 1983 has been posed by many[52]. They argue that the state has failed to implement 'good policies'[53] favourable to foreign and domestic private capital. Policies tended to ignore the interference of institutional forces hostile to markets which overshadowed the effects of market forces and disturbed the process of industrial development of the country. Lakshman (1997) in his 'introduction' to the book on "Dilemmas of Development" brought out the importance of non-economic factors which hindered the development momentum in Sri Lanka.

> ...it could be hypothesised that many institutional, cultural, political and other peculiarities of the country, not captured in the policy critique of mainstream economic discourse were behind Sri Lanka's failure to economically keep up with those other countries which, four decades ago were at either parallel or inferior conditions (Lakshman, 1997:16).

Meier (1995) also argues that forces hostile-to-markets would work counter to industrial development under neoliberal economic policies in 'new nations'. Discussing the relevance of neoliberal economic policies to developing countries, he argues that '...this calls for special care in identifying different institutional relations, in assessing the different quantitative importance of some variables... —such as population, "state of the art," institutions, and supply of entrepreneurs— (Meier, 1995:89). There can be at least two broad types of forces hostile to markets. One springs from the very behaviour of the firms. The other is the interference of certain non-economic variables that are external to the system.

In 'new nations', the state is the core institution that can interact with different forces in the system. It absorbs pressures coming from different segments specially, from the working class, political elite and the external environment (see Figure 1.1, chapter 1). The main responsibility of the neoliberal state, the 'facilitator', has been the provision of a cordial 'investment climate' to promote private industrial investment[54]. The neoliberal state can form new institutions to promote social relations among different groups in the system. It cannot guarantee the existence of a stable political and economic environment that would help to develop confidence among private entrepreneurs[55].

The question then arises as to whether the Sri Lankan state was able to provide a 'favourable investment climate' for the generation and accumulation of private surpluses in the economy. In other words, can Sri Lankan State be called as a neoliberal state? In fact, the state of Sri Lanka was not seriously bound by a broad doctrine like the neoliberal or the neoclassical theory in formulating its economic policies at least until the 1990s. Although Jayasuriya (2000) holds the view that government after 1977 followed 'the new ethos of laissez–faire growth, inspired by the ideology of economic rationalisation' others, however, take different stands about the Sri Lankan State. Moore holds that the package of economic liberalism implemented after 1977 was a package specific to the Sri Lankan politico–economic environment. For him, it was not bound by a broad theoretical economic foundation but by 'political mechanisms'. Neither, the party manifestos and budget proposals nor parliamentary debates give a clear insight into the true economic vision of the government after 1977. The state had persistently reiterated that industrial development was a natural process, and market forces would guide it in the course of time. But, the state appears to have failed to conceptualise comprehensively as to how it could facilitate market forces to achieve desired objectives.

Largely, political motives influenced economic behaviour of the state after 1977[56]. In the absence of a long-term vision of industrial development, the state distributed available resources among a few lead projects based upon political considerations. These included Mahaweli programme to provide irrigation and power and the urban development programme. '...[T]he greater part of the effort and the larger share of domestic and external resources went to the Mahaweli programme and the infrastructure for rice cultivation' (Gunatilake, 1999:203). These were all politically favoured projects, which helped the government in supporting its pressure groups (Dissanayaka, 2000,665;Moore, 1985).

At the same time, the Western donor agencies began to intensify pressure on the Sri Lankan State at different aid forums[57] for intensive use of neoliberal policies in the economy and streamlining of industrialisation as the main strategy of development. The state, which was increasingly becoming dependent upon foreign aid could not disregard these pressures for long while the domestic interest groups brought pressures for increasing welfare facilities in the system. Thus, two different forces were at work pressurising for achieving two different objectives that limited the autonomy of the government. The government was compelled to follow a dual economic policy reorienting its priorities for the promotion of industries as well as the provision of welfare services to targeted groups in society. This is reflected in the statement made by the Finance Minister in the Parliament in 1984: '[t]he time has come to focus on other important sectors –must re-orient our incentive structure to give the highest priority to production, employment and export'.

Export promotion was given high priority under the new strategy. Some new institutions were formed to monitor this process. One was the Export Development Board, EDB. This Board served as an intermediary to promote exports, but, later it was subject to political interference (Wignaraja, 1998). Others were the National Development Bank, NDB and Development Finance Credit Corporation DFCC which took certain 'remedial actions to provide medium and long term finance for product development and development of new exports on a high priority basis' (Budget Speech, 1983:35).

Under the neoliberal policy, institutional development was considered to be an integral part of the development of market forces in 'new nations'. This was an important requisite of the capitalist industrial society which promotes smooth generation and accumulation of surpluses in economies (Walsh, 1980). Sri Lanka under the state-centric development policy promoted a labour policy which was largely state-dependent (Uyangoda, 1992). The socialist regime did not solicit an institutional mechanism for the development of labour relations in workplaces. The President in his first address in the Parliament in 1977 emphasised the need of a new government policy regarding trade unions. He said that: 'unions should be truly democratic and free of control of outsiders'[58]. But, even after 1977, the state failed to make any constructive move in establishing an institutional framework for injecting the above values into the structure of trade unions. In reality, the unions, which were controlled by outside forces, have become stronger.

There were a few changes in the union structure after 1977. We noticed earlier that the working class had supported the UNP at the general election in 1977. This support, however, did not last for long; it gradually changed over time. The composition of the working class as well as their activities changed in the new market economic environment. In this new system, the majority of workers held temporary or contract employment in the newly emerging service and other sectors of the economy (Fernando, 1984)[59]. The previous state-dependent labour force, which was strong during interventionist regime, gradually transformed onto a private-dependent one under market-oriented economic policies. The employers also changed. The private firms —domestic listed and non-listed and foreign— employed those newcomers to the labour force on signals produced by the labour market. The private firm sector, under the influence of FDI, employed modern management practices for human resource development (HRD) in these organisations. Indeed, there was an absence of trade unions in the new industrial sector until the eruption of 'trade union organisaticn and agitation at Polytex Garments within the GCEC area'[60] in 1983 (Fernando, 1984:7).

The old trade unions resumed creating disturbances in the traditional industrial sector as well as in the state sector after 1979 (Fernando, 1984)[61]. This conflict grew and eventually ended up in a clash in July 1980. The general strike in 1980 was supported by thousands of public sector employees and private employees. 'This strike, which led to the dismissal of about 40,000 workers, has to be characterised as an ultimate failure. The failure of the July 1980 General Strike marked a long term recession of trade union activity and class struggles in the century' (Fernando, 1984:13). However, the strategy of UNP — the suppression of workers for weakening trade unionisation— continued until 1994[62]. Dissanayake (2000:669) describes it as '...one of the numerous curses introduced into Sri Lanka by President Jayewardene and President Premadasa was the brutal suppression of the right of Labour'.

Two other most crucial non-economic factors that disturbed the industrial growth process of the economy after 1983 were the multidimensional process of political decay, in Moore's words, and the 'ethnic violence' of the country. Moore provides a detailed account of events that took place in the system leading to a 'political decay' after 1983[63]. In brief, the political process changed with the extension of the period of the Parliament through a referendum. The ethnic tension, which was growing since the late 1970s, also culminated in 1983 with riots[64]. It has led the state to involve itself in a long war with

Tamil extremists in the North of the country after 1983. As ethnic tension continued, the state changed its priorities from economics to ethnic politics. Along with these, the activities of *Janatha Vimukthi Peramuna* ((JVP) in the South, a political party which was prohibited since 1983 by the government, disrupted the normal life of the people and the state. The state crushed this movement deploying armed forces in 1989. The other major disturbing events that took place at that time were the Presidential election in 1989 and the assassination of the President of the country by extremists in 1993.

The outcome of all this was the creation of an uncertain environment and, therefore, a 'poor investment climate' after 1983 (Moore, 1992: 69-80; Athukorala, 1995:547). 'All these created conditions of instability which held back private sector investment and hampered economic activity in all sectors' (Gunatilake, 1999:204). Two things apparently have contributed to the dismal investment climate of the country after 1983. One was the state's loss of interest in economic development which resulted in the transfer of resources to meet political objectives (Moore, 1990; Athukorala, 1998). The other is the increase in unplanned government expenditure on the war. Both have contributed to macroeconomic imbalances. The implementation of tough economic measures required for macroeconomic stability was difficult in the 1980s at a time when the country's political stability remained in doubt (Cass Alain, 1984).

The priorities of the state shifted to fulfil non-economic obligations after the violence in 1983. The government spent a huge sum of money on the rehabilitation of properties damaged by riots that took place after 1983. The 'direct damage to the economy at the time of the Peace Accord has been estimated at Rs. 55.6 billion'. Indirect and long-term damage is incalculable. Infrastructure alone, estimated to be valued at Rs. 20 billion, was destroyed (Budget speech, 1988:8). The Finance Minister in his budget speech revealed that 'the indirect effect of the general deterioration in business confidence has led to the abandonment of considerable new investment, both local and foreign' (Budget speech, 1988:8). The JVP also attempted to paralyse the administration and cripple the business sector attacking on a strategic, but non-military front (De Silva, 1989:4). Civil unrest and disturbances had disastrous effects on the economy. 'The extent of the losses resulting from the disruption of capital assets consequent to subversive activities so far have been estimated at around Rs. 2475 million. Losses in production of goods & services have been estimated to be around Rs. 6575 million' (Budget Speech, 1990:4). All these hampered the process of industrial development of the country further exacerbating political and economic instability and exhausting capital funds which otherwise could have been invested in the manufacturing industry.

6.7. New Conflicts

The new government in 1989 resumed reforms that were interrupted in 1988 for re-establishing political and economic stability in the country[65]. There was a close cooperation between the state and the private sector for the promotion of industrial accumulation in this new political environment. Neville Jayaweera, a prominent Civil Servant, provides a detailed account of the strategy adopted by the political leadership for developing a favourable 'investment climate' in the country[66]. In effect, industrial activities revived fast under the new 'investment environment' strengthening competitive forces in the system. The state was able to pay greater attention to economic development, especially, to the development of industry that was facing the challenges of 'globalisation'.

Under the new industrial policy of 1989, the state adopted certain measures to raise productivity of resources and economic competitiveness of industrial production[67]. Measures like liberalisation of the current account, acceleration of the privatisation process and provision of various micro stimuli to domestic and foreign capital helped in the development of a new investment climate. These measures aimed at stabilising the economy, rationalising the public sector, and introducing more effective welfare packages targeting the poor (Alailama et. al., 1997,245). Consequently, there was a considerable flow of foreign and domestic private funds towards industry (see figure 6.1, also Athukorala et. al., 2000).

New contradictions emerged once the 'Peoples' Alliance' (PA) government came into power in 1994. The PA administration was not very different from that of the previous UNP admistration, except in areas of 'governance and the style of management' (Gunatilake, 1999:204). This regime, however, was different from its predecessor 'socialist coalitions' though it had included many of the PA partners.[68] . Decision-making processes were also different[69]. The pressure groups behind the new regime were not those of 'lower middle class and working class', as was the case in the 1960s and the early 1970s. A 'new middle class'[70] dominated by the educated, both employed and unemployed, was behind the new regime. This new left-of- Centre regime departed from the rigorous interventionist policies of the old left regimes. It offered new policies in its manifesto for the General Election in 1994[71]. Under the influence of its new pressure groups, it insisted on the continuation of market-oriented economic policies, but with a 'human face'. Further, it pledged to adhere to the policy of transparency of the state —the modern social democratic approach (Pereira, 1993: 1338). Moreover, it strengthened some democratic institutions necessary for smooth functioning of the social democratic system of the country[72].

Achievement of macroeconomic stability of the country was one of the main objectives of this regime. It included reducing of budget deficits, bringing down interest rates and reducing cost of capital. It further intensified the privatisation process, and some micro stimuli were given to industrialists (Gunatilake, 1999:205). Deviating from the previous phase of socialist government, 1970-77, the regime provided all assistance to the development of the private sector. It continued to treat the private sector as the 'engine of industrial growth'. The Marxist parties and left-wingers in the SLFP brought pressure on the state against foreign investment but the government 'was very much in favour of foreign investors and was heavily dependent on such investment'[73]. The state was strong and bold enough to establish a separate institution, the PERC, to execute the privatisation programme recommended by the IMF-World Bank missions. Some large public enterprises have been privatised notwithstanding strong protests from the working class[74].

In spite of all this, industrial accumulation in Sri Lanka has got into low gear after 1994 (see Fig. 4.1). Hostile forces, which interfere in the process of capitalist industrial accumulation, were still powerful in the system, producing direct and indirect impacts on the investment environment. The labour disputes and ethnic violence have seriously retarded growth prospects of the industrial sector. There were also deficiencies in institutional developments hampering the capitalist development process (Lakshman, 1997). The quantification of the unfavourable impact produced by these different forces on investment climate, however, is difficult. Some of these have continued from the past, and others were newly added to the system.

The labour unrest in workplaces, which was relatively insignificant prior to 1994, began to spread fast in the system soon after the new regime came into power in 1995. '...[T]he workers who were suppressed for seventeen years went on the rampage' (Dissanayake,2000:669). These have affected foreign direct investment in FTZs adversely. '...[T]here was a spate of labour unrest specially in Korean factories in the Biyagama Zone and surrounding areas, which dampened the investment momentum which had built up'[75]. Dissanayake (2000:669-73) provides a long list of disturbances, harassment and disappointments of local and foreign management in FTZ firms after the new government came into power in 1994[76]. 'There were about thirty one strikes in foreign owned companies in Sri Lanka during the four months, September to December 1994', substantially reducing the number of working days in manufacturing firms (Dissanayake, 2000:670). Figure 5A3.1 provides a comparison of number of workdays lost between pre- and post- 1994 periods. Workdays lost after 1994 were alarmingly high. The worker unrest in the industrial sector hampered the growth processes in the manufacturing and other sectors of the economy[77]. The Central Bank Annual report (1995) describes this development as follows:

> Although the dynamism of Sri Lanka's leading growth sector, manufacturing, was laudable, during the year this sector was affected by labour unrest which was later resolved by government intervention. While an attempt was made to codify the working conditions and rights of labour in the form of a Workers' Charter, employers and investors expressed misgivings about the move, entirely influenced by the spate of strikes[78].

The new regime, nevertheless, proposed an institutional mechanism for establishing a democratic process of industrial relations between employers and employees in the system. A "Workers' Charter" to promote industrial relations in workplaces was proposed by the government to minimise worker unrest. This was meant to facilitate the process of negotiations, i.e., 'collective agreements' and 'collective bargaining', between the employers and employees in workplaces. However, the class of organised employers expressed reluctance to come to a compromise with the government on the 'charter'[79]. They bargained for "an investors' charter after workers' charter"[80]. The Central Bank (1995:15) reported that 'employers and investors expressed misgivings about the move'. This mistrust between the employers and employees and the inflexible attitudes of both parties created conflicts and industrial insecurity in work places. This trend continued throughout the period which was injurious to the industrial development of the country.

We saw earlier that the ethnic violence was the major factor that hindered the industrial development of the country after 1983. Therefore, the vision of the new government was to establish peace and harmony for economic and political stability of the country. But, the recommenced armed-conflict in 1995 disturbed this peace process of the government. "Peace was shattered in April (1995) by the unilateral action of the LTTE (to recommence hostilities) and the country was brought to the lamentable situation where invaluable lives and property of many Sri Lankans are placed at risk" (Budget Speech, 1996:6). There were many violent attacks on civilian and economically vulnerable targets in the principal city of Colombo. The Finance Minister expressed the gravity of this problem in the Budget Speech in 1998 as follows.

> " In late 1995, the oil storage tanks were set on fire and a few months later the Central Bank was destroyed. Only three weeks ago, the country's emerging Commercial Centre was attacked. These are a few instances of how the LTTE attempted to disrupt our economy in their desperation" (Budget Speech, 1998:1).

The escalation of the armed-conflict in the North was the end-result of the above. This shifted the attention of the state more and more towards military rather than economic objectives. The government's defence expenses[81] grew fast over this period upsetting all macroeconomic targets of the country[82].

Many have attempted to measure the costs of this war taking into account both direct and indirect costs of the war (Richardson et. al, 1991; Groba et. al., 1993; Marga, 1998: Goonetileke, 1998; Kelegama, 1999; Sarvananthan, 2001, National Peace Council, 2001, Arunatilake, 2001). Direct cost includes military costs borne by the state and the LTTE, and the costs of damage to physical and social infrastructure. Indirect costs include the lost income due to foregone investment, reduced tourist arrivals, forgone foreign investment, lost human capital which resulted from deaths, injuries etc. and output forgone due to displacement of people. According to the calculations of Arunatilake et al. (2001:1495) "...the accumulated total cost of the war up to 1996 [including direct and indirect] was at least Rs.

1,135 billion at 1996 prices (168.5 % of the 1996 GDP (which was) equivalent to US$ 20.6 billion)".

The attacks targeting tourist industry have severely weakened the inflow of foreign exchange to the country. Sri Lanka has apparently lost foreign exchange worth US $ 200 Million annually as a result of the drop in tourism. Additionally, the tourist industry was unable to create annual employment opportunities to about 90,000 people of the country (Budget Speech, 1997). The dislocation of businesses, drop in production, rise in expenses at firm level security and increase in risk premium in insurance on businesses have contributed to the rise in cost of production at firm levels weakening comparative advantage so far enjoyed by firms internationally (Budget Speech, 1997).

The other major hostile factor was the slow change in institutional prerequisites fundamental to the process of capitalist development. Critics (Moore, 1990; Lakshman, 1997) 1990; Lakshman, 1997) have highlighted the presence of some significant forces, which surface from time to time, through social, political and cultural ethos of the system disturbing the process of economic development. These forces are detrimental to the capitalist development process, especially, to the promotion of market forces in the system. They operate in the system to weaken the process of decision-making via creating 'soft states', weakening conditions pertaining to law and order, property rights and investment friendly tax policies.

Generally, the government after 1994 was characterised as a 'soft state' finding it difficult to bring in necessary changes to political and economic conditions affecting investment. The Parliamentary electoral system in operation makes the state depend upon the support of a few minority political parties. Critics are of the view that 'an unstable government is not likely to take important decisions needed for an improvement of business conditions. A government lacking a clear majority in Parliament is likely to favour popular short-term policies rather than to adopt realistic sound policies'[83].

All these appeared to have been responsible for the loss of confidence of foreign investors in investing funds in Sri Lanka. For such capital, countries like China and Vietnam offer a variety of incentives. Local investors also have lost confidence in the 'investment climate' of the country. The businessmen postponed big investment decisions for some time immediately after the new regime came into power in 1994 (Lanka Guardian, 1994:7). Even after a few years of functioning of the present 'coalition', the private sector maintained the same stringent policy of 'wait-and-see'[84]. The share market was in disarray and foreign participation gradually slowed down. The net purchases of shares by foreigners were Rs. –89.7 million in 1995, Rs. –1560.0 million in 1998 and Rs. – 950.8 million in 1999 (Colombo Share Exchange Fact Book, 2000:18). Domestic investment was low in the share market. The net purchases of shares by domestic companies were Rs. 668.7 million in 1995, Rs. 1834.0 million in 1998 and Rs. 1228.7 million in 1999 (Colombo Share Exchange Fact Book, 2000:18). Foreign Investors 'continued to be net sellers' of shares especially after 1997[85]. The share price indexes of different sectors of the economy fell drastically (Fact Book, 2000: 15-28). This sluggishness in the share market is a clear reflection of entrepreneurs' loss of confidence in the system.

6.8. Summary

The path of industrial accumulation in Sri Lanka experienced many vicissitudes over the last fifty years. It passed through three main phases enriched by different political ideologies, both capitalist and socialist. It finally reached the territory of liberal economics in 1977.

Many prerequisites, ranging from private property rights to free trade zones, were provided to promote market forces[86]. The 'tripod structure' —the 'alliance' of local, foreign and state capital— was the outstanding feature of the market economy. The 'alliance' responded favourably to market signals fostered by neoliberal policies. There was accumulation of capital in manufacturing, finance, construction, services and trade sectors. Domestic and foreign capital took the lead in investing in manufacturing. State capital entered the process of infrastructural development to boost private investment activities. The investment climate as shaped by the neoliberal policy framework enhanced the confidence of the private entrepreneur.

There were changes again in the post-1983 period. First, the 'investment climate' reversed and began to be unfavourable for private investment. The institutional forces hostile to markets began to dominate policy decisions. Ethnic violence and the subversive activities of the JVP created an unstable 'investment climate'. Second, there was disarray in the 'alliance'. Domestic capital partially withdrew from capital formation and the state concentrated more on defence and less on the provision of infrastructural facilities. The resources tended to move out of manufacturing towards finance and service sectors.

The unusual performance of the market economic structure after 1983 may be due to the weak adaptive capacity of the political economic structure to accommodate changes. These drawbacks were the products of overwhelming interference of institutional forces hostile to markets in the system. After 1994, in particular, labour unrest impaired the process of neoliberal industrial development. This suggests that the forces hostile to markets, which had interfered in the Sri Lankan economic structure in the early post-independent period, as identified by Myrdal, have not fully disappeared from the economic scene. They continue to interfere with the market economy even after 50 years of Independence!

The state of a 'new nation' like Sri Lanka can contribute a great deal to the development of an environment conducive to the promotion of competitive market forces in a system of capitalist industrial development. The state may be required to perform as a 'hard state' to defeat forces antagonistic to market forces and to overcome disturbances coming from institutional forces hostile to markets in the system. The state can establish new institutions like bargaining mechanism to ensure harmonious labour-capital relations in the workplace to resolve industrial disputes.

This chapter has provided an explanation of industrial investment in a 'disturbed investment climate' where institutional forces hostile to markets interrupt the economic system. This analysis reveals that a favourable 'investment climate' is a necessary condition for a self-generating growth process under a market economic environment. It is the responsibility of the state of a 'new nation' to create such an environment in the system. Such environment may encourage the active participation of the 'tripod structure': the force that will instantaneously promote the capitalist industrial development in a 'new nation'.

Notes

1. Perkins (1991) provides a detailed analysis on this objective and practical significance in the concept of privatisation (quoted in Meier, 1995:542).
2. A part of investment fund in developed countries has moved

out of these countries because of 'the drive for increased efficiency [which] has involved breaking up the production process into discrete segments, each located in the best place in terms of cost and productivity considerations' (World Bank (1997:92).

3. The new Finance Minister Mr. Felix R. Dias Bandaranaike in the Budget Speech announced these measures in 1976 (Hansards, 1977:2233-2235).
4. Amongst, the non-implementation of (1) wealth tax schedules (2) the withdrawal of tax-holidays granted to dividends of exempted companies and (3) gift tax and estate duty rate schedules proposed in the Budget speech of Dr. N.M. Perera for 1975.
5. Some of the concessions were as follows: Security of Investment, Tax holidays, Incentives for Industrial Undertakings, Capital Allowances, Lump Sum Depreciation, Incentives for Export of Manufactured Products, Tax Incentives for the Promotion of Tourism, Tax of capital expenditures, Carry forward of losses, Investment relief for companies, Investment relief for individuals, Customs Duty concessions, Exemption of foreign contractors, Exemption of foreign personnel, Relief under Double Tax Agreements, Application Procedure, (Hansards, 1977: 2237).
6. Among the members of the committee, the presence of Dr. N.M. Perera, Mr. Peter Keuneman and Dr. Colvin R.de Silva, the members of the Cabinet, was significant because they represent Marxist parties (Hansards, 1977:2240).
7. The 'majority of the workers enthusiastically supported this regime in the hope that it would create a "socialist society" (Fernando, 1984:15).
8. Mr. J.R. Jayawardene brought these changes after he became the Party leader in 1973 bringing in Young men, some are unemployed and of relatively low social status (Moore, 1990:21).
9. New intelligentsia comprised educated ministers like Lalith Athlathmudali, Ronie de Mel, Gamani Dissanayake who led the cabinet. 'Athulathmudali was made minister of trade and commerce, a key ministry in the implementation of J.R.Jayewardene's new economic policy'. Ronnie de Mel, the new comer to Cabinet office is an excellent technocrat' (De Silva, 1994: 300,451).
10. In his book K.M.de Silva provides details about this study. The complete report appears to be available in J.R.Jayewardene MSS. De Silva, in his analysis, argues that the suggestions

that Shenoy put forward were unrealistic that he has not given enough thought to the political and economic environment in 1966. He seems over-valued the private sector in recommending the private sector as the engine of growth (De Silva et al., 1994:169 –170).

11. De Silva points out that Shenoy's report is influenced by 'the views of Ludwig Von Hayek, Milton Freedman' (De Silva et al., 1994:168).
12. The approach of the authorities thus to reiterate the concept of 'just and fare society' "society where the man who works feels he is entitled to the fruits of his labour". And by naming the country, as a 'Socialist Democratic Republic of Sri Lanka' govt. may have expected to make this transition frictionless and sober. The transition was assisted by popularising the 'People's sector', object of which was to ensure the production, ownership and distribution belong to the people (National Assembly Debates, 1977:107).
13. The macro stimuli included: '(i) unification of the exchange rate and adoption of a floating exchange rate system with an effective devaluation carried out in 1977; (ii) restructuring of import tariffs to reduce import controls and import duty rates; (iii) decontrol of prices of previously price-controlled products and provision of greater freedom even to government enterprises to charge economic prices; (iv) ending of licensing requirements and state monopolies from most types of imports; (v) replacement of food subsidies with a food stamp scheme for the benefit of lower income groups, while allowing the prices of most previously subsidised goods and services to rise according to market forces; (vii) the establishment of remunerative prices for several agricultural products like paddy and (vii) interest rate reforms involving a substantial upward revision in deposits and loan rates' (Peiris, 1997:34)
14. Later, these institutions were subject to different pressure came from interest groups. (See Wignaraja, 1998: 105 for details).
15. (Ministry of Finance and Planning, 1987).
16. These transfers were made not only for public manufacturing corporations but also for other government institutions. The table 4.5.3 in page 216, in *Economic Progress of Independent Sri Lanka,* provides detailed information on the size of these transfers from 1985 to 1996. For example, the magnitude of these transfers was about 42.2 per cent of govt. revenue in 1985 and it was only 17.9 in 1996.
17. 'In rationalising taxes, the maximum personal income tax rate

was reduced from 50 per cent to 35 per cent while the corporate income tax rate was unified at 35 per cent with a lower tax rate of 15 per cent on export income. The Wealth tax was removed in 1990 and the 100 per cent tax on share transfers between residents and non-residents was abolished' (Jayasundera, 1998:2).

18. In addition to the change in the entire constitution from West Minister system to a presidential system, some private sector friendly clauses were included in the new one. One such was Investment Protection agreement to gain and retain the confidence of investors. This refers to the clause 157 of the new constitution. See for details (De Silva et al., 1994:454).
19. The strategy, objectives, the policy instruments and the institutional framework employed by this new regime were explicitly stated in the 'Pattern of Industrialisation', by Upananda Vidanapathirana summarising the work done by Balakrishnan .N (1977), Dahanayake P.A.S (1979), Lakshman W.D (1979), Premachandra. A (1984, 1985). Also (Ministry of Finance and Planning, 1986:165 – 193).
20. Established in 1991 under the Security Exchange Commission Act No.26 of 1991.
21. New financial instruments and institutions were introduced. Private sector commercial Banks were permitted to introduce various new items like Implicit money (i.e. Plastic credit cards), certificate of deposits, Automated Teller Machines, Secondary Debentures markets etc. Secondary markets for treasury bills and shares, Merchant banks, investment banks, unit trusts etc.
22 The methods of privatisation and performances of the privatisation programmes are given in Box 4.5.2 and 4.5.3 respectively, (Ministry of Finance and Planning, 1987: 216-218).
23. The private companies are the non-listed large companies where the number of equity shareholders can be up to 50. The family based companies are normally dominated by family members or relatives. These can accommodate as mush as 50 members, but, in practice, these contain only a few members. The former employ profession managerial staff for the management functions of the firm. The latter may employ the family or relatives to the managerial positions. It was noticed that the board of directors has been the same for many consecutive years in the latter but the boards of directors are not the same in the former.

24. Many provide information on the role of the 'tripod structure' in different countries. In Brazil for example, 'consensus between local and foreign capital around the issues of accumulation is a fundamental part of the explanation of the successes of Brazilian industrialization'. Evans uses the word "the triple alliance"(Evans, 1979:11-12). In Thailand '(1) state and public enterprises including military-related firms, (2) multinational enterprises (MNEs), and (3) Thai (ethnic Chinese) private groups. These three groups have constantly been the major agents of Thai capitalism and have supported corporation activities like the three legs of a tripod' (Akira, 1989:275).
25. Economic Progress, 1998:128-169. Also in "Infrastructural Development" by K.D. Ranasinghe (1998).
26. For details of actions taken by the government under this new strategy, see Athukorala (1995:547)
27. But, Roemer et al (1991) suggests that under the neoliberal set up, the government should promote private institutions to improve market performance and should invest in infrastructure that supports private activity.
28. This includes exchange policies, currency devaluation, import liberalisation, elimination of foreign exchange controls, tariff reforms etc.
29. Some States are sometimes called 'hard States' or assertive States, which exercise authoritative powers and play dynamic roles in the process of economic development. Thus, terms "soft State" and "hard State" come, on and off, in the development literature which highlight the conceptual relevance of them even in present economic analyses, especially, on South Asian countries (Myrdal, 1970:211-51; Suriyakumaran, 1984: 32; Hasan at el., 1989: 45; Wade, 1990: 253-54; Streeten, 1993:1290).
30. Cowen et al. (1996:427) provides Japan and S. Korea as examples for Development State. For Chalmers Johnson the Development state 'gives its first priority to economic development' (quoted, Cowen et.al, 1996:427).
31. Wade (1990:52-72) talks about the measures taken by Taiwan and their toughness and the role of the state to make the measures to be successful. Pei (1998:40) states that Chalmers Johnson, Alice Amsden, and Robert Wade argue on '...the effectiveness of state intervention in the economy through industrial policy, credit control, and investment targeting' have highly contributed to the dramatic economic transformation of East Asia.

32. Foreign investors are attracted to Sri Lanka 'as a low-cost base in terms of both the availability of cheap, and trainable labour and its investment climate'. 'Sri Lanka's overseas investment promotion campaign has courted assembly producers in high-tech industries' (Athukorala, 2000:106).
33. For Athukorala (2000:122), direct skill and technology transfers are not very significant. 'Many of the industries apply only universally available technology. Even in electronics —generally considered a high-tech industry—the assembly activities transferred to Sri Lanka are simple labour-intensive processes'.
34. Both Athukorala and Wignaraja (1998) discuss the types of technology and managerial skills employed by the FDI firms. According to Athukorala, '[D]irect skill and technology transfer does not seem to be significant. Many of the industries do not possess any technology that is not universally available. In the electronic industry, which is generally considered a high-tech industry, most of the production assembly activities transferred to Sri Lanka appear to be simple labour intensive processes' (Athukorala, 1997: 421).
35. Athukorala et al. (2000:128) find the same trend but at dissimilar proportions. To them 'the share of clothing in total manufacturing exports declined from 72 per cent in the early q980s to 60 percent in the mid-1990s'.
36. This trend got weakened after the mid-1990s.
37. See Figure 6A.3, Appendix 5.
38. Athukorala at el., (2000: 133) provide a detailed explanation on this shift. They see the 'changes in the export pattern confirm closely to the pattern predicted by the conventional (Heckscher –Ohlin) trade model. They argue that resource intensive exports have dropped from 69.3 in 1978-89 to 32.2 in 1990-5. Labour intensive exports have risen from 26.2 to 58.6 during same periods. Capital intensive exports have risen from 4.5 to 9.1 per cents. 'The changing structured of production and exports implied changes in comparative advantage...
39. Domestic industrialist experienced only limited transfer of technology. But,'[m]arket information gained through joint-venture operations and contact with international buyers has invariably contributed to the export success of local firms'. 'The introduction of efficient management, inventory systems, worker training, or incentives may result in applications in other industries' (Athukorala et. al., 2000:123).
40. See p. vvi in Wignaraja (1998).
41. Data in Annual Reports of Central Bank of Sri Lanka are used

to develop this diagram. The following procedures were adopted:

1. Real Export earnings of Foreign Firms = (Export Earnings of BOI enterprises/ GNPD).
2. Real Export Earnings of Local Firms = (Value of Industrial Exports/ GNPD) - Real Export earnings of Foreign Firms.
3. Sales (Real) Revenue of Local Firms at the Local Market = (Value of Industrial Production/ GNDP) - (Real Export earnings of Foreign Firms + Real Export Earnings of Local Firms).

   Where, GNPD - GNP Implicit Deflator.

42. The government set minimum wage as Rs. 2000 per worker during President Premadasa's period. He instructed the 200 garment factories to be set up in remote areas to generate employment to rural people. The latter produced high transport costs. Nominal wage rate were growing fast in the structure and also the worker unrest was growing in work places (see Figure 6A.3, Appendix 5).
43. Commercial Bank lending rates secured by stock in trade and immovable property were in the range of 13 - 18 per cents after 1977 (Central Bank of Sri Lanka, 1998:294).
44. The macroeconomic adjustment is to change in the structure of aggregate demand and supply to restore growth while generating a sustainable medium term current account position which is consistent with external capital flow. The structural changes would entail raising real savings and real investments and the efficiency of investment. (Rajapatirana, 1986:60).
45. The capacity utilisation of firms was in the range of 30%-40% prior to 1977 (National State Assembly Debates, 1977:61-62).
46. The demand generated by heavy government spending in irrigation, urban development and housing were largely absorbed by the import sector as local industrial firm s failed to respond promptly.
47. See chapter 5 for the origin of this class and refer to the National State Assembly Debates (1977:2232). Also, Wignaraja (1999:114) for rent-seeking practices of public firms before 1977.
48. 'This [neoclassical view] implies a very conscious and urgent attempt by the state to bring about a rapid expansion of the private over the public economy, of market over non-market resource allocation, and of competitive over hierarchically-determined economic decisions'. But, the economic liberalisation in Sri Lanka was an involuntary economic liberalisation especially with 'a large volume of resources were allocated to the public sector through political mechanisms'

leads to economic distortions favouring the Sri Lankan public sector' (Moore, 1990:20-2).

49. Kelegama questions whether the transnational corporations like Unilevers, Coca Cola and Walls would allow local substitutes like soap, and beverages produced by local firms like Pure Beverages and Elephant House to grow in the local market.
50. The DSI Shoe Company is the second largest shoe producer who holds a large share in the local shoe market. The interview with the management revealed that they find hard to compete with shoes coming from Hong Kong and China of which the quality is improved using new technology and the styles are new and the prices are moderate.
51. The non-listed company sector was unable to fulfil certain requisites to reach the listed company status, especially the maintenance of reasonable profit margins and the maintenance of a stable dividend policy for a specified period, because of poor business conditions.
52. The good examples are the recent books edited by W.D. Lakshman (1997,1999) in which authors like Gunatilake, Athukorala, Attapatu, Kelegama etc. argue in those lines.
53. As mentioned in Chapter 5, these include policies to maintain macroeconomic stability, openness, better allocation of resources, availability of physical and human capital, accessibility of new technology via MNCs (Rowen, 1998: 5-7).
54. Many examples in this nature can be found in the literature where successful governments, some called, developmental States' in other countries have performed to push the private sector into the forefront in the industrial development. Taiwan and South Korea are best examples of East Asia. (Cowen et al, 1996: 427-32; Bell,1995; Jenkins, 1995).
55. Many discuss the role of a neoclassical State. "The role of the public sector is seen as the creation of a favorable enabling environment for economic activity." (Meier, 1995:525) (quoted in Stanley Fischer and Vinod Thomas, "Policies for Economic Development" *American Journal of Agricultural Economics* (August 1990): 809-13.
56. The political importance of such projects and the necessity of giving priority to complete Mahaweli in seven years (compared to the opposition's period of completion of thirty years) have been spelt out by many Ministers in the Cabinet (National Assembly Debates, 1977:1547, 2005, 2161).

57. At the Aid Group Meeting Donor nations strongly insisted Sri Lanka to launch reforms like interest rate policy encouraging private sector investment, rationally assured profit margins for export industries, exchange rate policy etc. They warned that 'the budget for next year will be watched closely by us for signs of a strong and determined government willing to make the effort to bring the economy into line with long term growth requirements' (Lanka Guardian, 1984:10).
58. President Jayawardena wanted to change the structure of trade unions allowing the union members to determine the management of the union outside influence as opposed to the influence of political parties (National Assembly debates, 1977:107).
59. Women labour was prominent in the Garment sector, banking and educational institutions who were resisting to union activities (Fernando, 1984).
60. Greater Colombo Economic Commission GCEC is responsible for foreign direct investment in that area.
61. 'The growing frustration of the workers was mostly reflected when the JTUAC sponsored a trade union delegates convention in early March' (Fernando, 1984:12).
62. For example, in 1991, about 54 workers in three firms, —Vinail, Vinail Products, best food—were thrown out of work because of the strike launched demanding better facilities. The Courts decided that this action of firms was illegal and ordered to re-employ them paying compensations (Divayina, 297th paper, Dec. 13, 2000, p.9).
63. He explains in details the nature of the new political system that: '[t]he government began to repress democratic opposition parties in a harsh and extra-legal fashion. The life of the existing Parliament was extended for a further full six-year term in 1982 through a referendum marred by force and fraud. In Sinhalese- Tamil ethnic conflict, which had long been simmering, burst into open warfare after major civilian violence against Tamil in July 1983.Resort to violence for political and criminal purposes became widespread. Bu late 1987 the state system itself had begun to disintegrate in an alarming fashion: control of the Tamil north and east of the country was divided between an Indian military 'peacekeeping' force and remnants of the main Tamil separatist guerrilla army; in the south the radical Sinhalese JVP youth movement was in open armed conflict with state agencies and the cadres of the ruling party ... The government was deeply unpopular and sustained in

power in part by the force of a much-expanded military –cum-political intelligence apparatus ...(Moore, 1990:21).

64. Some commercial and business properties of minority community were destroyed by riots.
65. See Gunatilake (1999:204) for details about the measures taken by the government in this regard.
66. He writes that President Premadasa 'is acceptable to big business to the wholesaler and small retailer to a contractor, to petit and national bourgeoisie, and above all, to the foreign investor'.
67. The measures taken by the state are given, in detail, in Lanka Guardian under *1989-92 The IMF Scenario* (Lanka Guardian, 1990,12(19): 13). Also *Sri Lanka: Policy Matrix 1989-92, IMF Report.* describes all industrial and trade reforms.
68. See Dissanayaka on the people, their characteristics, values etc. of the members of the new Cabinet (Dissanayaka, 1994:170).
69. It was a widely discussed matter that major decisions were made in an inner-Cabinet comprising a few powerful Ministers. The left-wing partners did not have a big say in the decision making process. This is reflected in the way the Cabinet re-shuffle was made in 1997 when the left-oriented Ministers were removed from important ministries. For example, the former Minister of Labour, Mr. Mahinda Rajapakse, whose Workers Charter was extremely controversial, was transferred to a less sensitive ministry. The Media Ministry was taken away from a left-wing sympathiser, Mr. Dharmasiri Senanayake and given to a person close to leadership.
70. The concept of the 'new middle class' is spelt out by Arthur J.Vidich editing the book 'The New Middle Class: Life-style, status claims and political orientation' (Basingstoke; Macmillan, 1995).
71. A team of top professionals -the new elite group– prepared this manifesto. See pp. 187-190, The Politics of Sri Lanka, Vol. II, T.D.S.A. Dissanayaka, 1994.
72. Institutions related to press, judicial autonomy, market autonomy and human rights etc. were strengthened.
73. The Prime Minister Chandrika Bandaranaike Kumaratunga addressing the nation on Television has explained in July 1994. (Dissanayaka, 1994: 187).
74. Telecommunication, salt, Gas, Steel etc. The protest launched by the working class against the privatisation of Telecomm-unication and the Steel Corporation was very strong.

75. Extracted from an interview given by former ambassador of Sri Lanka to the Republic of South Korea, Lalith Pedris to Dinesh Weerakkody. This was published under ' Korean Investments drop after 1994' in The Sunday Leader, June 09, 1996.
76. He cited a few such incidences that '... a senior executive of Prima Mills of Singapore was "captured" by his workforce and held prisoner on top of the roof of their three storey building in Colombo. The threat directed at Prima was that either the Company meets the demand of the workers or else their executive would be thrown down from the rooftop! That scene was televised and was shown abroad on BBC and CNN news Programmes. It enraged people in Singapore and shocked prospective investors throughout the world. In like manner BBC and CNN news programmes showed the Free Trade Zone in Katunayake where strikes were banned by law, but where the on going strike at the biggest single factory there, Ansell from Australia was going from bad to worse. That Australian Company manufactures rubber goods ranging from contraceptives to surgical gloves for their worldwide market' (Dissanayake, 2000:669-70).
77. A prominent Businessman, H.N.Gunawardene, the Chairman of Aitken Spence Group, commenting on the 'harsh business environment' created by political and economic factors argued that 'away from the battle front industrial unrest continued to affect industry. A strike by the garment workers affected the Company's performance contributing to a decline of profits by as much as 65 % over the previous year'. 'Business', *The Sunday Times*, August 25, 1996.
78. Problems and Issues (Annual Report, 1995:14).
79. The private sector itself faces the dilemma of how to co-oporate with the government while the latter treats both groups i.e. employers and workers more or less in equal terms. Some Industrialists tend to oppose this kind of industrial policy of the government while other are optimistic about it.
80. Charitha Ratwatte, Managing director, Sri Lanka Business Development Centre had discussed this idea in detail, *The Sunday Times Business*, November 19, 1995, p.4.
81. The defence expenditure of the government rose to about 5 per cent of GDP over this period (see curve 3 in fig.6.2).
82. The following table shows the worsening trends in macroeconomic targets over time.

Year	1993	1994	1995	1996	1997	1998	1999	2000
Budget Deficit/GDP	-8.7%	-10.5%	-10.1%	-9.4%	-7.9%	-9.2%	-7.5%	-9.9%
Govt. Debt /GDP	96.9%	95.1%	95.2%	93.3%	85.8%	90.8%	95.1%	97.1%
Current A/C Balance/GDP	-4.8%	-7.3%	-6.0%	-4.9%	-2.6%	-1.4%	-3.65%	-6.4%

Source: Annual report, Central Bank of Sri Lanka, 2000.

83. The Business pages of The Sunday times (Oct. 15, 2000).
84. The chairman of the Vanik Incorporation Limited, the former Secretary to the Treasury and Planning, Dr. W.M.Tilakaratna 'called upon the private sector to snap out of its wait-and-see policy attitude and act with long term objectives in mind'. See *Island*, August 04, 1996.
85. Colombo Stock Exchange provides the following information:

Foreign Participation Rs. Million

Year	*Purchase*	*Sales*
1998	5645	7205
1999	5050	6000
2000	1379	4623

86. Number of institutions established to deal with the industrial sector has gone up to 28 according to the 'Economic Progress of independent of Sri Lanka' see page 112, Box 3.2.2.

7

Concluding Remarks

The task of 'new nations' primarily has been to transform their static primary production bases in to dynamic industrial production processes in a short period of time. 'Development Economics' offered the 'new nations' a 'fast and compressed' path of industrial development associated with capitalist industrial accumulation. The state was assigned an important role in this process of transformation. It was expected to take measures to mobilise resources towards industry and, if necessary, participate directly in industrial activity. It must provide a 'favourable investment climate' required for private investment. The state needs to implement policies to promote market forces and weaken forces-hostile-to-market in the system. In the process of transformation, as some argue, 'development economics' would eventually cease to exist once full-pledged market forces take over control of the economy under a neoclassical or neoliberal economic foundation of capitalist economics.

Most 'new nations' formulated ambitious economic development programmes in line with 'development economics' to achieve 'fast and compressed' industrial development. Some 'new nations', in the East Asian bloc, were able to achieve their economic objectives within about three to four decades. Sri Lanka in South Asia has performed quite differently from the manner in which the above nations progressed. Sri Lanka's fifty years of industrial growth is slower and longer than that of most other countries in the South East Asian bloc. Besides, the path also has been cyclical with different degrees of vicissitudes. This study endeavoured to understand the nature and the causes for the above pattern of industrial development in Sri Lanka.

Historically, the 'investment climate' has been the main determinant of product cycles and patterns of investment in the country. Sri Lanka has experienced two such product cycles under two different 'investment climates'. One was the plantation product cycle, which extended to a period of almost a century, and the other is the industrial product cycle, which has continued for almost half a century already. The plantation product cycle thrived under the 'classical economic environment'. Its 'investment environment' was shaped by the doctrine of *laissez–faire*. Foreign and domestic capital engaged in plantations, on a large scale, attracted by relatively high profit margins and a favourable 'investment climate'. State capital participated only in infrastructural activities. The 'tripod structure' contributed to the success of the 'plantation enterprise' in this economic environment[1].

The industrial product cycle commenced after the end of the plantation product cycle, especially, after World War II. The new product cycle began to thrive under 'development economics', different from the previous policy of *laissez faire*. This transition has led to three important empirical enquiries. One is about the whereabouts of entrepreneurial skills that thrived in the system during the colonial period. The other is on the whereabouts of the huge capital base that had accumulated in the system before independence. The last is about the successful engagement of the above two factors in the industrial product cycle. The post- independence economic history of Sri Lanka provides a wealth of information to develop hypotheses regarding the above issues. This study examines the third issue as to whether the above forces have successfully been integrated into the post-independence process of industrial accumulation. It is interesting to know whether 'development economics', and subsequently the 'neoliberal policies' have been able to expedite the process of transformation from plantation to an industrial-based economy.

There were two factors that hindered the mobility of productive resources towards industrial formation in the early phases. One was the lack of a competitive economic advantage in the manufacturing sector compared with other sectors of the economy. This resulted in relatively low profit margins in manufacturing compared with other sectors of the economy. The other was the unfavourable 'investment climate'. These two produced different disincentives for private capital accumulation in manufacturing. What type of 'investment environment' did the private entrepreneurs anticipate? Two historical occasions provide explanations to this question. One was the *laissez faire* classical economic environment that existed in the nineteenth century. Other was the period during WW II where the private sector had engaged in large scale manufacturing activities, for the first time, in Sri Lanka.

The process of industrial development after 1956 passed through two distinct investment environments, one under 'development economics' and the other under 'neoliberal' policies. The pre-1977 investment climate was predominantly planning-oriented while the post–1977 was primarily market-oriented. Each of them provided different incentives to the process of industrial accumulation. The initiation of industrial accumulation under the planning-oriented industrial strategy was found appropriate for countries like Sri Lanka where the level of industrial infrastructure and entrepreneurial skills were inadequate for any private initiation[2]. Sri Lanka's state directly participated in manufacturing after 1956. It helped the country to broaden its industrial capacity speedily. This process of accumulation, however, failed to move towards a self-generating growth path because of the failure of state enterprises to generate adequate surpluses for large-scale reinvestment. Industrial accumulation, therefore, had become state-fund dependent.

The private sector was found quite slow off the blocks, albeit, some new industrialists who sprang up in the system after 1960 with the support of the state. It did not respond positively to higher profit margins produced by excessive protection and other micro stimuli of the state. There were many limitations and obstacles to their effective participation in the industry. Largely, the interest groups, the forces-hostile-to-market, tended to dominate the environment which weakened market forces, the dynamic force in the capitalist system. These developments slowed down the industrial growth of the country.

The neoliberal regime in 'investment environment' after 1977 encouraged market forces to determine the reallocation of resources among alternative needs. Trade liberalisation intensified international trade which helped the active involvement of market forces in the economy. The domestic private, foreign and state capital played an integral role in this system, contributing to the achievement of relatively high rate of capital accumulation at least until 1983. The supportive services like trade, finance, insurance and others played their respective roles in the economy.

The neoliberal industrial regime experienced certain drawbacks. The manufacturing sector was able to attract a relatively low volume of resources compared to other sectors like trade, construction and finance. Though there was a considerable increase in industrial capital between 1977 and 1983 and again between 1990 and 1994, the long-term industrial growth was generally low. The events that took place after 1983 were responsible for the discouragement of the 'tripod structure' in industrial accumulation. All in all, the weak market forces in the neoliberal economy were able to produce only limited pressure for change towards industrial accumulation. Industrial accumulation under neoliberal economic policies was not 'fast and compressed' to the extent that other NICs experienced in a relatively limited period.

This study identified possible causes for the failure of these two approaches, statist and neoliberal, of industrial accumulation in Sri Lanka. The main impediment, as uncovered by this study, has been the interference of forces-hostile-to-market, the non-price axis[3], which grew in the above two environments and hindered market forces in the system. The interest groups brought in excessive pressure for the provision of welfare facilities, which disturbed the planning-oriented approach of industrial accumulation prior to 1977[4].

The anti-market forces disturbed the neoliberal economic strategy of industrial development after 1977. These forces overshadowed the gradually growing market forces in the system interfering in the allocation of resources. These forces brought pressure on the state with regard to the distribution of a large magnitude of foreign aid in favour of politically popular projects while discouraging the allocation of funds for industrial development. The UNP government, continuing with the old industrial vision of the 1950s, acted on the presumption that industrial accumulation was a natural process of the private sector[5]. Its policy of trade liberalisation counteracted with the infant industry argument. The anti-market forces like 'political decay', ethnic violence, industrial disharmony, mistrust between the state and the private sector etc. contributed greatly to the slow growth of private industrial accumulation.

Myrdal's (1970) assertion is still valid for explaining current dilemmas faced by some 'new nations' today. His thesis pointed out the necessity of weakening 'non-economic factors', initiating some forms of 'modernisation' in systems of 'new nations', which was considered to be the main prerequisite for economic development of these nations[6] (Streeten, 1993:1282). He argued that attitudes and institutions should be changed radically to promote speedy development (Myrdal, 1970:33). Meier (1995:89) insisted that 'some institutional changes and modifications in the value structure are necessary if the inhibiting institutions and values are to be removed'. Even after 50 years of warnings by economists, South Asia still remains a region of ethnic and religious bias. Pockets of ethnic and religious dogmas and attendant cults are basically market-hostile, just as some leadership traditions. They interfered with the economic policies of these societies (Corbridge, 1995:1-27).

Sri Lanka's journey towards capitalist industrial development lacked the liberty to develop institutions for maintaining good 'business-government relationships' in the system. There are, at least, three broad types of institutions that need to be established by the state of a 'new nation'. The first involves the development of institution guaranteeing private property rights, establishing law and order etc., in the process of capitalist accumulation. Secondly, the development of supportive services like transport networks, communication facilities, power generation, financial institutions, insurance institutions etc., for the acceleration of the progress of already operating industries. The third involves the institutions necessary for counteracting non-market forces in the system (Meier, 1995:89).

Lakshman (1999:15) holds that 'Sri Lanka has the necessary foundation already laid' to provide 'the required institutional background'. However, this foundation appears to have met only the first two institutional requisites. The last institutional requirement has not been adequately addressed, one which is crucial to the development of an unhindered capitalist economic system in Sri Lanka. One such hindrance is the weak employer-employee relations in state and private organisations[7]. The state has failed to introduce an institutional mechanism to promote employer-employee relations[8].

What are the alternative paths open to an economy which is stuck in a state of chaos? There are two broad options open to an economy which faces a 'disturbed investment climate'. One is the intensive use of neoliberal policies to stimulate private investment, lessening simultaneously all possible disturbances coming from institutional forces-hostile-to-market. This may be the best option. The possible outcomes of this policy can be visualised: Let us assume that the country had implemented this policy, 'strategy I', after 1983. 'Strategy I' refers to the creation of a favourable investment climate by the state, defeating all hostile forces that hinder neoliberal policies.

Under such circumstances, we can assume that local private industrialists would continue to perform in the same way that they did prior to 1983 (in the undisturbed investment climate). The extrapolation of private industrial accumulation for the period after1983, at an annual rate of growth that prevailed prior to 1983 is made in curve 3 in fig. 7.1[9]. The curve 7 (adding the curve 3 to curve 5) gives the possible levels of fixed industrial investment effected by the 'tripod structure' that could have prevailed after 1983 had there been a favourable investment climate in the country. Curve 7 describes an average annual long run rate of growth of 1.6 percent of industrial fixed investment per GDP (see logarithmic regression results in Regression 7A2.1 in Appendix 2). A polynomial trend curve is fitted to the data in curve 7, which is labelled as curve 8 in figure 7.1. Curve 8 provides the long-term trend of capitalist industrial accumulation under a possible positive 'investment environment'.

Curves 7 and 8 are useful indicators that demonstrate possible effects of a good 'investment climate' under neoliberal policies on long-term manufacturing fixed investments of the country. This provides some evidence about the capacity of domestic private capital as the potential main partner of industrial development in Sri Lanka[10]. Figure 7.1 tends to suggest that the vision of 'domestic private industrial capitalism' is apparently too ambitious a goal to be achieved in the medium term without the support of foreign capital. The total manufacturing fixed investment would grow only at an average annual rate of 3.6 percent in such circumstances. We cannot therefore, underestimate the contribution of FDI in the process of industrial capitalist development of Sri Lanka in the foreseeable future.

The second-best option may be the state's partial withdrawal from neoliberal policies. Alternatively, the state can actively participate in the economy either through intensifying industrial activities or providing infrastructural facilities during periods of disturbances. This is meant to fill the vacuum of industrial-related-investment created by the withdrawal of the other two 'pods' because of political and economic instability of the country. Tanzi (1997: 255) makes a similar suggestion for countries, which are undergoing 'post chaos' economic problems. He suggests that the role for the states in countries 'with poor functioning of markets should be to supplement market activities'[11].

The state may take part in industrial investment during unstable environments to keep up with the long-term trend of industrial formation in the country. This possibility can be studied referring to

'Strategy II', curve 6 in fig. 7.1. The long-term general trend of industrial accumulation of the country (curve 8 in fig. 7.1) could be maintained only if the state incurs an additional manufacturing investment at least equal to 30 percent of its total expenses in 1983. Therefore, the policy implication for 'disturbed investment climate' would be the active state participation in economic activities within the neoliberal policy framework. State capital would serve as a buffer to counterbalance the drop in private capital during 'disturbed investment environment'. Thus, state capital as the main 'pod' can play a dual role, one in the stable environment and the other in the unstable environment, as a balancing force for successful implementation of neoliberal economic policies.

Figure 7.1 Behaviour of the 'Tripods' under different Investment Environments

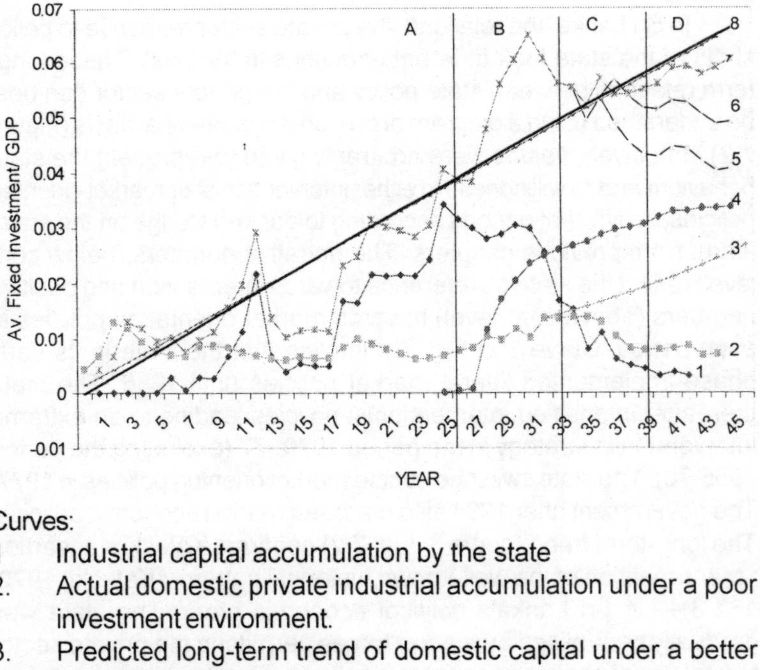

Curves:

1 Industrial capital accumulation by the state
2. Actual domestic private industrial accumulation under a poor investment environment.
3. Predicted long-term trend of domestic capital under a better investment environment.
4. Actual foreign capital accumulation.
5. The actual domestic, foreign and state capital accumulation —'the tripod structure'.
6. The predicted long-term total industrial accumulation under

"Strategy II" assuming the state after 1983 increased its industrial investment by about 30 per cent of 1983 level.

7. The predicted long run total industrial investment of the 'tripod structure' under "Strategy I" if the country is able to provide with a better investment environment under neoliberal policies.
8. Long-term trend curve with good policies.

Finally, the change in the state–private sector relations is an important trend to be understood in the process of capitalist industrial accumulation. This will help policy planners to understand the extent of capitalist industrial accumulation in the country concerned. The 'close business-government relationship' is always salutary to industrial development under neoliberal policies (Haggard, 1998:78). The cordial state-private sector relations would undoubtedly encourage the private sector to participate extensively in the accumulation process.

In Sri Lanka, the relations, the private sector response to policy shifts of the state took different directions in the past. These long-term relations between state policy and the private sector can best be understood using a diagram drawn on a hypothetical basis (Figure 7.2). Intuitively, values were arbitrarily given to represent the state behaviour and its willingness to either interventionist or market-oriented policies, in different periods according to our knowledge on the state, learnt from previous chapters. The negative numbers (below zero level) reflect the state's preference towards intervention and positive numbers (above zero level) towards market orientation policies in each period. Curve 3 in Fig. 7.2 implies that the state in its early phase implemented liberal market policies until 1956. The state thereafter intensified interventionist policies leading to an extreme interventionist strategy in the period 1970 -77 (excluding the period 1965-70). The state switched over to market oriented policies in 1977. The government after 1994 also practised market economic policies. The long-term trend (curve 3, Fig. 7.2) confirms Kalecki's assertion –the "repetition of the well-known historical pattern" (Kalecki, 1972: 162-3)— in Sri Lanka's political economic order. The state was gradually neutralised by market forces permitting the private sector to implement neoliberal economic policies. The Sri Lankan economy has eventually entered the process of capitalist industrial development.

The response of the private sector to policy shifts of the state has been quite favourable. Private investment has gone up whenever the state has been in favour of market-oriented policies. Curve 2 in fig. 7.2 confirms that the private investments are on the upturn along with the market oriented economic policies of the state, especially after 1977. This suggests that all forces (actors in each cells of our diagram in figure 1.1, chap. 1) are now in agreement with the new capitalist development process in Sri Lanka. The only 'Achilles heel' in the Sri Lankan industrial development process has been the interference of forces-hostile-to-market. The state has a great responsibility in minimising the effects of such forces.

Figure 7.2 Relationships between fixed Investments and Degrees of Market Orientation

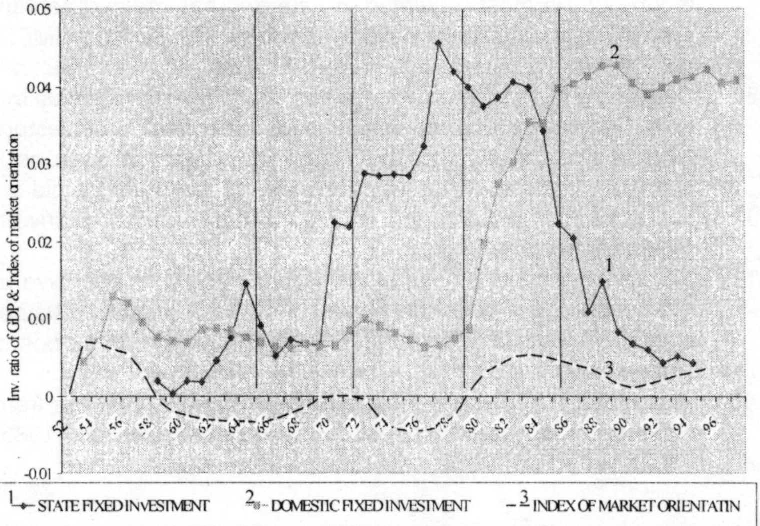

Notes

1. Ferguson's Directory (1925) has made an assessment on the success of this 'plantation enterprise'.
2. Many NICs commenced their industrial accumulation with a path emphasising planning-centric strategy For example, South Korea, Taiwan, Japan and newly emerging countries like India, China.
3. The terminology used by Colclough (1993:4) for explaining the same concept.
4. ...[These] were so explicitly unfavourable to the private sector' (Gunatilake, 1999:195).

5. The behaviour of a neoliberal state ought to be 'designing the industrial policy with a view to building up a modern, structurally diversified economy'. The state should target to provide directed and subsidised credit to particular sectors like in S. Korea (Sobhan, 1999:49). Sri Lanka did not follow the above practices.
6. Modernisation theorists held that developed societies were distinguished by their economic, social, cultural and political *modernity,* which contrasted sharply with the traditional values of underdeveloped, developing, backward, Third World or latecomer societies' (Corbridge, 1995:2).
7. Chanakya Dissanayake in the Special report writes that 'Sri Lanka's over regulated labour market is seen as a major deterrent to attract FDI's into the country'. The labour market is 'one of the most regulated in Asia and has created serious growth constraints to the nation'. Business, The Sunday TIMES, vol. 07, No. 82, Sunday, January 28, 2001.
8. Chanakya Dissanayake describes that the approach of the government 'the Charter, which came under fire from investors when it was initially introduced few years back, is seen as a competitive disadvantage by the investor community', ibid.
9. We assume that the period 1977-83 was the heyday of private industrial accumulation.
10. The proposition of Athukorala is that the long term objective of the nation ought to be the elevation of the domestic industrial capital class while encouraging FDI for medium term purposes (Athukorala, 2000).
11. This type of 'bringing the state back in' is quite different from what was suggested by neoliberal revisionists (Skocpol, 1985: 28; Boyer, 1996: 108).

Appendix 1

Table 2A1.1 Expenditure on Imports and Items Imported

Item	*1911* *Rs.*	*1921* Rs.
1. Soap	1,266,434	680,196
2. Paper	512,453	1,498,445
3. Rubber Manufactured	8,071,230	585,592
4. Bricks and Tiles	256,322	290,294
5. Brushes	160,169	71,322
6. Matches	n.a	603,478
7. Perfumes	241,268	189,471
8. Tea Chest	2,295,969	1,839,887
9. Umbrella	356,394	417,454
10. Hardware	2,287,591	2,253,897
11. Candles	207,222	37,456
12. Cement	465,722	394,542
13. Earthenware	291,971	578,656
14. Embroid	101,856	84,909
15. Glass	461,721	944,141
16. Brass	n.a	242,072
17. Furniture	137,232	365,132
18. Mats	52,156	33,938
19. Ceramics	551,641	n.a
20. Leather	810,594	n.a

Sources: The Ceylon Blue Books, 1911 and 1921.

Table 2A1.2. Industries Providing Items for Final and Intermediate Use

Nature of Industry	*No. of Factries In urban areas*	*No. of Factries In other areas*
1. Final use		
Ice and soda water	8	2
Weaving and spinning	1	13
Steam Laundry	1	-
Brass Foundries	-	117
2. Intermediate Use		
Gas work	1	-
Saw mills	12	3
Iron foundries	5	-
Coir mills	11	53
Tiles and brick manufacturing	143	280
Cane basket manufacturing	6	5
Lime kilns	22	145
Fiber Mills	7	-
Electrical installing engines	2	-
Bulk petroleum oil tanks	2	-
Tanneries	4	1
3. Printing, ruling etc		
Machines	100	6

Source: Ferguson Directory, p. 676, 1875.

Table 2A1.3. Number of Industries Formed in Different Periods

Type	*1875*	*1916*	*1928*	*1938*
Total number of industries existed each year.	8	20	29	44
New industries added in each interval		12	9	15

Compiled using the Ferguson Directories related to each period.

Table 2A1.4. Annual Average Growth Rates of Urban Population in Sri Lanka

1871	*1881*	*1891*	*1901*	*1911*	*1921*	*1931*	*1946*	*1953*	*1963*
10.8	10.2	10.7	11.6	13.2	14.2	13.2	15.4	15.3	19.1

Sources : Population of Sri Lanka, Country Monograph Series No. 4, United Nations, 1976. Kalra, B.R. (1967) 'Data on Occupational Structure in Cities', 1901-61, Bose (ed), Pattern of Population Change in India – 1951-61, Bombay, Allied Publishers, pp. 287-314.

Table 2A1.5. Export and Import Price Indices and Terms of Trade

Year	*1926*	*1928*	*1930*	*1932*	*1934*	*1936*	*1938*
Export Price index (Av. 1934-36 =100)	193	141	105	65	86	103	99
Import Price index Av. 1934-36 =100)	194	183	145	106	101	97	102
Terms of Trade	100	77	72	61	85	106	97

Source : Table in page 95, *The Instability of An Export Economy* by Gamani Corea, 1975.

Table 2 A 1.6. Per Capita Import of Consumer Goods at 1938 Prices

Year	*(Rs.)*	*Year*	*(Rs.)*
1928	27.09	1942	18.29
1931	24.04	1943	19.26
1932	23.70	1944	22.31
1933	22.37	1945	22.39
1934	25.31	1946	23.21
1935	25.28	1947	26.39
1936	25.05	1948	24.29
1937	26.23	1949	25.23
1938	25.35	1950	27.02
1939	25.90		
1940	24.94		
1941	23.51		

Source : Economic and social development of Ceylon. 1926-51, issued by the Ministry of Finance, 1951.

Table 2A1.7. Economic Indicators

Year	*Cost of living index*	*Average Rate of Inflation %*
1938	100	
1939	104	4.0
1940	112	7.7
1941	122	8.9
1942	165	35.2
1943	196	18.8
1944	200	2.0
1945	221	10.5
1946	228	3.2

Source : p. 9, Ceylon Year Book, 1948.

Table 3A1.1 Industries Operated Before WW II

Established	*Types and Names of Industries*	*Established*	*Types and Names of Industries*
	Food, Beverages and Tobacco		***Chemicals and Chemical products***
1906	Sedawatta Mills ltd.	1891	Apothecaries Co. ltd.
1910	Ceylon Brewery ltd.	1917	Ceylon Match ltd
1932	Ceylon Tobacco Co.	1934	Lanka Light ltd.
1937	Abraham Industries	1913	Colombo Pharmacy Company Limited
1938	Lever Brothers ltd.	1929	E.B Creasy & Company Limited
	Leather, Rubber, Wood, Paper		***Non-metallic Mineral Products Petroleum and Coal***
1909	American Engraving Works,	1936	Shaw Industries Ltd.
1917	Nissei Trading Co. ltd		***Machinery - Transport equipment***
1923	Ceylon Boot Manufactory	1934	General Auto Works Ltd.
1926	Jainu Deen and Co Ltd		***Miscellaneous items***

(Countd.)

	Base Metal Industries and Metal Products	1891	Apothecaries Co Ltd.
1905	Jinasene Ltd.	1894	Ceylon Cold Stores
	Construction and Engineering	1937	Abraham Industries
1892	Brown and Company Limited	1911	Hunter and Company Limited
1922	Samuel Sons and Company Limited	1910	Walkers and Greig Limited
1888	Wellawatta Spring and Weaving Mills ltd	1919	Shaw Wallace and Hedges Limited
1909	Heyleys ltd		

Sources : Ferguson Directories 1875, 1935, 1938, and 1941.
Census and Statistics 1901, 1911, and 1921.
Ceylon Blue Books 1900, 1901, 1925, and 1938.

Table 3A1.2 Industries Operated after WW II

Established	*Types and Names of Industries*	*Established*	*Types and Names of Industries*
	Food, Beverages and Tobacco		***Chemicals and Chemical products***
1944	Rockland distilleries ltd.	1943	Parfum ltd.
1945	Modern Confectionery Works	1941	South Chemical Industries
1946	Midland Chocolate Manufacturers	1939	J.L Morrison Son and Jones Ltd.
1946	Sri Lanka Distilleries	1941	Swadeshi Industrial Works Ltd.
1943	Harischandra Mills Ltd.		
	Leather, Rubber, Wood, Paper		***Non-metallic Mineral Products Petroleum and Coal***
1940	Richard Pieris and Company Ltd.	1941	The Colombo Memorial Stone Company
1939	Don Somapala Corporation Ltd.	1944	Ceylon Mirror Industry

(*Contd.*)

(*Contd.*)

1941	Cane Furniture	1949	ACME Printing and Packaging Ltd.
			Metal Products
1943	West Ceylon Co.		
1944	Excelsior Trading Co.	1946	Francis Perera Co. Ltd.
1946	City Foot Wear	1947	Ceylo Tin Manufacturers Ltd.
	Electrical Machinery apparatus		***Miscellaneous Items***
1941	United Electrical Ltd.	1949	Associated Motorways Ltd.
1941	Sirrul Kadheer and Co. Ltd	1945	United Motor Lanka Ltd.
1945	Silvertone Radio Service	1946	Cargills (Ceylon) Ltd.
		1945	Eastern Merchants Ltd.
		1949	Ceylon and Foreign Trades Ltd.

Sources : Ferguson Directories 1944, 1946, 1947, 1948 and 1949.

Table 3A1.3. Average Fixed Investment (Real Values: 1952=100) (Rs.)

	Plantation	*Manufacture*	*Construct*	*Trade*	*Finance*
1952	1,892,203	1,311,853	1,128,574	3,327,801	8,343
1953	2,009,044	2,117,093	1,343,542	3,224,724	11,121
1954	2,128,409	3,728,946	1,351,587	1,964,032	12,475
1955	2,285,822	3,315,957	1,358,766	2,118,873	14,402
1956	2,236,530	2,170,800	1,362,626	2,116,267	18,567
1957	2,264,868	2,297,343	1,327,735	2,091,492	27,738
1958	2,856,124	2,473,253	1,488,858	2,320,562	268,067
1959	2,923,804	2,546,396	1,820,802	2,273,069	279,307
1960	2,331,346	3,222,659	2,548,246	2,636,020	278,195
1961	2,229,728	3,456,981	2,824,776	2,392,285	262,406
1962	2,293,592	3,427,945	3,684,253	2,602,449	241,592
1963	2,248,149	3,267,752	3,601,095	2,411,303	401,108

(Countd.)

1964	2,110,554	3,047,668	5,771,025	2,474,049	224,743
1965	2,240,511	2,904,922	7,885,988	2,992,894	221,949
1966	2,280,296	2,936,813	8,996,029	3,092,609	483,655
1967	2,417,870	3,504,948	10,261,616	3,067,663	473,141
1968	2,243,730	3,504,402	12,272,598	2,188,554	487,116
1969	1,958,783	3,694,350	13,435,945	2,042,620	571,257
1970	1,949,071	4,825,776	12,333,595	2,628,601	560,217
1971	1,895,123	5,886,674	11,111,424	3,087,314	560,456
1972	1,688,838	5,496,403	9,692,045	3,008,761	599,426
1973		5,126,650	9,556,640	2,710,403	610,542
1974		4,687,748	8,287,721	2,516,637	686,376
1975		4,185,392	7,700,602	1,812,758	631,579
1976		4,436,570	8,300,199	2,875,602	576,781
1977		5,213,793	9,715,134	4,452,319	971,339
1978		6,294,533	4,282,031	4,498,873	1,365,898
1979		7,019,417	5,443,401	3,232,017	2,209,811
1980		9,233,236	18,190,839	2,837,146	2,395,277
1981		9,189,044	15,334,273	4,025,628	4,734,735
1982		11,594,772	9,050,329	4,835,556	4,997,053
1983		10,615,235	8,066,520	4,466,925	5,556,915
1984		14,961,106	9,107,704	4,141,967	5,378,577
1985		15,521,539	50,250,231	4,422,801	11,681,295
1986		15,997,213	49,265,858	4,332,342	11,444,783
1987		16,408,976	33,668,041	5,131,223	11,470,209
1988		15,742,727	42,606,735	4,907,149	10,606,989
1989		13,439,098	33,668,041	4,744,609	11,085,738
1990		11,118,037	35,556,743	4,582,069	11,496,363
1991		11,135,469	30,232,471	4,795,881	11,284,309
1992		11,941,438	24,277,017	5,140,862	11,182,402
1993		13,010,620	21,738,198	5,051,560	10,569,135
1994		14,470,921	32,102,091	11,850,124	12,947,945
1995		11,988,000	41,287,000	9,613,000	16,723,000
1996		13,112,000	37,252,000	8,893,000	16,577,000
1997		15,030,000	34,219,000	9,951,000	17,373,000
1998		12,556,000	31,764,000	11,906,000	20,813,000

Source : Based on Author's Database. See page 97 and 100 for further information.

Table 3A1.4 Earnings Per Share (EPS) of Industries (Rs.)

Year	*Plantation*	*Manufacturing*	*Construction*	*Finance*	*Trade*
1941	n.a	18.4	n.a	n.a	n.a
1943	n.a	4.49	n.a	n.a	n.a
1952	47.04	3.15	3.76	1.03	1.70
1953	24.60	0.57	3.85	0.49	1.35
1954	22.33	0.70	1.67	0.38	2.38
1955	10.88	1.61	1.41	0.53	1.73
1956	10.95	1.61	0.73	0.75	1.54
1957	10.48	1.44	0.96	1.06	0.89
1958	7.41	1.76	0.59	1.03	1.52
1959	6.63	1.25	0.92	0.70	0.89
1960	7.12	1.10	1.20	0.72	0.56
1961	7.62	0.84	1.39	0.72	0.37
1962	8.90	0.99	1.39	0.90	0.54
1963	8.59	1.35	1.02	0.76	1.14
1964	6.91	1.63	1.09	0.87	1.49
1965	5.62	1.72	2.60	1.12	1.82
1966	7.42	1.86	3.94	0.97	1.76
1967	6.80	2.16	3.10	1.36	5.49
1968	5.19	1.72	1.34	1.54	1.83
1969	7.56	1.58	1.83	1.43	1.96
1970		1.17	1.49	1.20	1.08
1971		1.19	1.48	1.55	1.38
1972		1.51	2.35	2.10	1.22
1973		1.65	1.91	3.41	1.26
1974		1.66	2.13	1.87	1.94
1975		1.65	2.02	2.58	2.61
1976		1.65	2.08	2.21	2.98
1977		2.37	9.44	5.46	2.54
1978		3.09	8.30	7.15	3.47

(*Contd.*)

(*Contd.*)

Year	*Plantation*	*Manufacturing*	*Construction*	*Finance*	*Trade*
1979		4.59	4.28	2.58	2.49
1980		4.59	1.35	9.09	5.55
1981		1.79	0.15	3.64	8.26
1982		1.99	0.22	2.97	6.89
1983		0.66	0.08	3.39	5.43
1984		0.70	0.28	3.79	4.17
1985		0.56	0.53	4.93	8.14
1986		1.39	0.76	7.10	6.25
1987		0.24	0.53	9.10	6.95
1988		0.62	2.19	6.07	6.75
1989		1.48	0.62	7.91	6.54
1990		3.28	11	9.8	1.78
1991		4.46	21.5	14.9	5.41
1992		4.18	6.43	15.09	4.71
1993		5.12	4.94	6.68	4.77
1994		2.90	3.05	2.36	8.48
1995		1.84	2.01	3.46	9.75
1996		2.15	2.64	4.51	7.05

Source : Author's Database and Hand Books of Rupee Companies, 1941 and 1943.

Table 3A1.5. List of Names of Industrial Establishments (Old Firms)

ISIC	*Name of firms*	*Year of Establishment*
313	Ceylon Cold Store Ltd.(311, 312)	1894
352	Ceylon Match Co. Ltd.	1918
313	Ceylon Brewery Ltd.	1910
314	Ceylon Tobacco Co. Ltd.	1932
353	Ceylon Oxygen Ltd.	1938
355	Richard Pieris and Co. Ltd. (381)	1940
352	Swedeshi Industrial Work Ltd.	1941

(*contd.*)

Year Plantation Manufacturing Construction Finance Trade

355	Associated Motorways Ltd.	1949
372	Acme Aluminium Co. Ltd.	1949
351	Hayleys Ltd. (353, 382)	1953
311	Pure Beverages Com. Ltd. (313)	1955
352	Glaxo Ceylon Ltd. (311)	1956
382	Associated Electrical Corp. Ltd.	1962
352	Reckitt and Colman (Ceylon) Ltd.	1962
383	Acl Cables Ltd.	1962
321	Ceylon Synthetic Textile Mills Ltd.	1962
351	Chemical Industries (356)	1964
351	Lankem Ceylon Ltd. (356)	1964
	Muller and Phipps (Ceylon) Ltd.	1964
322	Asian Cotton Mills Ltd.	1967
321	Kandy Textiles Industries Ltd.	1967
	Lambretta Ceylon Ltd.	1967
352	Parquet (Ceylon) Ltd.	1967
324	Bata Shoe Co. Of Ceylon Ltd.	1950
321	Ceylon Textile Manufacturers Ltd.	1971
321	Wellawatta Spinning and Weaving Mill Ltd.	n.a
383	Associated Cables Ltd.	1962
383	Elephant Lite Corporation Ltd.	1956
351	Industrial Asphalts (Ceylon) Limited	1964
352	J.L.Morrison Son and Jones (Ceylon) Ltd.	1939
341	Kalamazoo Systems Ltd.	1958
341	Paragon Ceylon Ltd.	1958
313	W.M. Mendis and Co. Ltd.	1960

Sources : Ferguson Directories, Census of Ceylon, Ceylon Blue Books, Hand Books of Rupee Companies.

Table 3A1.6. List of Names of Industrial Establishments (New Firms)

SIC	*Name of firms*	*Year of Establishment*
372	Alufab Ltd.	1979
383	Kelani Cables Ltd.	1969
382	Singer Industries (Cey) Ltd.	1974

(*Contd.*)

(*Contd.*)

SIC	*Name of firms*	*Year of Establishment*
355	Statcon Rubber Co. Ltd.	1974
321	Chemanex Ltd. (351)	1974
321	Ceylon Silk Ltd.	n.a
383	Siedles T.V Industry Ltd.	n.a
311	John Keells Ltd.	1973
341	Haycarb Ltd.	1973
381	Bonars (Ceylon) Ltd.	n.a
383	Abans Electricals Ltd.	1981
355	Associated Rubber Products Ltd.	1982
390	Blue Diamonds Jewellery Worldwide Ltd.	1991
356	Central Industries Ltd.	1984
312	Ceylon Grain Elevators Ltd.	1983
341	Compak Morison (Lanka) Ltd.	1982
355	Dipped Products Ltd.	1976
383	Kelani Cables Ltd.	1969
372	Lanka Aluminium Industry Ltd.	1983
369	Lanka Cement Ltd.	1981
369	Lanka Tiles Ltd.	1984
372	Metal Packing Ltd.(381)	1983
	Mikechris Ltd.	1978
311	Pelwatta Sugar Industries Ltd.	1983
382	Regnis (Lanka) Ltd.	1987
369	Tokyo Cement Co.	1982
324	Korea Ceylon Footwear Manufacturing Company Ltd.	1980
321	Kuruwita Textile Mills Ltd.	1981
321	Pugoda Textiles Lanka Ltd.	1990
390	Ceylon Gems Ltd.	1984
311	Nestle Lanka Limited	1980
390	Rainbow Gems Ltd.	1979
351	Union Carbide Ltd.	1988
313	International Distillers (Lanka) Ltd.	1980
313	Ceylon Tea Services Ltd	1981

Source : Hand Books of Rupee Companies.

Table 3A1. 7. Average Fixed Investment by Three Classes of Investors

(Real Values: 1952=100) **(Rs.)**

Period	*Old Firms' Average Real Investment*	*1960s Firms' Average Real Investment*	*1977sFirms' Average Real Investment*
1952	1326946		
1953	2072278		
1954	4529763		
1955	5244570		
1956	2645222		
1957	2651991		
1958	2838526		
1959	2895936		
1960	3774522	1363503	
1961	4228833	1581491	
1962	4359614	1902861	
1963	3989849	2335865	
1964	3906479	1779911	
1965	4150177	1174461	
1966	4177994	1214629	
1967	4792610	1549516	
1968	5013797	1644317	
1969	5072915	2521547	
1970	6227358	3813339	
1971	6513270	5731840	
1972	6304380	5192638	
1973	5966998	4832326	
1974	5410445	4295460	
1975	5344687	3689005	
1976	5377566	3992232	
1977	5361127	3840619	
1978	8771242	4279932	1004213
1979	12181358	4719246	2008426

(*Contd.*)

(*Contd.*)

Period	*Old Firms' Average Real Investment*	*1960s Firms' Average Real Investment*	*1977s Firms' Average Real Investment*
1980	17989591	6151248	2244755
1981	17326075	7179951	2122852
1982	16640792	6780683	4958242
1983	17942685	6041262	5806690
1984	15888445	12393901	7009272
1985	18916859	13453698	11362029
1986	20354654	13573432	14000805
1987	20019833	13645769	18207170
1988	18435908	11943991	14469570
1989	19052364	10219267	13604249
1990	19668819	8494544	12738927
1991	21683601	8741031	12507169
1992	25355167	27070610	8617670
1993	10262104	12528736	12550985

Table 4 A1.1. Periodic Average Rates of Growth

Period	*GDPAverage Growth Rate: (%)*	*Govt's. Capital expenditure/ (%)*	*Incremental CapitalOutput Ratiosof*	*Our Results # Growth Rate Fixed Assets (all sectors)*
1951 –55	4.5	3.9	3.04	14.0
1956- 65*	3.0	5.2	4.77	3.6
1966 –70	5.4	6.6	2.67	5.6
1971 –75	2.9	6.4	6.10	-2.2
1976 –80	5.5	12.2	4.00	5.9
1981 –85	5.2	14.1	4.30	10.0

Source : Table IV, Fiscal Policy in Sri Lanka since Independence, P.B. Jayasundera.

* Average values were calculated for the period 1956 –65 using figures of 2.0 and 4.0 in Jayasundera's table for periods 1956 -60 and 1961 –65, respectively.

Semi-log function was used for aggregate data in Author's database.

Table 3A1. 8. Average Fixed Investment According to Types of Products

(Real Values: 1952=100) (Rs.)

Year	Very Old Firms			Firms After 1960			Firms After 1977		
	(F, B, T)	(C, P)	(CMG)	(F, B, T)	(C, P)	(CMG)	(F, B, T)	(C, P)	(CMG)
1952	1959290		1010773						
1953	3254228		1481303						
1954	7403087		2614213						
1955	7665251		3792161						
1956	3680655		2201465						
1957	3936179		2170421						
1958	4665754		2153315						
1959	4995996		2108413						
1960	5302486		3010539	1363503					
1961	6594386		3215024	1581491					
1962	6397322		3486311	1536047		2269675			
1963	6145702	1151413	3471403	1425000		3246730			
1964	5849475	1078781	3477724	1311306	494847	3533581			
1965	7184404	945103	3765530	1276958	277337	2020337			

(*contd.*)

Year	Very Old Firms			Firms After 1960			Firms After 1977		
	(F, B, T)	(C, P)	(CMG)	(F, B, T)	(C, P)	(CMG)	(F, B, T)	(C, P)	(CMG)
1966	6867708	1157003	3888400	1427675	283658	2039076			
1967	7265155	1147609	4774377	1409715	1192939	2154280			
1968	7647249	1547335	4875592	1341874	1514082	1817605			
1969	7107518	2152096	5020481	1185211	1630560	3189762			
1970	7212056	2099513	7287678	1124909	1735653	5646536			
1971	8028606	2201971	7328587	1131975	1842654	9739471			
1972	8239649	1983776	6871460	1036438	1638332	8325170			
1973	8172106	1785133	6316679	2637742	1436942	7884625			
1974	7338592	1636616	5763089	3346555	951095	6955408			
1975	7220787	1580320	5724774	4177157	940256	5905603			
1976	7279690	1608468	5743931	3761856	945676	6430505			
1977	7250238	1594394	5734352	3969506	942966	6168054			
1978	13638069	2776319	7044041	4318559	1415086	7153201			1049323
1979	20025900	3958245	8353729	4667612	1887206	8138347			2098646
1980	34690255	3123762	9180550	15391592	1807682	7667389			2355901

(*contd.*)

(*contd.*)

Year	Very Old Firms			Firms After 1960			Firms After 1977		
	(F, B, T)	(C, P)	(CMG)	(F, B, T)	(C, P)	(CMG)	(F, B, T)	(C, P)	(CMG)
1981	33259380	3101487	12488390	13793959	3149988	9917890	2551169		1460013
1982	29330574	3606564	13640568	13564568	3511016	7990729	11360520	6883357	12387794
1983	35310398	3270488	12253000	14676601	3389308	5701523	16109361	9832069	11332542
1984	31687319	2875836	10545595	17555720	3080417	19986778	16502519	14844148	17279049
1985	41085852	2816619	10340234	22305416	4186952	19769871	16074160	14378310	19611228
1986	45111456	2835036	10546861	21233854	4188612	20404778	15248312	13002225	22400497
1987	44051480	2771824	10620101	20100864	4667909	20471931	14262595	9422184	19379350
1988	37294889	2580940	12219155	19228593	4071203	17388577	12464904	8394027	15009388
1989	37455101	2959577	13296704	21627379	4202857	12432974	10437757	8467187	13718166
1990	37615312	3338214	14374253	24026164	4334511	7477370	8410611	8540347	12426944
1991	38369521	3144086	18438918	24136555	5377385	6972836	9015219	12286529	11483131
1992	43281510	3241548	22967220	22696884	5518455	7023813	9865630	13368319	11122723
1993	37227521	4020579	30977942	22951510	7595851	8385845	14178428	11765187	11560174
1994	30782565	4111210	31198668	20701225	10032108	9500227	14578904	16308829	12121241

Source: Based upon Author's Database.

Table 3A1.9 Selected Structural Information (1998)
(Sectoral and product-wise distribution of firms)

ISIC		*# manufacturing Firms*	*# Export Firms*	*ISIC*		*# manufacturing Firms*	*# Export. Firms*
3112-3116	Meat, dairy, fish, grain, etc.	**120**	**154**	**3620**	Glass and Glass Products	**13**	**37**
	Dairy Products	5			Bottles	2	
	Fish	3			Fibreglass	2	
	Flavourings and Fragrances	2			Fbreglass Products	4	
	Food Industry equipment	1			Fibreglass Furniture	2	2
	Food Items	27			Glass	2	1
	Fruits	11	31		Opticals and Optical Accessories		1 1
	Milk	4	1	**3691-3699**	**Cement, Lime Plasters etc.**	**15**	**4**
	Sea food	3	3		Asbestos Products	2	
	Cashew	3			Flooring Materials	7	1
	Cocoa	1	12		Flour	2	
	Coconuts	5	33		Tiles	4	3

(contd.)

(*contd.*)

ISIC		*# manufacturing Firms*	*# Export Firms*	*ISIC*		*# manufacturing Firms*	*# Export. Firms*
	Coconut Products	8	30	**3720**	***Non-ferrous Basic Metal***	**65**	**44**
	Desiccated Coconut	9	15		Aluminum and Aluminum Extrusion	5	4
	Coffee	2	12		Aluminum Products	9	4
	Oil	4	4		Boxes	2	
	Bakery Equipment	5	2		Granite	3	5
	Confectionery	9	7		Graphite	1	1
	Flowers	3			Steel Furniture	9	2
	Foliage and Plants	8			Matches	3	1
	Sugar	1			Metal	2	1
	Poultry and Poultry Products	6	4		Galvanized Steel	3	1
					Stainless Steel	5	3
3121	***Spices, Animals, Feeds etc.***	**3**	0		Steel Fabricated Items	7	6
	Aquatic Products	1			Steel Scrap		4
	Breading and Weatherstrips	2			Steel and Steel Products	16	5
				3811-	***Cutlery, Handtools,***	**55**	**37**

(*contd.*)

(*contd.*)

ISIC		*# manufac-turing Fims*	*# Export Fims*	*ISIC*		*# manufac-turing Fims*	*# Export. Fims*
				3819	***Hardware etc.***		
3131-3133	*Beverages*	**9**	**8**		Bolts and Nuts	4	2
	Beer	4	4		Building Materials	8	6
	Beverages	4	2		Fencing Materials	4	
	Liquor	1	2		Hardware	4	3
	Household Items	7	7				
3140	*Tobacco*	**1**	**1**		Indistral Accessories	4	1
	Tobacco and Tobacco products	1	1		Industral Equiment	1	
3211-3220	*Textiles and clothing*	**182**	**133**		Insulation Materials	1	2
	Apparel Accessories	14	19		Refrigerator Equipment and Component	3	2
	Apparels	65	68		Sanirary ware	4	4
	Bags	15	18		Tableware	5	5
	Batik Products	6	10		Toiletries	5	5
	Linen	5	4		Tools	2	2

(*contd.*)

(*contd.*)

ISIC		*# manufac-turing Firms*	*# Export Firms*	*ISIC*		*# manufac-turing Firms*	*# Export. Firms*
	Bylon Products	2	4		Woodwork tools	1	1
	Telephones and telephones systems	1		**3822-3829**	Agricultural Machinery	**5**	**8**
	Textiles	4			Agricultural Equipment and Machinery	3	
	Upholstery Products	4			Tractors and Trailers	2	2
	Footwear	4	3	**38313839**	Electrical Machinery	**97**	
	Fabrics	7	7		Air conditioning Equipment and Parts	1	2
	Handicrafts	16			Antennas	1	1
	Interior Decorative Items	21			Batteries	1	1
3231-3233	Leather and Fur	**18**	**42**		Cables	4	2
	Gloves	7	26		Carbon	4	4
	Leather and Leather Products	11	16		Cookers and Cooker Accessories	1	

(*contd.*)

(*contd.*)

ISIC		*# manufac-turing Fims*	*# Export Fims*	*ISIC*		*# manufac-turing Fims*	*# Export. Fims*
3320	**Wooden, Furniture and Fixtures, cane**	**63**	**33**		Electrical appliances	3	
	Antiques	2	5		Electrical Componentsand Accessories	10	1
	Brassware	7	9		Electrical Conductors	5	1
	Brooms	6	7		Electrical Equipment	2	1
	Brushes	12	12		Electrical Fittings	14	1
	Cane and Cane Products	3			Electrical Equipment and Devices	1	
	Plywood and Plywood Products	2			Fire Fitting Equipment	1	
	Coir and Coir Products	31			Fire Protection and Detection Eqip.	2	
					Fire Works	1	
3511-3529	***Industrial chemicals***	**66**	**35**		Lighting Systems and Fixtures	7	4
	Chemicals –Agro	3			Machinery	3	2

(*contd.*)

(*contd.*)

ISIC	*# manufacturing Fims*	*# Export Fims*	*ISIC*	*# manufacturing Fims*	*# Export. Fims*
Chemical for Paints	1		Garment Industry Machinery	2	1
Chemical for Soap Industry	2		Food and Beverage Machinery	1	1
Detergents	49	4	Grinding and Milling Machinery	1	1
Dyes and Pigments	2		Industrial Machinery	2	1
Industrial Chemicals	7	5	Jewellery Industry machinery	2	1
Fertilizer	3	3	Tea industry Machinery	2	1
Paints	12	1	Machinery Components and Spare Parts	1	1
Primers and Fillers	5	1	Marine Industry equipment	2	1
Raw material for Paints	1	4	Marine Products	4	4
Thinners	6	3	Safety equipment and Accessories	3	
Wood Preservatives and Finishers	7	6	Security Equipment and systems	2	1
Paper	6	5	Sewing Machines	1	1

(*contd.*)

(*contd.*)

ISIC		# manufac-turing Firms	# Export Firms	ISIC		# manufac-turing Firms	# Export. Firms
	Petroleum Products	6	3		Solar Power Heating system	1	1
	Printing Industry Requisites	5			Telecommunication Equipment	3	1
3522-3528	Industrial chemicals, Medicine, Soap, Cosmetic	**23**)	**57**		Fab systems	1	
	Laundry Soap and Washing Powder	9			Transformers	6	
	Detergents and Disinfectants	5	6	**3841-3844**	Transport equipment	**14**	**8**
	Baby Care Products	5	5		Automobile Accessories	5	3
	Cleaning and Janitorial Equipment	1	16		Automobile Components	4	
	Health Care Products	4	14		Automobile Spare Parts	2	2
	Herbs and Herbal Products	9			Automobiles	2	2
	Horticulture Requisites	13	2		Bicycles	1	1
	Medical and Surgical equipment	3	5	**3851-3853**	Scientific Equipment	**17**	**7**
	Medical and Surgical Requisites	3	1		Audio Equipment	2	2

(*contd.*)

(*contd.*)

ISIC		*# manufacturing Firms*	*# Export Firms*	*ISIC*		*# manufacturing Firms*	*# Export. Firms*
	Pharmaceuticals	6	2		Clocks	2	2
	Veterinary	2	6		Communication Equipment	2	1
	Soap	7			Computer Software	6	
3421-3240	Printing and Publishing	**47**	**15**		Photographic Equipment and Accessories	1	1
	School Requisites	5	15		Watches	1	1
	Advertising and promotional materials	10	5		Generators	2	1
	Stationary	18		**3911**	Manufacturing NEC	**3**	**2**
3551-3559	Rubber Products	**47**	37				
	Umbrella and Umbrella spares	3	2				
	Rubber	7	7	**3560**	Plastic Products	**98**	**54**
	Rubber Products	26	23		Headwear	4	4
	Tyres	5	4		PVC and PVC Products	10	5

(*contd.*)

(*contd.*)

ISIC	*# manufac-turing Firms*	*# Export Firms*	*ISIC*	*# manufac-turing Firms*	*# Export. Firms*
Industrial tyres	3	3	Packing/ Packaging materials	24	14
Rebuilt tyres	6		Plastic Packing / Packaging	5	1
			Plastic and Plastic Products	17	8
			Drinking Straws	1	
			Plastic sheets	1	
			Polythene and Polythene Products		28 19
			Polythene Films	8	3
Grand Total				**972**	**624**

There were 212 types of products produced by the corporate firm sector in1998.

Source: Colombo Stock Exchange has listed all firms according to product; manufacturing and export. See pages 81 –119. Hand Book of Listed Companies, 1998.

Table 3A1. 10 Average Price Levels Prevailed in Two Environments #

Average Price Levels during Planning-Oriented Environment (%)

1959	60	61	62	63	64	65	66	67	68	69	70	71	72	73	74	75	76	77
0.2	-1.6	1.3	1.4	1.8	3.7	0.3	-0.2	2.2	5.8	7.4	5.9	2.7	6.3	9.6	12.3	6.7	1.2	1.2

Average Price Levels during Market Economic Environment (%)

1978	79	80	81	82	83	84	85	86	87	88	89	90	91	92	93	94	95	96
12.1	13.1	26.1	18	10.8	14	16.6	1.5	8	7.7	14	11.6	21.5	12.2	11.4	11.7	8.4	7.7	15.9

Calculated the percentage changes in CCPI (1952=100)

Source: Data based on Economic Progress of Independent SRI LANKA, Central Bank of Sri Lanka, Table 10, P280.

Table 5A1.1 List of Manufacturing Establishments

ISIC	*Old Firms*	*Year of Establish*	*Year of Quotation*
313	Ceylon Cold Store Ltd.(311, 312)	1894	n.a
352	Ceylon Match Co. Ltd.	1918	1976
313	Ceylon Brewery Ltd.	1910	n.a
314	Ceylon Tobacco Co. Ltd.	1932	1966
355	Richard Pieris and Co. Ltd. (381)	1940	1951
352	Swedeshi Industrial Work Ltd.	1941	n.a
355	Associated Motorways Ltd.	1949	1969
372	Acme Aluminium Co. Ltd.	1949	1956
351	Hayleys Ltd. (353, 382)	1953	n.a
311	Pure Beverages Com. Ltd. (313)	1955	1959
352	Glaxo Ceylon Ltd. (311)	1956	1963
382	Associated Electrical Corp. Ltd.	1962	1977
352	Reckitt and Colman (Ceylon) Ltd.	1962	1967
383	Acl Cables Ltd.	1962	1976
321	Ceylon Synthetic Textile Mills Ltd.	1962	1981
351	Chemical Industries (356)	1964	1964
351	Lankem Ceylon Ltd. (356)	1964	1970
	Muller and Phipps (Ceylon) Ltd.	1964	1965
322	Asian Cotton Mills Ltd.	1967	1969
321	Kandy Textiles Industries Ltd.	1967	1969
	Lambretta Ceylon Ltd.	1967	1969
352	Parquet (Ceylon) Ltd.	1967	
324	Bata Shoe Co. Of Ceylon Ltd.	1950	1984
321	Ceylon Textile Manufacturers Ltd.	1971	1984
321	Wellawatta Spinning and Weaving Mill Ltd.		
383	Associated Cables Ltd.	1962	1976
383	Elephant Lite Corporation Ltd.	1956	1982
351	Industrial Asphalt (Ceylon) Limited	1964	1978
352	J.L. Morrison Son and Jones (Ceylon) Ltd.	1939	1964
341	Kalamazoo Systems Ltd.	1958	1958
341	Paragon Ceylon Ltd.	1958	1974
313	W.M. Mendis and Co. Ltd.	1960	1978
	New Firms		
372	Alufab Ltd.	1979	1981
383	Kelani Cables Ltd.	1969	1974

(*Contd.*)

ISIC	*Old Firms*	*Year of Establish*	*Year of Quotation*
382	Singer Industries (Cey) Ltd.	1974	1981
355	Statcon Rubber Co. Ltd.	1974	1981
321	Chemanex Ltd. (351)	1974	1974
321	Ceylon Silk Ltd.		
383	Siedles Tv Industry Ltd.	n.a	n.a
311	John Keells Ltd.	1973	1974
341	Haycarb Ltd.	1973	1975
381	Bonars (Ceylon) Ltd.	n.a	n.a
383	Abans Electricals Ltd.	1981	1984
355	Associated Rubber Products Ltd.	1982	n.a
390	Blue Diamonds Jewellery World-wide Ltd.		1992
356	Central Industries Ltd.		
312	Ceylon Grain Elevators Ltd.	1983	n.a
353	Ceylon Oxygen Ltd.		
341	Compak Morison (Lanka) Ltd.		
355	Dipped Products Ltd.	1976	1982
383	Kelani Cables Ltd.	1969	1974
372	Lanka Aluminium Industry Ltd.	1983	1987
369	Lanka Cement Ltd.	1981	1982
369	Lanka Tiles Ltd.	1984	1986
372	Metal Packing Ltd.(381)	1983	n.a
	Mikechris Ltd.	1978	1981
311	Pelwatta Sugar Industries Ltd.	1983	1983
382	Regnis (Lanka) Ltd.	1987	1987
369	Tokyo Cement Co.	1982	n.a
324	Korea Ceylon Footwear Manufacturing Company Ltd.	1980	1981
321	Kuruwita Textile Mills Ltd.	n.a	n.a
321	Pugoda Textiles Lanka Ltd.		
390	Ceylon Gems Ltd.	1984	n.a
311	Nestle Lanka Limited	1980	
390	Rainbow Gems Ltd.	1979	
351	Union Carbite Ltd.	1988	1988
313	International Distillers (Lanka) Ltd.		
313	Ceylon Tea Services Ltd.		

Source: Ferguson Directories, Census of Ceylon, Ceylon Blue Books, Hand Books of Rupee Companies.

Table 5A1. 2. Companies Prevailed Prior to the Mid-1950s

Year of Establishment	*Name of the Company*
1909	Colonial Motors ltd.
1910	Walkers and Greig ltd.
1911	Hunter and Company Ltd
1913	Colombo Pharmacy Company Ltd
1919	Shaw Wallace and Hedges ltd.
1921	Millers ltd
1929	E.B. Creasy and Company ltd
1939	J.E Morison, Son and Jones (Ceylon) ltd.
1945	Eastern Merchants Ltd
1945	Diesel and Motor Engineering Company ltd.
1945	United Motors Lanka ltd.
1946	Cargills (Ceylon) ltd
1949	Ceylon and Foreign trades ltd
1949	Associated Motorways ltd
1952	Hayleys ltd
1953	Autodrome ltd.
1956	Glaxo Ceylon Ltd
1956	Elephant Lite Corporation ltd.

Sources : Ferguson Directories, Census of Ceylon reports, Ceylon Blue Books, Hand Books of Quoted Companies.

Table 5A1. 3. Names of Public Enterprises (1956-77)

National Milk Board	*Ceylon Steel**
National Paper*	Sri Lanka Tyre*
Ceylon Ceramics	Ceylon State Hardware*
Ceylon oils and Fats*	State Fertiliser Manufacturing*
Ceylon Plywood*	Ceylon Fisheries
Ceylon Leather Products*	Sri Lanka State Flour Milling*
Paranthan Chemicals*	Petroleum*
Ceylon Cement*	State Timber*

(*Contd.*)

National Milk Board	*Ceylon Steel**
Sri Lanka Sugar	State Printing*
Ceylon Mineral Sands*	Sri Lanka Ayurvedic Drugs
National Salt	State Distilleries (Seeduwa)
Jute Industries.	State Graphite*
Sri Lanka Tobacco	State Rubber Manufacturing*
National Textile*	

The companies marked by asterisks are by and large intermediate input manufacturing or processing industries, a fraction of which may go as final goods. *Source* : Lakshman (1979).

Table 5A1. 4 Surpluses Generated by Sectors

(In nominal values)

	Manufature Rs.	*Finane Rs.*	*Trade Rs.*	*Construction Rs.*
1953	4,973,000	4,757,722	1,618,098	1,468,183
1954	96,718,312	55,808,847	34,180,611	(367,696)
1955	57,325,261	45,630,024	(1,561,048)	778,636
1956	15,761,898	26,415,388	11,814,222	3,414,387
1957	18,570,849	23,234,597	1,572,503	310,258
1958	21,762,730	22,952,255	3,246,823	469,164
1959	26,069,925	30,118,253	4,723,609	781,042
1960	16,982,108	20,176,114	(351,769)	2,480,419
1961	19,984,456	46,370,599	497,058	429,108
1962	68,053,711	30,348,292	(1,769,071)	1,173,762
1963	34,546,820	35,013,711	2,515,981	705,109
1964	34,424,484	35,186,670	4,051,422	277,333
1965	48,318,163	53,825,953	12,759,085	4,999,96
1966	9,314,724	44,619,168	10,617,039	4,229,142
1967	11,844,611	48,359,249	4,954,787	4,078,792
1968	3,786,251	75,366,438	2,114,103	5,459,587
1969	57,051,996	37,604,986	1,268,149	2,699,076
1970	88,448,770	97,870,113	19,564,995	2,903,883
1971	56,834,022	65,007,612	6,485,918	1,076,373

(Contd.)

(Contd.)

	Manufature Rs.	*Finane Rs.*	*Trade Rs.*	*Construction Rs.*
1972	12,873,937	66,440,333	2,643,625	(4,115,008)
1973	26,539,802	83,257,932	10,387,476	1,719,700
1974	12,789,892	87,360,210	2,629,864	5,166,751
1975	(32,551,127)	61,249,617	954,296	123,871
1976	(66,751,266)	(7,460,336)	19,086,554	2,336,774
1977	153,644,873	238,726,265	10,488,904	12,053,453
1978	98,580,393	328,435,256	(4,021,048)	40,162,006
1979	443,043,618	21,790,688	43,670,626	(27,332,332)
1980	399,471,818	418,144,248	19,645,110	6,566,391
1981	547,775,306	609,952,893	46,201,855	113,795,755
1982	1,510,606,853	873,439,688	63,926,748	(8,068,311)
1983	339.249,269	705,130,731	57,596,590	397,906,039
1984	1,760,274,193	433,374,770	66,970,325	130,115,027
1985	1,716,054,691	905,081,499	43,965,707	301,034,647
1986	1,052,106,923	(548,215,404)	75,913,040	(561,655,036)
1987	1,243,276,072	3,062,748,320	38,160,795	(228,628,910)
1988	536,930,581	580,110,677	4,202,118	(154,090,069)
1989	1,159,353,924	1,908,710,566	3,310,723	(145,631,798)
1990	2,122,543,999	(78,312,754)	79,353,316	(137,173,526)
1991	1,230,921,999	3,974,894,040	117,525,738	400,894,322
1992	3,438,406,385	4,052,867,671	116,440,659	167,669,731
1993	3,727,355,630	4,792,230,243	162,572,855	(717,415,154)
1994	1,890,561,703	5,841,962,101	439,407,099	1,111,102,528

Sources : Author's database. Estimated according to the formula proposed by Scott Henderson and Graham Peirson (1984:116).

Table 5A1. 5. Performance of State Industrial Enterprises

	Capital Employed Rs.	*Profits/Loss (Mn.) Rs.*	*Profits/Capital Employed %*
1964	328.7	7.3	2.2
1965	402.1	8.7	2.2
1966	144.5	7.1	4.9

(*Contd.*)

	Capital Employed Rs.	*Profits/Loss (Mn.) Rs.*	*Profits/Capital Employed %*
1967	53.3	2.2	4.1
1968	753.5	38.6	5.1
1969	924.5	65.1	7.0
1970	1172.9	62.2	5.3
1971	929.0	63.5	6.8
1972	2159.2	62.4	2.9
1973	1923.7	84.1	4.4
1974	2180.5	203.1	9.3
1975	2120.9	129.3	6.1
1976	2557.3	93.0	3.6

Source: Central Bank: Annual Reports and Reviews of the Economy.

Table 6A1.1 Share of Product Categories in Total Exports of Foreign Firms

Year	*Food. Beverages Tobacco %*	*Textile Appare Leather products %*	*Petroleum, Rubbe, Plastic products %*	*Non-Metallic Mineral products products %*	*Metal products Machinery, Transport equipment %*
1979	0	97	3	0	0
1980	0	96	4	0	0
1981	1	82	4	0	2
1982	1	79	5	0	1
1983	2	79	4	0	2
1984	3	82	4	0	2
1985	0	80	4	3	1
1986	1	81	5	4	1
1987	2	79	4	4	2
1988	2	73	4	7	4
1989	3	74	3	6	5
1990	5	67	3	10	4
1991	6	66	5	8	3

(*Contd.*)

(*Contd.*)

Year	Food. Beverages Tobacco %	Textile Appare Leather products %	Petroleum, Rubbe, Plastic products %	Non-Metallic Mineral products products %	Metal products Machinery, Transport equipment %
1992	4	62	5	7	2
1993	4	74	5	4	0
1994	3	69	9	5	0
1995	3	65	11	5	1
1996	4	61	11	5	1
1997	4	63	11	4	1
1998	5	63	11	3	2
1999	4	63	11	4	1

Source: Annual reports, The Central Bank of Sri Lanka.

Table 6A1.2 Share of Product Categories in Total Exports of Domestic Firms

Year	Food. Beverages Tobacco %	Textile Appare Leather products %	Petroleum, Rubbe, Plastic products %	Non-Metallic Mineral products products %	Metal products Machinery, Transport equipment %
1	2	3	4	5	6
1979	12	20	62	3	1
1980	7	19	69	3	2
1981	7	34	55	2	1
1982	9	33	52	2	2
1983	8	44	41	2	2
1984	6	52	37	2	1
1985	5	47	41	1	3
1986	5	53	31	6	2
1987	5	56	25	9	2

Contd.

1	*2*	*3*	*4*	*5*	*6*
1988	6	56	24	10	1
1989	4	53	21	18	0
1990	2	56	22	10	6
1991	1	66	15	7	6
1992	1	66	12	8	5
1993	1	44	16	17	10
1994	3	53	8	12	11
1995	2	63	6	10	13
1996	1	65	6	9	16
1997	0	72	4	6	16
1998	0	78	0	7	11
1999	0	73	0	8	16

Source: Annual reports, The Central Bank of Sri Lanka.

Appendix II

Regression 3A2.1 Growth Rate Of Per Capita Real Income (GNPD:1952=100) 1957-77

Summary Outpur

Regression Statistics	
Multiple R	0.98
R Square	0.97
Adjusted R Square	0.97
Standard Error	0.01
Observations	19

ANOVA

	df	*SS*	*MS*	*F*	*Significance F*
Regression	1	0.069	0.069	525.047	0.000
Residual	17	0.002	0.000		
Total	18	0.071296 6			

Coeffici-	*Standar ents*	*t Stat d Error*	*P-value*	*Lower*	*Upper 95 %*	*95 %*
Intercept	2.864	0.033	87.403	0.000	2.795	2.933
X Variable1	0.011	0.000	22.914	0.000	0.010	0.012

Source : Semi-log Regression based on data in Economic Progress of Independent SRI LANKA, Central bank of Sri Lanka, 1998.

Regression 3A2.2 Growth Rate of Per Capita Real Income (GNPD: 1982=100) 1977-97

SUMMARY OUTPUT

Regression Statistics	
Multiple R	0.98
R Square	0.95
Adjusted R Square	0.95
Standard Error	0.03
Observations	22

ANOVA

	df	*SS*	*MS*	*F*	*Significance F*
Regression	1	2.93E-01	2.93E-01	4.09E+02	8.76E-15
Residual	20	1.43E-02	7.16E-04		
Total	21	3.07E-01			

	Coefficients	*Standard Error*	*t Stat*	*P-value*	*Lower 95 %*	*Upper 95 %*
Intercept	1.51	0.08	19.75	0.00	1.35	1.66
X Variable 1	0.02	0.00	20.22	0.00	0.02	0.02

Source: Semi-log Regression based on data in Economic Progress of Independent Sri Lanka, Central bank of Sri Lanka, 1998.

Regression 3A2.3 Growth Rate of Per Capita Real Income (GNPD): 1982=100) 1990-99

Summary Outpur

Regression Statistics	
Multiple R	1.00
R Square	0.99
Adjusted R Square	0.99
Standard Error	0.00
Observations	11

ANOVA

	df	SS	MS	F	Significance F
Regression	1	0.031	0.031	1703.180	0.000
Residual	9	0.000	0.000		
Total	10	0.031			

	Coefficients	Standard Error	t Stat	P-value	Lower 95 %	Upper 95 %
Intercept	1.61	0.04	41.99	0.00	1.53	1.70
X Variable 1	0.02	0.00	41.27	0.00	0.02	0.02

Source : Semi-log Regression based on data in Economic Progress of Independent Sri Lanka, Central bank of Sri Lanka, 1998.

Regression 4A2.1 Model of Fixed Asset Determination in Manufacturing

Summary Outpur

Regression Statistics	
Multiple R	0.915
R Square	0.838
Adjusted R Square	0.818
Standard Error	23.106
Observations	29

ANOVA

	df	SS	MS	F	Significance F
Regression	3	68965.28	22988.426	43.059	0.000
Residual	25	13346.94	533.877		
Total	28	82312.21			

	Coefficients	Standard Error	t Stat	P-value	Lower 95 %	Upper 95 %
Intercept	22.811	7.678	2.971	0.006	6.998	38.624
X Variable 1	0.886	0.089	9.907	0.000	0.702	1.070
X Variable 2	0.281	0.053	5.294	0.000	0.172	0.390
X Variable 3	-27.308	9.022	-3.027	0.006	-45.888	-8.728

Source : Based on Author's Database.

Regression 4A2.2 Relations between Fixed and Other Assets (1956 – 1977)

(log Functional results)

SUMMARY OUTPUT

Regression Statistics	
Multiple R	0.553
R Square	0.306
Adjusted R Square	0.263
Standard Error	0.196
Observations	18

ANOVA

	df	*SS*	*MS*	*F*	*Significance F*	
Regression	1	0.27	0.273	7.069	0.017	
Residual	16	0.61	0.038			
Total	17	0.89				
	Coefficients	*Standard Error*	*t Stat*	*P-value*	*Lower 95 %*	*Upper 95 %*
Intercept	10.76	1.066	10.096	2.41	8.505	13.02
X Variable 1	-0.407	0.153	-2.65	0.017	-0.73	-0.08

Source : Author's Database.

Regression 4A3.3 Rate of Growth of Investment in All Sectors of the Economy

SUMMARY OUTPUT

Regression Statistics	
Multiple R	0.88
R Square	0.77
Adjusted R Square	0.76
Standard	0.13

Contd.

Error						
Observations						42

ANOVA

	df	*SS*	*MS*	*F*	*Significance F*
Regression	1	2.28	2.28	134.38	0.00
Residual	40	0.68	0.02		
Total	41	2.96			

	Coefficients	*Standard Error*	*t Stat*	*P-value*	*Lower 95 %*	*Upper 95 %*
Intercept	-2.24	0.13	-17.64	0.00	-2.49	-1.98
X Variable 1	0.02	0.00	11.59	0.00	0.02	0.02

Source : Author's Database.

Regression 4A2. 4 Rate of Growth of Internal Savings (1957-77)

SUMMARY OUTPUT

Regression Statistics	
Multiple R	0.88
R Square	0.77
Adjusted R Square	0.76
Standard Error	0.14
Observations	22

ANOVA

	df	*SS*	*MS*	*F*	*Significance F*
Regression	1	1.26	1.26	67.81	0.00
Residual	20	0.37	0.02		
Total	21	1.63			

	Coefficients	*Standard Error*	*t Stat*	*P-value*	*Lower 95 %*	*Upper 95 %*
Intercept	5.11	0.31	16.70	0.00	4.47	5.74
X Variable 1	0.04	0.00	8.23	0.00	0.03	0.05

Source : Author's Database.

Regression 4A.2.5 Rate Of Growth Of Private Equity Capital In Manufacturing (1957 –77)

SUMMARY OUTPUT

Regression Statistics	
Multiple R	0.73
R Square	0.53
Adjusted R Square	0.51
Standard Error	0.06
Observations	22

ANOVA

	df	*SS*	*MS*	*F*	*Significance F*
Regression	1	0.08	0.08	22.76	0.00
Residual	20	0.07	0.00		
Total	21	0.16			

	Coefficients	*Standard Error*	*t Stat*	*P-value*	*Lower 95 %*	*Upper 95 %*
Intercept	7.303	0.137	53.386	0.000	7.017	7.588
X Variable 1	0.010	0.002	4.770	0.000	0.005	0.014

Source : Author's Database.

Regression 4A2.6 Rate of Growth of Loan Capital in Manufacturing (1957 –77)

SUMMARY OUTPUT

Regression Statistics	
Multiple R	0.88
R Square	0.77
Adjusted R Square	0.76
Standard Error	0.13
Observations	22

ANOVA

	df	*SS*	*MS*	*F*	*Significance F*	
Regression	1	1.11	1.11	67.58	0.00000	
Residual	20	0.33	0.02			
Total	21	1.44				
	Coefficients	*Standard Error*	*t Stat*	*P-value*	*Lower 95 %*	*Upper 95 %*
Intercept	5.91	0.29	20.50	0.00	5.31	6.51
X Variable 1	0.04	0.00	8.22	0.00	0.03	0.04

Source : Author's Database.

Regression 4A2.6 Rate of Growth of Loan Capital in Manufacturing (1978 –94)

SUMMARY OUTPUT

Regression Statistics	
Multiple R	0.34
R Square	0.12
Adjusted R Square	0.05
Standard Error	5.10
Observations	16

ANOVA

	df	*SS*	*MS*	*F*	*Significance F*	
Regression	1	48.67	48.67	1.87	0.19	
Residual	14	364.28	26.02			
Total	15	412.94				
	Coefficients	*Standard Error*	*t Stat*	*P-value*	*Lower 95 %*	*Upper 95 %*
Intercept	35.25	23.69	1.49	0.16	-15.55	86.05
X Variable 1	0.38	0.28	1.37	0.19	-0.21	0.97

Source: Author's Database.

Regression 5A2. 1 Growth under Good Business Environment (1953 –76)

SUMMARY OUTPUT

Regression Statistics	
Multiple R	0.916
R Square	0.838
Adjusted R Square	0.830
Standard Error	0.100
Observations	21

ANOVA

	df	*SS*	*MS*	*F*	*Significance F*	
Regression	1	0.98	0.98	98.59	5.90E-09	
Residual	19	0.19	0.01			
Total	20	1.17				
	Coefficients	*Standard Error*	*t Stat*	*P-value*	*Lower 95 %*	*Upper 95 %*
Intercept	-4.39	0.23	-19.32	0.00	-4.87	-3.91
X Variable 1	0.04	0.00	9.93	0.00	0.03	0.04

Source : Author's Database.

Regression 5A2.2 Growth of Fixed Assets under Good Business Environment (1953 -76)

SUMMARY OUTPUT

Regression Statistics	
Multiple R	0.92
R Square	0.84
Adjusted R Square	0.84
Standard Error	0.10
Observations	21

ANOVA

	df	SS	MS	F	Significance F
Regression	1	1.022	1.022	102.932	0.000
Residual	19	0.189	0.010		
Total	20	1.210			

	Coeffici-ents	Standar d Error	t Stat	P-value	Lower 95 %	Upper 95 %
Intercept	-4.45	0.23	-19.56	0.00	-4.92	-3.97
X Variable 1	0.04	0.00	10.15	0.00	0.03	0.04

Source : Author's Database.

Regression 5A2.3. Growth Prospects of Fixed Investment under Tax Incentives (1953 –76) (Semi-log function)

SUMMARY OUTPUT

Regression Statistics	
Multiple R	0.97
R Square	0.95
Adjusted R Square	0.95
Standard Error	0.04
Observations	21

ANOVA

	df	SS	MS	F	Significance F
Regression	1	0.5991	0.5991	362.6847	0.0000
Residual	19	0.0314	0.0017		
Total	20	0.6305			

	Coeffici-ents	Standar d Error	t Stat	P-value	Lower 95 %	Upper 95 %
Intercept	-4.21	0.10	-42.14	0.00	-4.42	-4.00
X Variable 1	0.03	0.00	19.04	0.00	0.02	0.03

Source : Author's Database.

Regretion 5A2 .4. Growth Prospects of Investment in a Poor Business Environment (1956 –77) (Semi-log function)

SUMMARY OUTPUT

Regression Statistics	
Multiple R	0.95
R Square	0.91
Adjusted R Square	0.90
Standard Error	0.05
Observations	21

ANOVA

	df	*SS*	*MS*	*F*	*Significance F*
Regression	1	0.400	0.400	182.504	0.000
Residual	19	0.042	0.002		
Total	20	0.442			

	Coefficients	*Standard Error*	*t Stat*	*P-value*	*Lower 95 %*	*Upper 95 %*
Intercept	-3.54	0.11	-31.21	0.00	-3.78	-3.31
X Variable 1	0.02	0.00	13.51	0.00	0.02	0.03

Source : Author's Database.

Regression 7A2 .1. Potential Long Run Rate of Growth of Industrial Investment under Better Investment Environment (1952 –97)

SUMMARY OUTPUT

Regression Statistics	
Multiple R	0.911
R Square	0.831
Adjusted R Square	0.827
Standard Error	0.138
Observations	45

ANOVA

	df	*SS*	*MS*	*F*	*Significance F*
Regression	1	4.028	4.028	211.085	0.000
Residual	43	0.821	0.019		
Total	44	4.849			

	Coefficients	*Standard Error*	*t Stat*	*P-value*	*Lower 95 %*	*Upper 95 %*
Intercept	-3.303	0.121	-27.368	0.000	-3.546	-3.060
X Variable 1	0.023	0.002	14.529	0.000	0.020	0.026

Source : Author's Database.

Regression 7A2.2 Growth of Private Industrial Fixed Investment (1977-83) (Semi-log function)

SUMMARY OUTPUT

Regression Statistics	
Multiple R	0.930
R Square	0.865
Adjusted R Square	0.842
Standard Error	0.037
Observations	8

ANOVA

	df	*SS*	*MS*	*F*	*Significance F*
Regression	1	0.0539	0.0539	38.3540	0.0008
Residual	6	0.0084	0.0014		
Total	7	0.0623			

	Coefficients	*Standard Error*	*t Stat*	*P-value*	*Lower 95 %*	*Upper 95 %*
Intercept	-4.862	0.466	-10.438	0.000	-6.002	-3.722
X Variable 1	0.036	0.006	6.193	0.001	0.022	0.050

Source : Author's Database.

Bibliography

In addition to the major three types of references which are given below, the following non-official periodicals were also used, especially, for the Period after 1977.

Island, August 04, 1996

The Sunday Times Business, p.4, November 19, 1995

The Business pages of The Sunday times Oct. 15, 2000.

Business, The Sunday TIMES, Vol. 07, No. 82, Sunday, January 28, 2001.

The Sunday Observer, July 03, 1994.

1. Sri Lanka – Official Publications

Ceylon Sessional Papers (1911), Ceylon Government Press.

Ceylon Sessional Papers (1916), Ceylon Government Press.

Ceylon Sessional Papers, VI, (1921), Ceylon Government Press.

Ceylon Sessional Papers (1922), Ceylon Government Press.

Ceylon Sessional Papers (1953), Ceylon Government Press.

Ceylon Sessional Papers (1955), XV –XXV, Ceylon Government Press.

Ceylon Sessional Papers (1955), Report of the Taxation Commission, XVII, Ceylon Government Press.

Sessional Papers (1974), "Report of the Commission of Inquiry on Agency Houses and Brokering Firms", XII.

The Ceylon Blue Books (1900), Government Printer.

The Ceylon Blue Books (1901), Government Printer.

The Ceylon Blue Books (1925), Government Printer.

The Ceylon Blue Books (1938), Government Printer.

Ceylon Yearbook (1948), Ceylon Government Press.

The Ceylon *Hansard* (1926), Vol. 2, The Report of the Proceedings of Parliament, The National State Assembly.

The Ceylon *Hansard* (1932), Parliamentary Debates, The Ceylon Government Press. The Ceylon Hansard (1939), Parliamentary Debates, The Ceylon Government Press.

The Ceylon Hansard (1944), Parliamentary Debates, The Ceylon Government Press.

The Ceylon Hansard (1948), Parliamentary Debates, The Ceylon Government Press.

The Ceylon Hansard (1952 -53), Parliamentary Debates, The Ceylon Government Press.

The Ceylon Hansard (1953-54), 16 Parliamentary Debates, The Ceylon Government Press.

The Ceylon Hansard (1956-57), 24, Parliamentary Debates, The Ceylon Government Press.

The Ceylon Hansard (1957), Parliamentary Debates, The Ceylon Government Press.

The Ceylon Hanzard (1962), 29., Parliamentary Debates, The Ceylon Government Press.

National State Assembly Debates (1977), Official Report.

The Budget Speech, 1952 –53, Government of Sri Lanka, Government Press.

The Budget Speech, 1954 –55, Government of Sri Lanka, Government Press.

The Budget Speech, 1955 –56, Government of Sri Lanka, Government Press.

The Budget Speech, 1957: 28, Government of Sri Lanka, Government Press.

The Bulletin (1955), The Central Bank of Ceylon, 5, The Government Printer.

The Annual Reports, 1960 -68, Central Bank of Ceylon.

The Annual Report (1995), Central Bank of Sri Lanka.

Department of Economic Research (1970), *Survey of Private Investment*, Central Bank of Ceylon, Colombo.

Central Bank of Sri Lanka (1992), *Sri Lanka, An Economic, Financial and Investment Guide.*

Economic Progress of Independent Sri Lanka (1998), The Central Bank of Sri Lanka.

Survey of Private Investment, Department of Economic Research, Central Bank of Ceylon (1970).

Report on the Survey of Business Activities and Planned Investment in Sri Lanka, 1982/83 to 1985/86, Central Bank of Ceylon, Colombo.

Ministry of Finance (1951), *Economic and Social Development of Ceylon*, 1926 –1950 (A Survey).

Ministry of Finance and Planning (1986), *Facets of Development in Independent Sri Lanka.*

Ministry of Finance and Planning (1987), *10 Year Performance 1978 – 1987, 15 selected Manufacturing Corporation*, Public enterprises Division, General Tresury, 15th Sept.

Sri Lanka Census of Population (1963), All Island Tables, Department of Census and Statistics.

The White Paper on 'Government Policy on Private Investment', 1960.

Department of Census and Statistics, 1901, Census of Ceylon, 1901.

Department of Census and Statistics, 1911, Census of Ceylon, 1911

Department of Census and Statistics, 1921, Census of Ceylon, 1921.

Department of Census and Statistics, 1946, Census of Ceylon, 1946.

Economic and Social Development of Ceylon, 1926 -1950, (a Survey).

The Banking Commission (1935).

Report of the Presidential Tariff Commission (1985), Colombo.

2. General

The United Nations (1976), Country Monograph series No.4, Economic and Social Commission for Asia and Pacific.

India Quarterly, A Journal of International Affairs, Indian Council of World Affairs, (1980), XXXVI (2).

Ferguson's Ceylon Directory (1875), The Ceylon Observer Press, Colombo.

Ferguson's Ceylon Directory (1935), The Ceylon Observer Press, Colombo.

Ferguson's Ceylon Directory (1938), The Ceylon Observer Press, Colombo.

Ferguson's Ceylon Directory (1941), The Ceylon Observer Press, Colombo.

Ferguson's Ceylon Directory (1944), The Ceylon Observer Press, Colombo.

Ferguson's Ceylon Directory (1946), The Ceylon Observer Press, Colombo.

Ferguson's Ceylon Directory (1947), The Ceylon Observer Press, Colombo.

Ferguson's Ceylon Directory (1950), The Ceylon Observer Press, Colombo.

Handbooks of Listed (Quoted) Companies, Colombo Stock Exchange, from 1942 to 1999.

OECD (1969), "Report on the Investment Climate in Ceylon".

Lanka Guardian (1983,1984, 1985, 1987, 1989, 1993), Lanka Guardian Publishing Co.

Colombo Stock Exchange (2000), Fact Book.

The Ceylon Economists (1954, 1957,1958, 1959, 1961, 1962).

The Ceylon National Congress (1919).

3. Sri Lanka – Non- Official Publications

Abeyratna, Sirimal (1993), *Anti-Export Bias in the 'Export-Oriented' Economy of Sri Lanka, VU* University Press, Amsterdam.

Abeyratna, Sirimal (1997), "Trade Strategy and Industrialisation" in W. D. Lakshman (ed.) *Dilemmas of Development, Fifty Years of Economic Change in Sri Lanka*. Colombo: Sri Lanka Association of Economists: 341-383.

Abeyratne Sirimal (1996), "The Role of the State in `Developing' Economies", *Upanathi*: The Journal of the Sri Lanka Association of Economists, 7 (1&2):1-21.

Abeyratne, Sirimal (1989), "Industrialisation in the NICs and in Sri Lanka: Why the NICs Succeeded and Sri Lanka failed?", *Upanathi*: The Journal of the Sri Lanka Association of Economists, Colombo, 4(1&2): 45-72.

Abeyratne. Sirimal (1992), *Anti-Export Bias in the Export-Oriented Economy of Sri Lanka*, Institute of Social Studies, The Hague, Netherlands.

Abramovitz, Moses (1986), "Catching Up, Forging Ahead, and Falling Behind", *Journal of Economic History,* 46 (2, June): 385-406.

Adelman Irma (1975), "Development Economics- A reassessment of Goals", *development Economics,* (2) 302-309.

Adelman Irma (2001), "Fallacies in Development Theory and Their Implications for Policy" in Meier M. Gerald and Stiglitz Joseph E (2001), (eds.), *Frontiers of Development Economics,* The World Bank and Oxford University Press, new York: 103-130.

Agarwala, A.N and Singh S.P (Eds.) (1963), *The Economics of Underdevelopment*, New York, Oxford University Press.

Akira Suehiro (1989), *Capital Accumulation in Thailand, 1855-*

1985, The Centre for East Asian Cultural Studies.

Alailama Patricia and Sanderatne Nimal (1997), "Social Policies in a Slowly Growing Economy: Sri Lanka" in Mehrotra Santosh and Jolly Richard (eds.), *Development with Human Face; Experiences in Social achievement and Economic Growth*, Oxford, Clavendon Press: 235-263.

Amarasinghe Ranjith Y (1998), *Revolutionary Idealism and Parliamentary Politics: A Study of Trotskyism in Sri Lanka,* Social Scientists's Association, Colombo, Sri Lanka.

Amsden A.H (1990), "Third World Industrialisation: "Global Fordism" or a New Model?", *New Left Review*, (182):5-32.

Amsden A.H. (1989), *Asia's New Giant: South Korea and Late industrialization*, New York, Oxford University Press.

Amunugama Sarath (1994), "Bandaranaike and the the *Sihala Maha Sabha"* , Part Two, Review of Books, The Sunday Observer, July 03, 1994.

Arnold Wright (ed.) (1907), *Twentieth Century Impressions of Ceylon, Its History, People, Commece, Industry and Resources*, Lloyd's Greater Britain Public Co.

Atapattu, Danny (1997), "Capital Formation and Its Financing" in W. D. Lakshman (ed.) *Dilemmas of Development, Fifty Years of Economic Change in Sri Lanka",* Sri Lanka Association of Economists: 55-96.

Athukorala Premachandra (1984), "Direct Foreign Investment and Manufactured Export Expansion: The case of Sri Lanka", *Vidyodaya Journal*, 12 (Silver Jubilee issue): 21-41.

Athukorala Premachandra (1986), "The Impact of 1977 Reforms on Domestic Industry", *Upanathi*, Special Issue on "Adjustment with a Human Face" 1(1): 69-105.

Athukorala Prema-chandra (1987), "Foreign Direct Investment and Manufacturing for Export" in (ed.) W .D. Lakshman, Dilemmas of *Development*, fifty Years of economic Change in Sri Lanka, Sri Lanka Association of Economists: 386-421.

Athukorala Premachandra (1987), "Industrialisation: Its Policies and Achievements", in Dunham David and Abeysekera Charles (eds.), *Essays on the Sri Lankan Economy 1977-83*, Social Scientist's Association, Colombo.

Athukorala Premachandra and Rajapathirana Sarath (2000), *Liberalisation and Industrial Transformation, Sri Lanka in International Perspective*, New Delhi, Oxford University Press.

Athukorala Premachandra and Rajapatirana Sarath (1998),

"Economic Liberalization and Industrial Transformation in Sri Lanka", Paper presented at the conference on *Independent Sri Lanka: Economic Developments 1948-1998 and Prospects,* Central Bank if Sri Lannka, Colombo, 23-24.

Athukorala, Premachandra (1989), 'Export-Oriented Foreign Investment in New Exporting Countries: Patterns and Determinants with Evidence from Sri Lanka', *World Competition*, 13:63-81.

Athukorala, Premachandra (1995), "Foreign Direct Investment and Manufacturing for Export in a New Exporting Country: The Case of Sri Lanka", *The World Economy,* 18 (4), 543-64.

Athukorala, Premachandra and Sisira Jayasuriya (1994), *Macroeconomic Policies, Crises and Growth in Sri Lanka, 1969-90,* Washington D.C, World Bank.

Athukorala. Premachandra (1997), *Labour Productivity in the Manufacturing sector in Sri Lanka*, Colombo, Department of National Planning.

Athukorala. Premachandra and Jayatilaka S. Bandara (1989), "Growth of Manufactured Exports, Primary Commodity Dependence and Net Export earnings: Sri Lanka", *World Development*, 17(6): 897-904.

Bagchi, Amiya Kumar (1987), "The Characteristics of Industrial Process" Eatwell John, Milgate Murray and Newman Peter (eds.) *The New Palgrave A Dictionary of Economics*, E to J series :819-829.

Balakrishnan, N (1977), "Industrial Policy and Development Since Independence" in K. M. de Silva (ed.), *Sri Lanka, A Survey*, C. Hust and Company:192-212.

Balogh .T (1966), "Economic Policy and the Price System", Chapter I, *The Economics of Poverty*, Weidenfeld and Nicolson.

Bardhan, Pranab (1984), *The Political Economy of Development in India*, Basil Blackwell, Oxford.

Bardhan, Pranab (1989), "Alternative Approaches to Development Economics", Chenery, Hollis and Srinivasan T.N, (eds.) *Handbook of Development Economics* I, Elservier B.V:39-68.

Bardhan, Pranab (1993), "Economic of Development and the Development of Economics", *Journal of Economic perspectives*, 7(2): 129-42.

Basu Gautam Kumar (1991), *The State, Development and Military Intervention,* South Asian Publishers Pvt. Ltd.

Basu Kaushik and Pulin Nayak (ed.) (1992), *Development Policy and Economic Development*, Oxford University Press.

Behrman Jera and Srinivasan T.N (eds.)(1995), *Handbook of Development Economics,* Vol. 3A, Elservier Science B.V.

Bell Stephen, 1995, "The Politics of Economic Adjustment: Explaining the Transformation of Industry-State Relations in Australia", *Political Studies*, XLIII, 22-47.

Bell, Clive (1987), "Developing Economics", Eatwell John, Migate Murrey; Newman Peter, (eds.) *The New Palgrave, A Dictionary of Economics*, The Macmillan Press ltd.:818-825.

Bert G. Hickman (1959), "Diffusion, Acceleration, and Business Cycles", American Economic Review, XLIX (4, September): 535-565.

Bhambhri, C. P (1989), "The Indian State: Conflicts and Contradictions" in Hasan Zoya, Jha S. N and Khan Rasheeduddin (eds.) *The State, Political Processes and Identity, Reflection on Modern India*: 73-87.

Bhargava, Pradeep (1987), *Political economy of Sri Lanka,* Navrang, New Delhi.

Birch Anthony H. (1993), *The Concepts and Theories of Modern Democracy, London, Routledge*.

Bischoff C.W (1971), "A Comparison of Models", Brookings *Papers on Economic Activity* 1.

Bischoff Charles.W, 1971, "Business Investment in the 1970s: A comparison of Models", Brookings Papers on Economic Activity,1: 13 –63.

Boyer, Robert (1996), "State and Market; A new engagement for the twenty-first century?" in Robert Boyer and Daniel Drache (eds.) *State against Market; The limits of globalization*: 84-114.

Branson William H (1972), *Macroeconomic Theory and Policy*, Harper & Row, Publishers, New York.

Carl Iverson (1956), "The Role of the Central Bank in the Ceylon Economy", Bulletin, Central Bank of Ceylon, 6(1): 8-11.

Cass Alain (1984), "IMF & Political Stability", *Lanka Guardian,* 7(5), July.

Chakravarty Sukhamoy (1992), "Development Economics and Indian Experience" in Basu Kaushik and Nayar Pulin (eds.) *Development Policy and Economic Theory,* New Delhi,Oxford University Press: 1-13 .

Chandrasekhar S.S (1946), *India's Population: Fact and Policy*, Asia Press.

Charles P. Kindleberger and Bruce Herrick (1977), *Economic Development*, -Hill Book Company.

Chaudhuri. R (1939), *The Evolution of Indian Industry*, University of Calcutta.

Chenery, Hollis. B (1975), "The Structuralist Approach to Development Policy", *The American Economic Review*, LXV(2):310-316.

Clark, Cal and Steve, Chan (1996), "MNCs and Developmentalism: Domestic Structures as an Explanation for East Asian Dynamism" in Steve Chan (ed.), *Foreign Direct Investment in a Changing Global Political Economy'*, London, Macmillan Press Ltd:84-103.

Clark, John J (1963), *Business Fluctuations, Growth, and Economic Stabilization: a reader*, (ed) John J. Clark and Morris Cohen, Random House, Inc.

Colclough, Christopher (1991), "Structuralism versus Neo-liberalism: An Introduction", Institute of Development Studies.

Colclough, Christopher (1993), *States or Markets? Neo-liberalism and the Development Policy Debate*, Colclough, Christopher and Manor, James, (eds.) Oxford, Clarendon press.

Collignon, Stefan, Jean Pisani-Ferry, and Yung Chul Park (1999). *Exchange Rate Regimes in Emerging Asian Countries.* New York: Routledge.

Corbridge Stuart (ed.), (1995), *Development Studies,* Oxford University Press Inc.

Corden W. M (1977), *Inflation Exchange Rates and the World Economy: Lecture on International Monetary Economics,* Oxford, Clarendon Press.

Corden W.M., (1980), "Trade Policies" in John Cody, Helen Hughes and Davis Wall (eds.), *Policies for Industrial Progress in developing countries,* Oxford University Press: 39-90.

Corea Gamani (1975), *The Instability of an Export Economy*, Marga Institute, Colombo.

Corea, Gamani (1998), "Relevance of Development Models of One Region for Another", Ghoshal, Baladas (ed.) *ASEAN and South Asia*, New Delhi, Sterling Publishers (P) ltd.

Corea, Gamani (1999), "Globalisation and its Implications for the Third World", A.D. V. de S. Indraratna (ed.) *Globalisation and South Asia: Retrospect and Prospect"*, Sri Lanka Association for the Advancement of Science: 27-36.

Cowen M. P and Shenton R .W (1996), *Doctrines of Development*, Routledge.

Cuthbertson, A. G and Khan M.Z (1981), *Effective Protection to Manufacturing Industries in Sri Lanka*, Ministry of Finance and Planning.

Dahanayake, P.A.S (1979), *Economic Policies and their Implications for the Foreign Exchange Resources Availability on Sri Lanka*, Central Bank of Ceylon.

Dan Usher (1980), *The Measurement of Economic Growth,* Basil Blackwell Publisher

De Silva Colvin R, 1975, "Sri Lanka in the Worsening World Economic Crisis", No.1, *STATE*.

De Silva K.M & Wriggins Howard (1994), *J.R.Jayewardene of Sri Lanka: A Political Biography, From 1956 to His Retirement (1989)*, vol. two.

De Silva K.M (1981), *A History of Sri Lanka,* New Delhi, Oxford University Press.

De Silva Mervyn (1989), "The Army –A new Actor", *Lanka Guardian,* 12(9, Sept) 4-5.

De Silva, S.B.D (1982), *The Political Economy of Underdevelopment*, London: Routledge & Kegan Paul.

Dissanayaka T.D.S.A (2000), *The Politics of Sri Lanka – The General Election -2000*, Vol. (V), Swastika (Private) ltd.

Dissanayaka T.D.S.A.(1994), *The Politics of Sri Lanka*, Vol. II, Swastika (Private) ltd.

Duncan, Ian (1995), "The Politics of Liberalisation in Early Post-Independence India: Deregulation in 1947", *The Journal of Commonwealth and Comparative Politics,* 33(1): 25-45.

Dunham david and Kelegama Saman (1998), "Stabilisation and Adjustment: Sri Lankan experience, 1977 –1993", *Economic and Political Weekly*, June 13.

Dunham David and Kelegama Saman (1997), "Does Leadership matter in the economic Reform Process? Liberation and Governance in Sri Lanka 1989-93", World Development, 25(2): 179-190.

Eccleshall Robert, Geoghegan Vincent, Jay Richard, Kenney Michael, Mackenzie Lain and Wilford Rick (1994), *Political Ideologies*.

Edwards C. (1993), *Industrial Policy Issues for Sri Lanka*, Industrialisation Series No.3, Institute of Policy Studies, Colombo.

Ees Hans Van, Kuper Gerald H and Elmer Sterken (1997), "Investment, finance and the Business Cycle: Evidence from the Dutch Manufacturing Sector, *Cambridge Journal of Economics*, 21:395-407.

Erich A. Helfert (1972), *Techniques of Financial Analysis*, Third edition, Richard D. Irwin INC.

Evans Peter, 1979, *Dependent Development: The Alliance of Multinational, State, and Local Capital in Brazil*, Princeton University Press.

Fei, J.C.H, and G. Ranis (1964), *Development of the Labour Surplus Economy*, Illinois: Richard D .Irwin, Inc.

Fernando Lloyd (1997), "Development Planning in Sri Lanka" in Lakshman (ed.), *Dilemmas of Development Fifty Years of Economic Change in Sri Lanka,* Sri Lanka Association of Economists, Colombo: 101-124.

Fernando M (1961), "The S.L.F.P - Capitalist or Socialist", *Ceylon Economist*, 5 (2): 165-174.

FitzGerald E.V.K, (1988), "State Accumulation and Market Equilibria: An Application of Kalecki – Kornai Analysis to Planned Economies in the third World", *Journal of Development Studies*, 24 (4), 50-75.

Fujita. N and James W.E (1989), "Export Promotion and the "Heavy industrialisation" of Korea 1973-83', *The Developing Economies*, XXVII (3) September.

Geoffred N. Walton (1987), *A review of Effective Protection and Comparative Advantage in the Manufacturing Sector of Sri Lanka*, Ministry of Finance and Planning, Colombo, 1987.

Gerschenkron Alexander (1962), *Economic Backwardness in Historical Perspective,* Cambridge, Massachusetts: Harvard University Press.

Ghosh Biswanath (1974), *The Changing Profile of India's Industrial economy*, The World Press Private ltd.

Ghosh Buddhadeb and Neogi Chiranjib (1996), "Liberalisation in India: Quality Differentials Between Public and Private Employees", *The Developing economies*, XXXIV (1): 61-79.

Ghoshal Baladas (ed.) 1998, *ASEAN and South Asia: A Development Experience*, Sterling Publishers (PVT.) ltd., New Delhi.

Goonetileke H (1998), "Counting the Costs of a Weary War", Kumar Rupesinghe (ed.) *Negotiating Peace in Sri Lanka: Efforts, Failures & Lessons*, International Alert of London, UK.

Goto Kazumi (1997), "Beyond the 'Structural Adjustment' and the 'East Asian Miracle' –Development Management Re-examined- ", OECF Journal of Development Assistance, 2(2):1-21.

Grobar Lisa M and Gnanaselvam S (2001), "Economic Effects of the Sri Lankan Civil War, *Pravada,* 7(7):395-405.

Grabowski, Richard (1998), "States Entangled in Markets: the process of Economic Development", *The Journal of Developing Areas*, 33:99-120.

Griffin, Keith. B and Enos, John. L (1970), *Planning of Development*, Addison-Wesley Publishing Company, Inc.

Guhu K.D (1935), "Industrial Problems of Ceylon", T*he Ceylon Economic Journal,* VII: 27-36.

Guimaraes J. P. C (1991), *Industrialisation in Sri Lanka: What can we learn from NIC?*, Institute of Policy Studies, Colombo.

Gunasinghe Newton (1990), "Capitalist Development in Sri Lanka – A Periodisation", *Economic Review*, Peoples' Bank, 16 (8): 3-4,17.

Gunatilake, Godfry (1999), "Development Policy Regimes"in Lakshman W.D and Tisdell C.A (1999) (eds.), *Facets of Development of Sri Lanka: socio-political, Economic, Scientific and Culture,* The University of Queens land: 177-209.

Gunatilleke Godfrey, Tiruchelvam Neelan and Coomaraswamy Radhika (1983), *Ethical Dilemmas of Development in Asia*, D.C Heath and Company.

Gupta Das (1952), "the Problem of Economic Development", *Bulletin*, Central Bank of Ceylon, 2(10): 12-16.

Gupta Das (1955), "The Economic Situation in 1954", at 11th Session of the ECAFE held in Tokyo, Bulletin, Central Bank of Ceylon, 5(5): 10-11.

Haavelmo T (1954), *A Study in the Theory of Economic Evolution,* Amsterdam, North-Holland Publishing Co.

Haggard Stephan. M (1998), "Business, Politics and Policy in East and Southeast Asia" in Rowen Henry S (ed.), *Behind East Asian Growth,* Salzbury Seminar, Routledge:78-104.

Haggard, Stephan and Kaufman Robert. R (eds.), (1992), *The Politics of Economic Adjustment: International Constraints, Distributional Conflict, and the State*, Princeton University Press, Princeton.

Hans Van Ees, Gerald H. Kuper and Elmer Sterken (1997), "Investment, Finance and the business cycle: evidence from the Dutch manufacturing sector", *Cambridge Journal of Economics,* 21:395-407.

Harberger, Arnold C (1998), "Policymaking and Economic Policy in Small Developing Countries" in Dornbusch Rudiger and Helmers Leslie C.H (eds.), *The Open Economy tools for Policy Makers in Developing Countries*, International Bank for Reconstruction and Development:249-306.

Harriss, John (1998), "Development and Significance of NIE" *in* Harriss, John, Hunter, Janet and Lewis Colin M (eds.), *The New Institutional Economics and the Third World Development*, London,Rautledge.

Harrod R (1948), *Towards a dynamic Economics,* London, Macmillan Press.

Hart-Lands berg, Martin (1993), *The Rush to Development: Economic change and Political struggle in South Korea,* New York: Monthly Review Press.

Heidenreich, Regine (1998), "Economics and Institutions: The Socioeconomic approach of K. William Kapp", *Journal of economic Issues*, XXXII (4): 965-984.

Helfert, Erich. A (1972), *Techniques of Financial Analysis*, Richard D. Irwin, Inc. 3rd edition.

Henderson Scott and Peirson Graham (1984), *Issues in Financial Accounting*, Third edition, Longman Cheshire Pty Limited.

Herring R. J (1987), "Economic Liberalisation Policies in Sri Lanka", *Economic and political weekly*,XX11(8).

Hettige, Siri (1999), "Transformation of Society" in W. D. Lakshman and C.A. Tisdell, (eds.), *Facets of Development of Sri Lanka Since Independence: Socio-Political, Economic, Scientific and culture,* Brisbane, University of Queensland: 40-45.

Hewavitharana B (1986), *Industrialisation, Employment and Basic Needs: The Case of Sri Lanka, Basic Needs and Employment*, Working Paper No. 60, ILO, Geneva, 1986.

Higgins, Benjamin (1959), *Economic Development, Principles, Problems, and Policies,* revised Edition, Constable and Company limited, London.

Higgins, Janice (1972), 'Switching on to Growth', *Central bank Staff Studies*, Central Bank of Sri Lanka, Vol. 2.

Hobday Michael (1995), *Innovations in East Asia – the Challenge to Japan,* Edvar Elgar, Aldershot.

Hoselitz Bert F (1952), "Non-Economic Barriers to Economic

Development", *Economic Development and Cultural Change*, 1(1): 8-21.

Hughes, Helen (1995), "Why Have East Asian Countries Led Economic Development", *the economic Record*, 71(212): 88-104.

Jayasinghe J. C de. S and Lakshman W. D (1979), "The Market Structure" in Lakshman W.D ed. (1979), *Public enterprises in the Economic Development of Sri Lanka*, National Institute of Business Management, Colombo: 157-171.

Jayasundara P.B (1986), "Fiscal Policy in Sri Lanka Since Independence", *Facets of Development in Independent Sri Lanka*, Ministry of Finance and Planning, Sri Lanka ;43-81.

Jayasundera P.B (1998), "Fiscal Policy Direction and Adjustment Issues", Monograph, The paper presented at the Seminar on *Independent Sri Lanka: Economic Developments 1948-1998 and Prospects*, March 1998, Central Bank of Sri Lanka.

Jayasuriya Laksiri (2000), *Welfarism and Politics in Sri Lanka, Experience of a Third World* Welfare *State,* The University of Western Australia.

Jayawardena A.S (1970), "Public Sector Industrial Enterprises in Ceylon", *Research and Industry*, Industrial Development Board.

Jayawardena A.S. (1978), *Public enterprise in Sri Lanka: Investment, Pricing and Performance*, Memo.

Jayawardena Kumari (2000), *Nobodies to Somebodies; The rise of the Colonial Bourgeoisie in Sri Lanka*, Social Scientist Association and Sanjiva Books.

Jayawardena, Kumari (1972), T*he Rise of the Labour Movement in Ceylon 1880-1933,*Durham, Duke University Press.

Jenkins, S. Roberts (1995), "Theorising the Politics of Economic Adjustment: Lessons from the Indian Case", *Journal of Commonwealth Politics*, 33(1): 1-24.

Jolly, Richard (1997), "Profiles in Success: Reasons for Hopes and Priorities for Action" in Mehrotra Santosh and Jolly Richard (eds.), *Development with Human Face; Experiences in Social achievement and Economic Growth*, Oxford, Clarendon Press:3-20.

Jorgenson D.W (1962), "The Development of a dual Economy", *Economic Journal*, 71:309-331.

Jorgenson D.W and Siebert. C.D, (1968), "Optimum Capital Accumulation and Corporate Investment Behaviour", *Journal of Political Economy*, November/December.

Jorgenson D.W and Siebert. C.D, (1968), Theories of Corporate Investment Behaviour", *American Economic Review*, LXIII (4): 681-712.

Jorgenson, D.W (1971), "Econometric Studies of Investment Behaviour: A Survey", *Journal of Economic Literature*, 9 (4): 1111 –47.

Joshi, Vijay and Little I. M. D (1997), "India -Reform on Hold", *Asian Development Review, Studies of Asian and Pacific Economic Issues*, 15(2): 1-30.

Kalecki Michal, 1972, *Selected Essays on the Economic Growth of the Socialist and the Mixed Economy*, Cambridge University Press.

Kalecki, Michal (1971), *Selected Essays on the Dynamics of the Capitalist Economy 1933-1970,* Cambridge University Press.

Kalecki, Michal and Kula, Maracin (1976), Bolivia- An intermediate regime in Latin America, first published in *Economia y Administration, 1970*, re-printed in *'Essays on Developing Economies'* p.198, The Harvard University Press.

Kalra B. R (1967), "Data on Occupational Structure", Base Asish (ed.), *Pattern of Population Change in India 1955-61.*

Karunaratna N.D. (1973), Techno-Economic survey of Industrial Potential in Sri Lanka, , ist edition, Industrial Development Board, Colombo.

Karunaratna N.D (1999), "The Export engine of Growth in Post-Independence Sri Lanka" in W.D. Lakshman & O. A. Tisdell (eds.), *Facets of Development of Sri Lanka since Independence: Socio-Political, economic, Scientific and Culture*, The University of Queensland: 235-250.

Karunatilake H.N.S *(1971), Economic Development in Ceylon*, Praeger Publishers Inc.

Karunatilake H.N.S (1987, *The Economy of Sri Lanka*, CDSS, Colombo.

Karunatilake, H.N.S (1986), " Public Enterprise and the Private Sector", *Sri Lanka Economic Journal*, 1(2): 89-113.

Karunatileke, H.N.S (1970), "Recent Development of the Economy and their Impact on Ceylon's Industrialisation", *Research and Industry*, Industrial Development Board.

Katzenstein, Peter (1985), "Small Nations in an Open International Economy: The Converging Balance of State and society in Switzerland and Austria", Evans B. Peter, Rueschemeyer

Dietrich and Skocpol Theda (eds.), *Bringing the state Back In*, Cambridge University Press: 227-256.

Kearney Robert N (1971), *Trade Unions and Politics of Ceylon*, the Regents of the University of California Press.

Kearney Robert N (1979), 'Politics and Modernisation in Modern Sri Lanka, A Society in Transition', Tissa Fernando and Robert N Kearney (eds.), *South Asian Series*

Kelegama, S (1993), *Privatization in Sri Lanka: The Experience during the Early Years of Implementation*, Sri Lanka Economic Association.

Kelegama, S (1994a), " Distributional Aspects of Privatization: The case of Sri Lanka", in V.V. Ramanadham (Ed.), *Privatization and Equity*, Routledge, London.

Kelegama, S (1997), " Privatization : An Overview of the Process and Issues, in W. D. Lakshman (ed.) *Dilemmas of Development, Fifty Years of Economic Change in Sri Lanka,* Colombo: Sri Lanka Association of Economists:456-493.

Kelegama, Saman (1998), *Privatization and the Public Exchequer: Some Observations from the Sri Lankan experience*, Paper presented at the conference on *Independent Sri Lanka: Economic Developments: 1948 –98 and prospects,* Central Bank of Sri Lanka, Colombo.

Kelegama, Saman and F.Foley (1996), *Policy Issues on Promoting Backward Linkages from the Garment Industry*, Colombo: Institute of Policy Studies.

Kelegama Saman (1999), "Economic Cost of Coflict in Sri Lanka", Robert I. Rotberg (ed.), *Creating Peace in Sri Lanka: Civil War and Reconstruction,* Brookings Institution Press, Washington D.C.

Khan Rasheeduddin (1989), "The Total State: The Concept and its Manifestation in the Indian Political System", Hasan Zoya, Jha S. N and Khan Rasheeduddin (eds.*) The State, Political Processes and Identity, Reflection on Modern India*: 33-72

Kindleberger, Charles, P and Herrick, Bruce (1977), *Economic Development*, Third Edition, McGraw-Hill, Inc.

Kubo Yuji (1989), "A model of Dual-Industrial Development in a Semi-Industrial Economy", *The Developing Economies*, XXVII (4):331-358.

Kuznets Simon (1961), "Long Term Trends in capital Formation Proportions" *Economic Development and Cultural Change,* IX (4): 25-248.

Lakshman W.D (ed.) (1979), *Public enterprises in the Economic Development of Sri Lanka*, Institute of Business Management, Colombo.

Lakshman W.D and Tisdell C.A (eds.), (1999), *Facets of Development of Sri Lanka: socio-political, Economic, Scientific and Culture,* The University of Queens land, 1999.

Lakshman W.D., 1986, "State Policy in Sri Lanka and its Economic Impacts 1970-85: Selected Themes with Special Reference to Distributive Implication of Policy", *Upanathi,* 1(1): 5-36.

Lakshman, W.D (1973), *Terms of Trade, Public Policy and Economic Development: 1948-58*, Unpublished Ph.D Thesis, Oxford University.

Lakshman, W.D (ed.), 1997, "Introduction", *Dilemmas of Development, Fifty Years of Economic Change in Sri Lanka of Development*", Sri Lanka Association of Economists, 1997:1-23.

Lal Deepak (1980), "Public Enterprises", in Cody John, Hughes Hellen and Wall David *Policies,* (eds.), *for Industrial Progress in Developing countries*, International Bank for Reconstruction and Development / The World Bank: 211-232.

Laski K. (1987, "On Kalecki Michal", *The New Palgrave, A Dictionary of Economics*, edited by John Eatwell, Murray Milgate and Peter Newman, Macmillan Press ltd 3: 8-14.

Lerski George Jan (1968), *Origin of Trotskyism in Ceylon: a documentary history of the Lanka Sama Samaja Party 1935–1942*, Stanford, Hoover Institute of war, Stanford University.

Lewis, W. Arthur (1958), *Economic Development with Unlimited Supplies of Labour,* The Manchester School: 139-91.

Lim, Timothy. C (1988) "Power, Capitalism and the Authoritarian State in South Korea", 1988, *Journal of Economic Issues*, XXXII (4): 1019-30.

Liyanage, Sumansiri, 1997, "State, State Capital and Capitalistic Development", in W D. Lakshman (ed.) *Dilemmas of Development" Fifty Years of Economic Change in Sri Lanka*, Sri Lanka Association of Economists: 423- 447.

Locke Richard M (1996), "The Composite Economy: Local Politics and Industrial Change in Contemporary Italy", *Economy and Society*, 25(4): 483-510.

Lucas Robert (1998), "Making a Miracle", Econometrica, 61 (2): 251-72.

MacEWAN, Arthur (1999), Neoliberalism or Democracy? Economic strategy, Markets, and alternatives for the 21st Century: 1-22.

McNALLY David (1993), *Against the Market: Political Economy, Market Socialism and the Marxist Critique*, London, Verso.

Marga Institute (1978), *Technology-Transfer & Reserve Flow, The Case of Sri Lanka,* Special Issue, 5 (2):

Marshall F. Ray, Cartter Allan. M and King Allan. G (1976), *Labor Economics*, Richard D. Irwin, Inc.

Masson, Paul, E. Jadresic, and P. Mauro (1999), "The Choice of an Exchange Rate Regime Revisited", paper presented at the conference on Exchange Rate Regimes in Emerging Market Economies organized by the ADBI, CEPII, and KIEP in Tokyo on 17-18 December.

Mayer, J. and Kuh, E. (1957), *The investment Decisions*, Cambridge University, Mass. Harvard University Press.

Meier Gerald. M (1995), *Leading Issues in Economic Development,* Oxford University Press, 6nd Edition.

Meier Gerald. M and Stiglitz Joseph. E (2001), (eds.), *Frontiers of Development Economics: The future in perspective,* A co-publication of the World Bank and Oxford University Press, New York.

Meier Gerald. M (1970), *Leading Issues in Economic Development, Studies in International Poverty*, Oxford University Press, 2nd Edition.

Mills Daniel Quinn (1978), *Labour* Management *Relations*, McGraw-Hill Book Company.

Moore Mick (1985), *The State and Peasant Politics in Sri Lanka*, Cambridge University Press.

Moore Mick (1990), "Economic Liberalization versus Political Pluralism", Lanka Guardian, 13 (8) 20-22.

Moore Mick (1991), "Rent-seeking and Market Surrogates: The Case of Irrigation Policy", Colclough, Christopher and Manor, James (eds.), *States or Markets? Neo-liberalism and the Development Policy Debate*, Institute of Development Studies, 1991:279-305.

Moore Mick (1992), "Retreat from Democracy in Sri Lanka", *The Journal of Commonwealth & Comparative Politics,* 30 (1): 64-84.

Moore Mick (1992), *What Type of Capitalism does Sri Lanka needs?*, Institute of Policy Studies, Sri Lanka.

Moore Mick, 1985, *The State and Peasant Politics in Sri Lanka*, Cambridge University Press.

Mouzelis, Nicos (1994), "The State in Late Development: Historical and comparative perspectives", Booth David (ed.), *Rethinking social Development: Theory, Research & Practice*, Longman Group Limited: 126-147.

Mukherjee, Sanjeeb (1989), "Class Struggles and the State in India", Hasan Zoya, Jha S. N and Khan Rasheeduddin (eds.) *The State, Political Processes and Identity, Reflection on Modern India,* 99-111.

Myint, H (1971), *Economic Theory and the Underdeveloped Countries*, Oxford University Press, Inc.

Myrdal Gunnar (1970), *The Challenge of World Poverty, A World Anti-Poverty Programme in Outline.*

Myrdal Gunnar (1968), *Asian Drama, An Inquiry Into the Poverty of Nations*, vol. 1, Twentieth Century Fund, Inc.

Nanayakkara Wifred S and Rodrigo P.C (1993), " Growth and Structural Changes in the Economy", (ed.) Patel Surendra J, *Technological Transformation in the Third World*, Vol. 1, Asia, Aldershot, Avebury: 197-318.

National Peace Council (2001), "The Economic Costs of the War", *The Economic, Social, Political and human cost of the War in Sri Lanka,* Colombo.

Naseem S. M (1999), "Globalisation, Technology and Asian Economic Development" in A.D.V.de .S. Indraratna (ed.) *Globalization and Asia, Retrospect and Prospect*, Sri Lanka association for the Advancement of Science; 208-235.

Nell Edward J. (1987), "Accumulation of Capital", Vol. 1, *The New Palgrave, A dictionary of Economics*, Mcmillan Press ltd.: 14-18.

Nicholas S.E.N (1933), *Commercial Ceylon,* Colombo, Times of Ceylon Co.

Nomura Michiaki (1997), "The Change in World Politics and Economy Brought about by Reaganomics", *in the Context of Asia's Prosperity-* Conference Proceedings, The Professors World Peace Academy-Korea: 61-69.

Okun, Arthur M (1970), The Political Economy of Prosperity, Brookings Institution.

Oliver R.L (1957), "The geological structure of Ceylon", *The Ceylon Geographer*, Bulletin of the Ceylon Geographical Society, 11(1-4): 9-16.

Parkin Michael, Powell Melanie and Matthews Kent (1997), *Economics*, third edition, Addison Wesley Longman Limited.

Peebles Patrick (1995), *Social Change in Nineteenth Century Ceylon,* New Delhi, Navrang.

Peiris Denzil (1958), *1956 and After: Background to Parties and Politics in Ceylon Today.*

Peiris G.H.(1996), *Development and Change in Sri Lanka: Geographical Perspectives*, International Centre for Ethnic Studies, Kandy, Sri Lanka.

Pereira Luiz Carlos Bresser (1993), "Economic Reforms and Cycles of State Intervention", *World Development*, 21 (8): 1337 -53.

Pieris. M. P (1997), "Economic Growth and Structural-Institutional Change Since Independence" in *Dilemmas of Development, Fifty Years of Economic Change in Sri Lanka* (ed.) W.D. Lakshman, Sri Lanka Association of Economists: 28-54.

Ponnambalam Satchi (1980), *Dependence Capitalism in Crisis: The Sri Lankan Economy, 1948 1980.*

Rajapathirana, Sarath (1988), "Foreign Trade and Economic Development: Sri Lanka's Experience", *World Development*, 16(10): 1143-56.

Rajapatirana Sarath (1986), "Some Policy Lessons from Macro Adjustment experiences: A Look at Six Countries", *Structural Adjustment and Growth*, Sri Lanka association of economists: 59-80.

Ram Rati (1986), "Government size and Economic Growth: A new Framework and some Evidence from cross-section and Time Series Data", *The American Economic Review*: 191-203.

Ramachandran M (1963), *Finance of Manufacturing Corporations in the Post-war Period*, Central Bank of Ceylon Bulletin, Dec.

Ramachandran. N (1963), *Foreign Plantation Investment in Ceylon 1889-1958*, Central Bank Research Series.

Ramanandham V.V (1963), *The Finance of Public Enterprises*, Indian Institute of Public Administration.

Ranasinghe K.D (1998), "Infrastructural Development", Seminar on Independent Sri Lanka: Economic Developments 1948 –1998 and Prospects, Central Bank of Sri Lanka.

Ranis Gustav and Schultz Paul T (1988), *The State of Development Economics, progress and Prospects,* Oxford, Basil Blackwell ltd.

Rao Bhanoji (1997), "Reflection on Reaganomics and Singapore Growth Experience", *in the Context of Asia's Prosperity-* Conference Proceedings, The Professors World Peace Academy-Korea:161-188.

Ratnasingham V. S (1976), *Urbanisation, Population of Sri Lanka,* a country Monograph, Series 4, United Nations.

Resnick, Stephen. A (1975), "State of Development Economics", The American Economic Association, LXV(2): 317-322.

Roberts, Michael (1979), "Elite formation and Elite 1832- 1931", *Collective identities, Nationalism and protest in Modern Sri Lanka,* Marga Institute, Colombo: 153-213.

Robinson Joan (1965), *Accumulation of Capital*, second edition, London, Macmillan.

Robinson, Richard (1986), *Indonesia: The Rise of Capital,* Allen & Unwin, North Sydney.

Rosenstein-Rodan, Paul .N (1943), "Problems of Industrialization of Eastern and South-Eastern Europe", *Economic Journal*, June-September: 204-7.

Rosovsky Henry (1965), "The Take-off into Sustained Controversy", *Journal of Economic History*, March: 271-275.

Rosovsky, Henry (1961), *Capital Formation in Japan 1868-1940*, The Free Press, a Corporation.

Rostow W .W (1960), *The Stages of Economic Growth,* Cambridge University Press.

Rowen Henry. S (ed.), (1998), *Behind East Asian Growth, the political and social foundations of prosperity*, Salzburg Seminar.

Rowthorn Bob (1982), *Demand, Real Wages, and Economic Growth,* Studi Economics

Samarawickreme N. D (1997a), "Can the Public Enterprise System Provide Growth Stimuli? -An Input-Output Approach on Structural Interdependence, The experience of Sri Lanka", Unpublished Monograph.

Samarawickreme N.D (1997b), "Changes in Economic Policy and Their Impact on Internal Trade in Sri Lanka", *Modern Sri Lanka Studies (New Series): A Journal of the Social Sciences,* University of Sri Lanka, Peradeniya, 1(2):49-81.

Sanderatne Nimal, (1995), *"The Economy", Sri Lanka Year 2000: Towards the 21st Century,* A CRDS Distinguished Authors contribution, in association with KVG & Sons, Colombo ltd.: 3-25.

Sarvananthan M (2001), "A social Cost of 'War for Peace'", *Pravada*, 7(7): 15-16.

Schneider, Friedrich and Frey, Bruno. S (1985), "Economic and Political Determinants of Foreign Direct Investment", *World Development*, 13(2): 161-175.

Schumacher E.F (1965), "Industrialization Though 'Intermediate Technology'" in Ronald Robinson (ed.), *Industrilization in Developing Countries*, Cambridge University Oversees Studies Committee Conference on Role of Industrialization in Development, Cambridge.

Seers Dudley (1963), "The Limitations of the Special Case", *Bulletin of the Oxford Institute of Economics and Statistics,* 25(2): 77-9.

Sen A. K (1972), *Choice of Techniques, An aspect of the Theory of Planned Economic Development*, Third Edition, Basil Blackwell.

Sen Amartya (1984), *Resources, Values and Development*, Blackwell.

Sen Anupam (1982), *The State, Industrialization and Class Formations in India; A Neo-Marxist Perspective on Colonialism, Underdevelopment and Development*, Routledge & Kegan Paul ltd.

Shapiro Helen and Taylor Lance (1990), "The State and Industrial Strategy", *World Development*, 18(6): 874-76.

Shastri Amita (1983), "Political Economy of Intermediate Regimes: The Case of Sri Lanka 1956 –70", *South Asia Bulletin*, III (2).

Sivalingam G (1997), "The Impact of Reaganomics on the Malaysian Economy", *in the Context of Asia's Prosperity*- Conference Proceedings, The Professors World Peace Academy-Korea:207-236.

Skocpol, Theda (1994), "Bringing the State Back In: Strategies of Analysis in Current Research" in Evans, Peter B., Rueschemeyer, Dietrich & Sckocpol, Theda (eds.), *Bringing the State Back In*, Cambridge University Press: 3-43.

Snodgrass, Donald R (1966), *Ceylon: An Export Economy in Transition*, Homewood, Ill: Richard D. Irvin Inc.

Sobhan Rehman (1999), "The East Asian Model in the Light of Contemporary Experience", Muchkund Dubey and Nancy Jetley (eds.), *South Asia and its Eastern Neighbours, Building a relationship in the 21st Century*: 40-55.

Srinivasan .T. N (1989), "Introduction to Part I", Economic development- Concepts and Approaches, Hollis Chenery & T. N. Srinivasan, *Handbook of development economics*: 1, Elservier Science B. V: 3-8.

Srinivasan T. N (1985), "Neoclassical Political Economy, the State and Economic Development" *Asian Development Review*, 3(2): 40-45.

Stanfield James Ronald (1999), "The Scope, Method, and Significance of Original Institutional Economics", *Journal of Economic Issues,* XXXIII (2): 231-255.

Stern Nicholas (1991), "Public Policy and the Economics of Development", reprinted in, *Leading Issues in Economic Development* by Meier Gerald M Sixth Edition: 548-52.

Streeten, Paul (1993), "Market and State: Against Minimalism", *World Development*, 21(8): 1281-1298.

Streeten, Paul. P (1967), "The frontier of Development Studies; Some issues of Development Policy", *Journal of Development Studies* 4(1): 2-24.

Sugiura Katsumi (1999), "Institutional Economics Needs Interdisciplinary studies of Social Sciences", *Journal of Economic Issues*, XXXIII (2): 253-283.

Suriyakumaran C (1980), "Debts, Deficits and the Development of Developing Countries", *South Asia Journal.*

Suriyakumaran C (1996), *The Wealth of Poor Nations*, new edition, Madras, T.R. Publications.

Tanzi Vito (1997), "The role of the State in Post-chaos situations", Szekely, Istvan .P and Sabot, Richard (eds.), *Development Strategy and Management of the Market Economy*', United nations, Oxford, Clarendon Press, 2.

Tewari, Meenu (1988), "Intersectoral Linkages and the Role of the State in Shaping the Conditions of Industrial Accumulation: A Study of Ludhiana's Manufacturing Industry", *World Development*, 26(8): 1387-1411.

Theil Henri (1971), *Principles of Econometrics*, John Wiley & Sons, inc.

Thirlwall A.P (1995), *The Economics of Growth and Development.* Selected essays of Thirlwall A.P, Hants, Edward Elgar Publication.

Tilakaratna W. M (1990), "Open economy in Sri Lanka: Some Observations", *Upanathi*, 15: 83-94.

Tongroj Onchan (1997), "Reaganomics and Economic Growth of Thailand", *in the Context of Asia's Prosperity*- Conference Proceedings, The Professors World Peace Academy-Korea :189-206.

Toye John (1993), "Is There a New Political Economy of Development", Colclough Christopoer and Manor James (eds.), *State or Markets? Neo-liberalism and the Development Policy Debate*, 1993,Clarendon Press, Oxford: 321-338.

Uyangoda Jayadeva (1992), "Economic Change, the State and Question of Security", P.V.J. Jayasekera (ed.), *Security dilemma of a Small State, Part I, Sri Lanka in the South Asian Context,* Institute of International studies: 179-203.

Vidanapathirana, Upananda (1986), "Pattern of Industrialisation; Strategies and Response", *Facets of Development in Independent Sri Lanka*, Ministry of Finance and Planning, Sri Lanka: 165-193.

Wade, Robert (1990), *Governing the Market, Economic Theory and the Role of Government in East Asian Industrialisation*, Princeton University Press.

Walsh, Vivian and Gram, Harvey (1980), *Classical and Neoclassical Theories of General Equilibrium*, Oxford University Press, Inc.

Walters, Alan (1999), "Globalisation – Past, Present and Future" in A.D. V. de S. Indraratna (ed.) *Globalisation and South Asia*, Sri Lanka Association for the Advancement of Science:37-50.

Walton Geoffrey. N (1987), *A Review of Effective Protection and Comparative Advantage in the Manufacturing Sector of Sri Lanka*, the Ministry of Finance and Planning, Colombo.

Warnapala, Wiswa W. A (1992), "Political Process and the Aspects of National Integration and Security in Sri Lanka, P.V.J. Jayasekera (ed.), *Security dilemma of a Small State, Part I, Sri Lanka in the South Asian Context,* Institute of International studies: 147-178.

Weeks, John (1985), *Limits to Capitalist Development: The Industrialization of Peru, 1950-1980,*Westview Press Inc.

White H. and Kelegama S (1994), "The Fiscal Implications of Privatization in Developing Countries: The Case of Sri Lanka", Institute of Social Studies, The Hague, Working Paper Series No. 179, The Netherlands.

Wickremaratna L. A (1973), "The Emergence of a Welfare Policy: 1931 – 1948", in K. M de Silva. (ed.) *History of Ceylon,* 3: 476-488.

Wignaraja Ganeshan (1998), *Trade Liberalization in Sri Lanka: Exports, Technology and Industrial Policy*, Basingstoke, UK, Macmillan Press.

Wijesinghe Mellory E (1976), *The Economy of Sri Lanka 1948 – 75,* President, Federation of Chamber of Commerce.

Williamson John (1998), "Sri Lanka's Search for the Right Economic Policies, 1948 –98", Seminar on Independent Sri Lanka: Economic Developments 1948 –1998 and Prospects, Central Bank of Sri Lanka.

Wilson A. Jeyaratnam (1975), *Electoral Politics in An Emerging State: Hthe Ceylon General Election of May 1970*, Cambridge University Press.

World Bank (1997), *Private Capital Flows to Developing Counties, The Road to Financial Integration,* A World Bank Policy Research Report, The International Bank for reconstruction, Oxford University Press.

Wou, Wei (1997), "Effects of Reaganomics on Taiwan Economy", *Rev.Sun Myung Moon & Reaganomics- in the Context of Asia's Prosperity-* Conference Proceedings, The Professors World Peace Academy -Korea: 127-159.

Wriggins Harward W (1960), Ceylon: *Dilemmas of a New Nation*, Princeton University Press, N..J.

Wright Erik Olin (1993), *Class, Crisis and the State*, London, Verso.

Yoo Ji- Sung (1997), "Repercussion Effects of Reaganomics on Korean Economy", *Rev.Sun Myung Moon & Reaganomics- in the Context of Asia's Prosperity-* Conference Proceedings, The Professors World Peace Academy -Korea: 92-123.

Zysman, John (1996), "The Myth of 'Global Economy': Enduring National Foundations and Emerging Regional realities", *New Political Economy,* 1(2): 67-184.

Index

A

Alternative industrial strategies,
adoption, 190, 245
Anti market forces impact, 244
Average Annual Rate of Fixed Assets in Four Categories of Firms, 107
Average Fixed Investment industry-wise
1952-98 figures, 256-57
investor class-wise, 262
Product-wise, 264
Average Price Levels,
Planning Oriented environments, 276
Market Economic environments, 276
Average Rate of Economic Growth (periodic), 263
Inflation 1938-46, 254

B

BOI (Board of Investment) Firms Performance, 210
British Colonialism
early era of accumulation, 51
later years, 57
objective, 51
in Sri Lanka, 17
Business Undertakings (Acquisitions) Act, 169

C

Capitalist accumulations practices, 172
Capitalist Class
domination, 194
investment practices, 67
Capital Employed Sectoral Share, 200
Capitalist industrial development
features, 204
class of investors, 205
Capital Formation long term trend, 94
Categories of goods manifactired, 107
Ceylon Blue Books, 56
Ceylon National Congress (CNC), 63
Coalition Government
1965, 164
change 1956 onwards, 155-56
Colebrook Commission The, 17
Colombo Stock Exchange listing, 93
Company list prior to 1956, 279
Compilation of a New Database: Methodology/Limitations, 91
Conflicts State Council Level, 61
Control Prices, 168
Controlled to Liberatise economy chages, 1977
Construnction sector, 97
Conservative Faction of Political elites, 63
Consumer goods supply, 53
Cost of living index 1938-46, 254

D

Development Theory of NICs, 21, 25
criticism, 28

change in, 29
Domestic Market for Industrial Products, 211
Domestic Private Capital Capacity, 246

E

East Asian miracle of World Bank, 30
Economic Policy Shift
effects, 133
private sector, 133-34
and private accumulation relationship, 138
phase 1, 149-50
phase 2, 154
phase 3, 164
phase 4, 165
Economic Conditions Changes, 102
Electoral Processes Problems, 63
Employer Employee relations, 58
Enterpreneures
types, 162-63
classes, 105, 108
Enterprise Sector Sri Lanka, 159
EPS (Earning Per Share),
different sectors, 102-103
of industries, 258
values of manufacturing industries, 163
Ethnic Violence in the country, 221
Export / Import / Price Indices / Terms of Trade, 253
External environment
changes, 190
influence, 59

F

Family based firms, 20
Fast and compressed growth path for 'New Nations', 22
Fergusons Directory of Private Firms, 152
Final / Intermediary goods industries, 252
Finance Sector, 98
Firms ownership product-wise, 202
Fixed Investment
rate of growth 1952-97, 98
Periodic Rate of growth, 133
and degrees of market orientation, 249
Foreign Direct Investment (FDI), 30
Policy, 168
measures, 206
inviting by new nations, 192, 197
Foreign Investors
attitude, 65
disinterest, 227
Foreign Industrialists, 112
Frontiers of Development Economics, 33

G

Gerschenkron's professional development theory, 26
Globalisation impact on domestic market, 215
Growth Prospects of Fixed Investments under Tax Incentives, 1953-76, 293
in a poor business environments, 294

H

Hostile Market Force, 217

I

Imports,
early 20th century, 53
substitution, 32
1911, 1921
items, 251
expenditure, 251
Inadequacy of state support to Industrial developmnet, 153
Indigenous
cottage Industries, 54
private venture industrial capital, 163
Industrial Accumulation
trends, 130
under ISI Policies, 172

post independent Sri Lanka, 189
patterns, 189
after 1994, 224
Industrial development progress-Sri Lanka, 20
Process, 48
Post 1956, 243
Post 1977, 206
1990s, 213
Industrialisation
idea of, 59
of new nations, 89
factors, 22
Sri Lanka, 89
Industrial Capital accumulation policy, 67, 74
Industrialist Classes, 104
growth, 104
Industrial Fixed Capital Formation of Private Sector, 142
Industrial Capital development directions, 158-59
Industrial
product cycle, 242
Industrial Changes under neoliberal economic policies
phase 1, 201
phase 2, 207
reasons of slowness, 208
Industrial establishments Old / New List, 259-61
Industrial investments
growht upto 1977, 147
policy shifts, 148
Industries numbers in different products, 252
Internal Economic Environment, 39
Internal Environment of Sri Lanka
changes, 192
conflicts, 193
Investment
behaviour factors, 135
term, 135-36
climate, 242
ISI Policies
Pro-market anti-market effects, 167

J

Jayawardance, J.R.,
on economic structure changes, 1977, 196-77
JVP (Janatha Vimukthi Peramuna), 222

K

Kalecki's investment model, 139, 143

L

Labour unrest post-1994, 225
Labour share in each industry, 56
Liberal Coalition (UNP)
view on industrial development, 150
political agenda, 152
Light Manufacturing sector, 53
LTTE hostilities, 226
cost of war, 226-27

M

Mahaweli and housing projects, 196
Manufacturing capital-Annual Growth Rate 1978-97, 207
Manufacturing Sectors, 99
Manufactories
coexistence of, 54
Market economic forces development of, 52
Market oriented
industrialization
transition to, 197
policies, 195
Marxist analysis on economic development, 35
Marxist influence, 64, 224
Marxist Conservative elite (class of), 67
Minimal State intervention in industrial development, 31
Model of determinants of investments, 142

MNCs role, 30
Myrdal
on socio-economic reforms, 27
thesis on dilemmas faced by new nations, 244

N

Nationalisation Policy, 168
Neo Liberal
economic policy, 29, 218
regime
drawbacks, 244
post 1977, 243
New Economic Strategies Sri Lanka, 157-58
Newly Industrialized countries (NICs)
achievements, 21, 149
New Industrialists
emerging of, 109
post 1960, 109
post, 1977, 111
'New Nations' in Asia,
economic/ political strategies, 129, 218, 241
tasks, 241
challenges, 191
New Monetarist School Policies (Shenoy on), 195
New Industrial Policy 1989, 223
Non-listed companies performance, 216
Non-listed large firms participation in industrial accumulation, 204

O

Old Institutional Economics (O.I.E), 27
Old Industrial Establishment list, 259-60
Old Manufacturing Establishments list, 277
Option open for economcy, 190, 245

P

PA (People's Alliance Government), 223
Performance of State Industrial Enterprises, 281
Plantation
enterpreneurs, 21
market economy, 17
avenues, pre-British, 47
early 20th century, 49
slow down, 58
accumulation strategy, 149
sector after WWI, 96
Policy of Industrialisation (1940s)
issues, 71
Political
decary post 1983, 221
elite
emergence, 58
divisions, 61
objectives, 63
change in 1956, 155
Parties formation, 69
post Independent growth, 18, 20
post 1931 developments, 62
forces, 62
Potential long run Rate of Growth of Industrial investment environment 1952-97, 294
Potential Industrial Processes, 24
Pre-British Period, 47
Price Policy, 28, 52
Private Sector
contribution, 19
oriented industrial development post WWI, 69
constraints in industrial formation, 154
enterprises
structure, 92
investments, 93
led structural changes, 114
in Sri Lanka, 129
Private Industrial
Accumulation, 65, 132
Entrepreneur development, 162
Fixed Investment growth 1977-83, 295
Privatisation of state institutions, 190
Private Investment
changing patterns, 96

patterns, 100
fixed assets, 100
Productive resources mobility, 242
Product categories share in Total exports
Foreign firms, 282
Domestic Firms, 283
Public Manufacturing Sector State dependence, 189
Public Sector
Investment, 131
Reformance 1978-87, 195

Q

Quasi Neo Liberal Policies
impact, 217

R

Radical Marxist Group, 63
Regression Growth Rate of Per Capita
Real Income
1957-77, 286
1990-99, 286
Model Fixed Asset Determination, 287
Growth of Fixed Assets under Good Business Environment (1953-76), 292
Relations between fixed and other Assets, 1956-67, 288
Rate of Growth of investments, 288
Rate of Growth of internal savings (1957-77), 289
Rate of Growth of Pvt. Equity Capital, 290
Rate of loan Capital 1957-77, 290
Growth under good bussiness environment, 292
Rent seeking practices, 171
Riots 1983 - rehabilitation, 222
Rostow, WW, Stage theory, 24

S

Sectoral Distribution of Local Manufacturing Firms 193, 115
Share Market, 169
Selected structural information, 267
sectoral / product-wise, 267
Slow-Industrial Growth, 172
Small nations vulnerability to international economy, 19
Small scale firms growth, 163
Socialist Oriented Policies, 166
Socialist Principle, 67
Socialist foundation to Capitalist foundation (changes), 196
South Asian / East Asian Countries
Performance, 21-22
Sri Lanka
as a neo-liberal state, 219
new economic strategy, 157-58
independence and after, 18
relations in the private sector, 129
Sri Lanka Freedom Party manifesto, 158
State Intervention forms, 33
State Theory of industrial development, 24
State Enterprises
Secondary benefits, 160
State Private Sector relations changes, 248
State and the economy of Sri Lanka, 35
States Participations in industrial accumulation, 156
Standard Product Group, 114
Strikes-post 1994, 225
Subsidised Pricing Policy of State enterprise sector, 161
Surplus Generated
by Sectors, 280
by Private and State sectors, 174

T

Taxation Policy, 170
Taxation cumulative effects of High Taxes and Poor investment climate on Fixed manufacturing investment, 177-78

Trade Liberalisation, 214
Trade Sector growth, 97
Trade Unions, 221
Transformation of economy, 49
    process, 50
Tripod
    structure, 205, 228
    under different investment climate, 247

U

UNP (liberal Coalition)
    Victory, 1977, 194
    Changed Policies, 194
    Industrial Policies, 151
United Left Front, 170
Urban Population
    growth, 64
    different periods
    average annual growth rate, 253

V

Venture Capital Firms, 119

W

Warnapala, 155
    on coalition victory, 155
World War I impact, 59, 62, 65
World War II,
    Industries before / after, 254-55
Workers Charter, 225